EDDIE ROBINSON

" ... he was the
Martin Luther King
of football"

A BIOGRAPHY BY
Denny Dressman

COMSERV BOOKS
LLC

DENVER

For information, contact
ComServ Books
P.O. Box 3116
Greenwood Village, CO 80155-3116
www.comservbooks.com

Dressman, Denny.
    Eddie Robinson : "-- he was the Martin Luther King of
football" : a biography / by Denny Dressman.
    p. cm.
    Includes bibliographical references and index.
    LCCN 2009910092
    ISBN-13: 978-0-9774283-3-5
    ISBN-10: 0-9774283-3-8

    1. Robinson, Eddie. 2. Grambling State Tigers
(Football team)--History. 3. Grambling State University
--Football--History. 4. Football coaches--United States
--Biography. 5. African American football coaches--
Biography.   I. Title.

GV939.R58D74 2010   796.332'092
                   QBI09-600182

Production Management by
Paros Press
1551 Larimer Street, Suite 1301   Denver, CO 80202
303-893-3332   www.parospress.com

Book Design by Scott Johnson

Printed in the United States of America
1   3   5   7   9   10   8   6   4   2

To all who share

Eddie's steadfast belief

that anything is possible in America,

"the greatest country in the world"

**Receiving the Tuss McLaughry Award from the American
Football Coaches Association in 1996, Eddie Robinson
joined former presidents, war heroes and astronauts
among recipients of the prestigious honor.** (Photo courtesy
of the American Football Coaches Association)

Table of Contents

"The only way they're going to know who
and what Eddie Robinson was, will be for us to tell them."

Doug Williams
April 9, 2007
Baton Rouge, Louisiana

Epitaph

LIFE ENDED for Eddie Robinson on April 3, 2007. By then, early in his eighty-ninth year, his legacy as a record-setting football coach had long been confirmed. Yet the fullness of his contribution as a historic black American role model in the context of the tumultuous Civil Rights Era had not been recorded for future generations. Upon the passing of "Coach Rob," writers everywhere tried to express what he meant to America along the sidelines as well as outside the stadium walls. News media across the nation sought reaction from his colleagues and former players, and many who admired him – even some who never met him in person – shared their personal appreciation with online responses to published commentary. Praise and admiration poured forth, tributes of every sort to a humble man whose reach was greater than he ever cared to claim or have emphasized.

"Nobody has ever done or ever will do what Eddie Robinson has done for the game," Joe Paterno has said, Paterno himself a legend after almost a half-century as Penn State's head coach. "Our profession will never, ever, be able to repay Eddie Robinson for what he has done for the country and the profession of football."

"As a person, he used the sport he loved to teach young men and women that sent the most players into the pros. And he will always be known as the first college coach to win more than four hundred games, the first black coach to become president of the American Football Coaches Association, and the man who put black college football on the map in the eyes of pro football scouts and coaches. Yet this is but one dimension of a remarkable figure. He helped his race achieve dignity and opportunity, as well.

Does any of this elevate Eddie Robinson to the stature of Dr. Martin Luther King? In the most literal sense there was, and can be, only one Martin Luther King. But maybe W.C. Gorden's sense is not overstatement; maybe it does not diminish or trivialize the role of America's acknowledged champion of racial progress to recognize another man's life in similar terms.

What follows is Eddie Robinson's life story as best this author can tell it. All who read it can decide for themselves if the facts fit the title.

PART ONE

Origins

1

AMERICA IN 1828 was a conflicted nation struggling mightily with the inherent contradictions between slavery and liberty, independence and unity. In the maelstrom of that time, which eventually led to war between the states, the words and deeds of two disparate men laid the foundation for the racially hostile way of life that dominated the South and negatively influenced the rest of America's collective attitude toward black citizens for nearly a hundred and fifty years.

John C. Calhoun, a first generation American, was born in South Carolina in 1782, near the end of the Revolutionary War. He served as vice president to John Quincy Adams and Andrew Jackson from 1825 to 1832, and also held the positions of Secretary of War, Secretary of State and U.S. Senator from South Carolina. Nicknamed the "cast-iron man" because of his steadfast defense of his beliefs, which included slavery, Calhoun died almost eleven years before the start of the American Civil War but still was acknowledged as a driving force behind the secession movement.

Thomas Dartmouth Rice was born in New York City in 1808, the year the U.S. Congress banned the importation of slaves – but did not make it illegal for U.S. citizens to obtain slaves and bring them into the country as their own or to sell. A carpenter's apprentice in a New York City shipyard, Rice aspired to be an entertainer. Specializing in comedy, song and dance, he began his theatrical career as an extra at the Park Theatre, New York City's only playhouse for the first quarter of the 19th century. He became "Daddy" Rice after he darkened his face with burnt cork and developed a black minstrel routine that became wildly popular in the United States and abroad. He has been called the "father of American minstrelsy" and is generally acknowledged as the first blackface performer to achieve international acclaim based on the enthusiastic reception his minstrel show received in England. Though he never set out to be, Rice also was the "father" of the manifestation of prejudice in the slave states. The worldwide exposure he gave his blackface caricature made Jim Crow a household name that came to stand for a way of life.

Calhoun, a lean, muscular man with chiseled cheekbones, angular jaw and jutting chin, was a rugged early American in every sense of the term. It is easy to picture him trudging behind a plow for countless hours, as he did in his youth and while he was a young man not yet elected to the U.S. House of Representatives. Formal education being rare in the South Carolina countryside in the late 1700s, John Calhoun, a Yale graduate, learned first at the feet of his father, who challenged his boy to think. Calhoun's piercing eyes in adulthood reflected a mind that rarely ever rested. It was said that he mastered reasoning before reading, and that being in his company compelled others "to think all the time," and inevitably left them "feeling inferior." Words appropriate to his description include intense, passionate, fiery, earnest, driven, brilliant and . . . humorless. Calhoun's father was preoccupied with the politics of the new nation, and passed his views on the independence of the states and the necessity of slavery to his son. When Patrick Calhoun died in 1796. it had been recorded a few years earlier that he "owned thirty-one Negroes."

It was in 1828 that 48-year-old Calhoun, an established politician and influential orator, and 20-year-old Rice, who was looking for his "break" while working as a stage carpenter and prop hand in Louisville, Kentucky, gave voice to a degrading view of blacks that endured for decades after slavery was outlawed. They weren't alone, of course. But their influence in shaping America's predominant attitude toward black citizens for much of the 20th century cannot be denied.

Objecting to what Southerners considered an onerous federal tariff on manufactured goods, and countering growing sentiment within the federal government in opposition to slavery, Calhoun authored *South Carolina Exposition and Protest*, an essay supporting the doctrine of nullification – the position that states could override federal legislation they deemed unconstitutional. Almost one hundred and thirty years later, segregationist states of the Deep South would adopt the doctrine of interposition – strikingly similar in principle to its forerunner, nullification – as a means of delaying or blocking the implementation of federal court orders and legislation outlawing discrimination and mandating racial integration.

As the culmination of an increasingly bitter feud with President Jackson, Calhoun resigned the vice presidency in 1832 for a seat in the U.S. Senate. In the senate he delivered what has been dubbed his "benevolence of slavery" oration. In it he declared: "Where two races of different origin, and distinguished by color and other physical differences, as well as intellectual, are brought together, the relation now existing in the slaveholding states between the two is, instead of an evil, a good – a positive good." Translated, the convoluted statement espoused the belief that blacks, as a race, were intellectually, and perhaps morally, inferior, and thus better off in bondage, with their masters responsible for their well-being. The acknowledged power of Calhoun's intellect and depth of his thought elevated the credibility of his words and attracted ready acceptance.

Calhoun's view was buttressed by the infamous Dred Scott decision, in which the United States Supreme Court ruled that people of African descent brought into the United States as slaves – as well as their descendants – whether or not they were slaves, were not citizens and could not become citizens, and thus were not covered by the Bill of Rights. The ruling also established that slaves were chattel – property – that could not be

The first known challenge to a Jim Crow law occurred in Louisiana the following year when Homer Plessy, who was one-eighth Negro, sat in a whites-only railroad car and was arrested. His court challenge eventually reached the U.S. Supreme Court, and in 1896 the Justices voted 7-2 in favor of upholding Louisiana's law, with the tortured reasoning that "racial separation did not necessarily mean an abrogation of equality." In practice, the "separate but equal" principle established in *Plessy v. Ferguson* legitimized two societies: one privileged and respected, the other disadvantaged and degraded.

With that, all conceivable obstacles to the Jim Crow South had been removed. By 1914, long-gone slavery had been replaced by a severe white-black caste system sustained by the force of law, personal intimidation and, as needed, clandestine violence. Relying on the *Plessy* ruling, southern states tightened their control of day-to-day existence under Jim Crow by controlling elections and political activism through an arsenal of poll taxes, literacy tests, primaries open only to Democrats – all of whom were white – and grandfather clauses granting the right to vote only to those people whose ancestors had voted before the Civil War.

The Jim Crow world was further regulated by a set of social customs and a rigid standard of racial etiquette that reflected the disrespect embodied in "Daddy" Rice's parody, and the bigoted views of John C. Calhoun and numerous segregationist politicians who followed him with dire warnings that integration would lead to the "mongrelization" of the white race. As a result, life under Jim Crow forbade Negro men from extending even the simplest forms of common courtesy to anyone of the "superior" race. A Negro man dare not hold a door for a white woman, nor even light her cigarette. Such gestures implied intimacy. Touch a white woman, and the black man would risk a charge of rape, for under Jim Crow it was fervently held that any form of contact could lead to sexual relations, which would corrupt the racial purity of future generations.

White men did not shake hands with Negro males because a handshake implied social parity; on the rare occasion when a black person rode in an automobile driven by a white person, the black was expected to always sit in the back. Proper Jim Crow etiquette specified that blacks could be introduced to whites, but never the opposite. Negroes were expected to address whites with courtesy titles, while whites spoke to blacks by first names only, rather than extend any semblance of social standing by acknowledging them with a respectful prefix. Eating together, of course, was unthinkable. Separate but hardly comparable water fountains and public restrooms . . . entrances and exits . . . waiting rooms and seating areas . . . hospitals, schools, churches and even cemeteries were the only way of life decades of Southern Negroes and whites knew growing up.

"I had two wonderful parents, and they told me and my brothers, 'It's our job to see that you reach adulthood,'" said R. L Stockard, who was born in Nashville, Tennessee in 1924 and became both a distinguished journalist and a respected professor of historical geography at Southern University in Baton Rouge. "In the South in the Twenties and Thirties you were not safe as an African American on the street AT ANY TIME. Even being legal, and surely if you were being illegal, your life wasn't worth a plug nickel. They would shoot you and leave you exactly where they shot you down. This is the way it was then, and our mother and father taught us that. So we learned very early about self-preservation and being able to survive. My middle brother was the 'off' one," Stockard continued. "You know, he was always asking my mother and daddy what we called off-the-wall questions. He said, 'Why can't I walk in the store and do like whites do?' And my mother and father simply said to him, 'Because you're not white.' And he said, 'What does that have to do with it?' And they said, very calmly, 'Those are the laws of Tennessee and the City of Nashville.' That's the way it was."

Goldie Sellers, who played for Kansas City when the Chiefs beat Minnesota 23-7 to win Super Bowl IV in January, 1970, met his wife while he played for Eddie Robinson at Grambling in the early 1960s. She was a cheerleader – named Peaches as an infant, she said, because of her honey-colored skin and peach-shaped face. They, too, learned at an early age the reality of growing up black in the Jim Crow South. "At that particular time," Goldie said, "we, as blacks, could not look a white man in the eye. Just like if you look certain animals in the eye, they'll fight you. There were just a lot of things you couldn't do. We had to be subservient people, bottom line. If we did not adhere to the rules and guidelines that governed us, then dire consequences would take place. It was just that simple."

Peaches recalled the role violence played in maintaining the Jim Crow way of life. "They would do things in a way that kept us scared out of our lives," she said. "In Tallulah (in northeastern Louisiana near the Mississippi line), there were probably three blacks to every one white. There was a young man – gorgeous. Anyone with what we called good hair and light complexion was pretty. This man was pretty. He was gorgeous. He had tried to vote in Tallulah, and they hemmed him up between Rayville and Tallulah." The details of what happened after the man was cornered are unknown, but the outcome isn't. "It was the first time I ever attended a funeral with a closed casket," Peaches said. "As black people we would always open the casket because it was our way of saying goodbye. They couldn't even open his casket. These were the kinds of things they did to keep us fearful."

Goldie and Peaches had been married about two years, and their daughter was a toddler, when Peaches returned to Rayville at Easter to visit her mother. "We went to a drug store that my mom had dealt with all my life," she said. "They had redone the whole store, but I knew even then I couldn't sit on a stool. So I went down and asked, 'May I please have an ice cream cone, and would you push it way down in the cone, so that my little girl won't waste it all over her dress?' My mom and I had been someplace and we had dressed her up really nice, and we didn't want her to get it all over her nice dress."

Peaches waited, and was ignored. "The woman behind the counter kept waiting on other people. So I said, 'Please forgive me. Maybe you didn't hear me.' And I wasn't being uppity. I just really thought she had not heard me. I said, 'Could I please have a single scoop ice cream cone, and would you push it way down in the cone.' She said, 'You are waited on down there. You want to get an ice cream for that little girl, you have to go down there and get waited on.' I said, 'You can take that ice cream . . .' And my mom said, 'Peaches. Peaches, we'll go down to Jitney Jungle – that was the biggest grocery store – and we will buy Gigi a whole half gallon of ice cream plus some cones. Because, when you go back to Denver, momma still has to live here.' We were programmed to be accepting of the way times were. I'm a full-grown adult, and my mom puts her hand on me and says don't go there. We had been raised as kids to be very respectful of our elders. And our elders had taught us to be respectful of white folks. You will keep your mouth closed and do what's expected of you."

In some situations it simply was not possible to maintain a low profile. Black college football teams traveled throughout the South by bus, and that made them easy targets for harassment. "You'd be traveling on the bus, and the sheriff would stop you and threaten to arrest the whole bus," said retired Alcorn State coach Marino Casem. "We were going from Alcorn to Jackson (Mississippi) on Highway 18 one time when the sheriff pulled us over. He said the bus driver was driving over the center line and he was going to arrest everyone on the bus. He wanted to know, 'Who's in charge of this bus?' I got out and talked with him, and it just so happened the president of the college was coming up behind us. The president stopped and asked the officer what happened. Our president acted like he was going to fire the driver. The sheriff was so impressed with how much hell we were taking from the president, he told us to go on. He figured we'd get more hell from the president than from him."

Growing up, Eddie Robinson experienced similar intimidating and humiliating incidents. Once, a white housewife accused him of stealing her husband's wristwatch after Eddie delivered ice to their home. Eddie was in a police car, wondering what might happen to him, when the woman told the officer she had spoken with her husband and was mistaken. Several times Eddie was denied admittance to public places, including the stadium where Louisiana State University's football team played. Somehow, though, he managed to avoid the bitterness these events could have seared into his personality. Rather than dwell on that past, Eddie chose to look optimistically ahead. What he saw was inevitable change and opportunity few others could even imagine under the oppressive circumstances.

2

EDWARD GAY Robinson came into the world on February 13, 1919, in Jackson, Louisiana, a plantation town about thirty miles north of Baton Rouge. He was the first and only child of Frank Robinson, a third-generation sharecropper, and his wife, Lydia Stewart. By the early 1900s, the boll weevil had devoured most of the cotton crop all the way to Texas, so Frank planted other crops, including corn and tobacco. Sharecropping, of course, was an almost impossible way to make a living, no matter what crops were planted. In a typical sharecropping arrangement, a former slave (and inevitably his descendants, because of the ultimately one-sided arrangement) agreed to provide his and his family's labor in return for a house, work animals, tools and seed. The deal at harvest was supposed to be that the landlord and sharecropper would split equally the income from the sale of the crops. The sharecropper, however, almost always had run up a big bill at the landowner's store – the original company store. The credit price of food and clothing was, by design, greater than the cash price, so the sharecropper owed at least the equivalent of his full share of crop sale proceeds. Often the debt was even greater, which resulted in a new form of servitude when the Louisiana State Legislature passed a law binding share-croppers to the land they worked until they could pay off their debt.

While Frank toiled to beat the stacked deck, Lydia worked as a domestic in the homes of well-to-do whites, who were plentiful in the town that called itself the "Athens of Louisiana" and nicknamed one of its streets "Silk Stocking Avenue." Turn-of-the-century Jackson was home to Centenary College, Feliciana Female Collegiate Institute, Millwood Institute and the East Louisiana State Hospital, and, according to a publication of the time, proudly counted "four churches for white people, three churches for colored people, eleven general merchandise stores, two well established drug stores, two millinery stores, two refreshment parlors, two first class hotels, one furniture store, two blacksmith shops, a first class barber shop, a wide awake newspaper and a railroad of our own." A century later the Jackson Historic District featured one hundred twenty-four structures, including a well-preserved historic commercial corridor.

Jackson was founded in 1815, just a few years after Louisiana became the 18th state in the Union. Originally a settlement called Bear Corners for the black bears that roamed the surrounding wilderness, the eventual town the State of Louisiana designated as the seat of justice for Feliciana Parish was named for Gen. Andrew Jackson. Old Hickory, it is said, camped with his soldiers along nearby Thompson Creek following the Battle of New Orleans, Jackson's historic triumph in the War of 1812. Fourteen years later Jackson would become the seventh U.S. President – with John C. Calhoun serving as his vice president until Calhoun resigned December 28, 1832 in bitter disagreement over the intertwined issues of states' rights and slavery.

With its share of plantations and slaves in the 1800s, Jackson and environs enthusiastically supported secession when Louisiana became the sixth state to withdraw from the Union on January 26, 1861. The Confederate spirit remained a part of Jackson's heritage when Eddie Robinson was born almost sixty years later, and continued beyond the day he died. The Battle of Jackson Crossroads, one of two Civil War engagements to occur in the Jackson area, was commemorated annually. And fifteen miles away Port Hudson battlefield, site of the longest siege in U.S. military history, was designated a National Historic Landmark in 1974. It was there, between May

23 and July 9, 1863, that 6,800 Confederate troops battled Union forces totaling more than 30,000 in fierce fighting that gave graphic meaning to battle sites with names such as Fort Desperate and Slaughter's Field. Control of the Mississippi River was at stake, and with the fall of Vicksburg and the surrender at Port Hudson, the Confederacy was cut in half. Military defeat was then inevitable, though almost two more years would pass before Generals Ulysses S. Grant and William Tecumseh Sherman, the industrial superiority of the North, and decisively greater manpower would force surrender at Appomattox.

Among the North's soldiers at Port Hudson were two regiments of southern blacks whose bravery and sacrifice won the respect of their comrades-in-arms. The First and Third Louisiana Native Guards were composed of former slaves and free men of color – slaves who had purchased themselves under Spanish law prior to statehood, and the offspring of the slave mistresses of white slaveowners who often emancipated these women and their children, an act called manumission. Even the limited freedom that made it possible for blacks from Louisiana to bear arms against the South would not last, however, and their service would ultimately justify new repression. By the time of Eddie Robinson's infancy, Louisiana had passed Jim Crow laws prohibiting manumission and miscegenation (interracial marriage or cohabitation), obstructing minority voter registration, and legalizing every imaginable form of segregation, including the Separate Car Law.

In addition to being the year of Eddie Robinson's birth, 1919 is remembered for several historic events. In Europe, negotiations to formally conclude the carnage that had been declared "the war to end all wars" were grinding excruciatingly toward completion, though the treaty that ended World War I would do little more than sow the seeds for the next, more far-reaching global conflict, one that would claim four times as many lives. Prohibition became law, but without effective enforcement it did little more than provoke rampant bootlegging until the manufacture and distribution of liquor was once again legalized more than a decade later. In the sporting arm those who are endeavoring to discredit our Race."

Under the heading, **"We Call Attention to Some Things Which Should Be Observed by Our People,"** the *Defender* listed twenty-seven statements, all beginning with Don't. Those dealing with such issues as "vile" language, discourteous behavior, respect for police officers, avoiding brawls and refraining from becoming a public nuisance could have gone without saying, or so it would seem. Others which spoke to the differences between rural and urban life, however, are more revealing of the adjustment newly arriving Negroes from the agricultural South had to make:

Don't congregate in crowds on the streets to the disadvantage of others passing along.

Don't spend your time hanging around saloon doors or poolrooms.

Don't be made a tool or strikebreaker for any corporation or firm.

Don't leave your job when you have a few dollars in your pocket.

Don't allow children to beg on the streets.

Don't appear on the street with old dust caps, dirty aprons and ragged clothes.

Don't forget street car conductors are bound by rules of the car company which the law compels them to obey.

And most important:

Don't use liberty as a license to do as you please.

Black newspapers achieved their greatest significance - in numbers, circulation and, above all, influence – between the early years of the new century and 1960. The *Chicago Defender* was the nation's largest with circulation of more than 250,000 per week at its peak. Publisher Robert S. Abbott shrewdly extended his publication's reach by enlisting black Pullman porters to smuggle copies south of the Mason-Dixon Line. As opposition to the *Defender* grew (word spread of a young boy who was arrested in Pensacola, Florida, in 1916 for selling the *Defender),* porters often pitched bundles of papers from moving trains into the bushes alongside the railroad tracks, to be retrieved and circulated when supporters felt it was safe to do so. Robert Vann's *Pittsburgh Courier* nearly equaled the *Defender* in circulation by producing fifteen regional editions tailored to specific big-city areas across the country. Also among the most prominent were *The Afro-American* in Baltimore, *The Amsterdam News* in Harlem and the *California Eagle* in Los Angeles.

By the 1920s, there were approximately five hundred black newspapers in America. Most vigorously advocated in numerous ways on behalf of black Americans; many are identified with particular campaigns. The *Defender,* with its editorials and stories that encouraged southern blacks to move to Chicago and other northern cities, is recognized as the driving force behind The Great Migration. The *Eagle,* whose publisher, Charlotta Bass, became a target of the anti-Communist McCarthy Hearings, campaigned aggressively against the racist film, *Birth of a Nation,* which celebrated Ku Klux Klan violence while demeaning African Americans. And the *Courier* initiated a nationwide campaign for equal rights during World War II, which led to an investigation by the FBI. While fighting bigotry and oppression (and enduring the consequences), black newspapers also tried to help their constituencies as much as possible. The *Defender's* advice to newcomers was but one example. Black papers printed train schedules to help readers make plans to start a new life outside the specter of Jim Crow, published listings of employers in northern cities that did not discriminate, and identified merchants in those cities where blacks could buy "safely."

more than fifty inches of rainfall per year, the frequent beat of raindrops on the roof often soothed everyone to sleep.

Little Eddie's early years were filled with experiences that no doubt helped shape the man he would become. His parents both worked hard, their example impressing on him the value of honest labor and its benefits. He held no fewer than seven jobs from adolescence through college, and as a coach emphasized the relationship between hard work and accomplishment. His great-grandfather owned his own horse and some land, both nearly unimaginable for a black man of his generation. He operated a syrup mill – demonstrating to Eddie that it was possible, even under Jim Crow, to achieve a measure of independence and prosperity in America, the land of opportunity for all. Daddy Frank didn't smoke or drink alcohol, and the whole family went to church without fail. Mama Lydia was an especially spiritual woman, who throughout her life spoke of her God who brought them through. No wonder, then, that Grambling football players didn't dare miss weekly services or make light of clean living.

An uncle whom Eddie admired because he was always well-dressed taught him how to cut hair and told him it was a "living" he could use forever, even though it turned out he didn't need the skill beyond his college years. From that uncle he gained an appreciation for communicating self-respect through a good personal appearance, which explains Eddie's insistence that Grambling football players always dress presentably when they traveled. His daddy was quick with the belt, disciplining with physical punishment that nonetheless imparted an acute awareness of right, wrong and responsibility. The consequences of trying to sneak into a theater to see the hottest new movie, *King Kong*, or into the football stadium at Louisiana State University – administered with sharp whaps and stern words – kept him out of the kind of trouble that could have threatened his well-being or even cost him his life in the racist world of his youth. As a result, accountability to teammates as well as to coaches was non-negotiable on Eddie's Grambling teams.

Divorce altered the landscape – literally – after Eddie's sixth birthday. He cried a little boy's torrent of tears as Mama Lydia left Jackson for Baton Rouge without him. She was less than thirty miles away but it might as well have been three hundred. Daddy Frank followed a short time later, though not to reconcile with Eddie's mother or even to get him closer to her. Having decided to escape sharecropping's stranglehold, Frank landed a job as a laborer at the Standard Oil refinery built in Louisiana's capital city in 1909 (later the largest oil refinery on the North American continent). Frank remarried, and Eddie lived with him and his new wife.

Being in Baton Rouge enabled Eddie to see Lydia regularly while he was in school; she lived on 12th Street near South Boulevard, only about a mile away. Allowed the option of living with his mama after eleventh grade, Eddie treated it as an opportunity to help her make ends meet by cutting hair and working other jobs. (When he moved in, Lydia was working for four dollars a week.) Eddie also liked the way his mama made his friends feel welcome in her humble home, bringing food from the residences where she worked to provide meals for them. In the end – even though his father was happily remarried, his stepmother was caring and supportive, and he was able to stay close to his mother – the disruption and heartbreak of his broken home had a lasting effect. Eddie resolved that, when he married, it would be for life.

Neither Frank nor Lydia finished elementary school, but both understood that education opened doors that otherwise would remain closed, especially to black men in the age of Jim Crow. In addition, Frank's new wife, Ann, was a teacher. Together they all made sure Eddie went to school. He earned not only a bachelor's degree from Leland College in 1941, but also a master's from the University of Iowa twelve years later. Ultimately the value placed on learning would guide his coaching philosophy, as both tactician and surrogate father to young athletes. He became a lifelong student of his game, and 80 percent of his football players earned their degrees, one of the highest graduation rates in college football history at any level.

day at 8:15 a.m., at 3:30 p.m. to signal the end of the school day, and at the direction of a teacher to announce lunch break, class changes and fire drills. McKinley's approximately five hundred students lived within a 40-mile radius that encompassed seven parishes: Point Coupee, Iberville, Tangipahoa, East and West Feliciana and East and West Baton Rouge. At that time, high school began in eighth grade and ended after the eleventh, and the curriculum included English, Latin, "commercial geography," history, civics, arithmetic, algebra, geometry, general science, biology, chemistry, teacher training, manual training, and "domestic science," another name for home economics. African-American teachers in Louisiana were paid about $400 per year, and they taught only in all-black schools.

A lot had happened between Eddie's first encounter with Julius Kraft in 1928 and when he entered McKinley five years later. Louisiana had tightened the grip of Jim Crow by passing statutes that expanded the separation of the races in transit from train cars to all public transportation, prohibited integrated apartment buildings, and instituted poll taxes and literacy tests to make it harder for Negroes to vote if they did succeed in registering. The illiteracy rate among blacks ten years of age and older had been reduced to slightly more than 23 percent, but that still was almost three times the comparable illiteracy rate for whites in the state. The stock market had crashed and the nation was in the grip of The Great Depression; one quarter of America's workforce was unemployed. Franklin Roosevelt had been elected president, but his New Deal economic revival was yet to come. McKinley's football team had won every game it played for six straight years through 1932. The Depression, however, would present an obstacle not even Julius Kraft could overcome. Lack of funds forced the suspension of football for two years just as Eddie started high school.

While Eddie waited for his chance to compete under Kraft's direction, he developed another sporting interest. Joe Louis began making boxing history in 1934, winning several amateur championships then turning pro and winning twelve straight bouts, ten by knockout. During his career he would participate in twenty-seven heavyweight championship bouts, a record that may never be surpassed. He became Eddie's hero, though there was nothing unusual about that. Joe Louis was the hero of nearly every black American male, especially in the 1930s as he fought his way to the heavyweight championship of the world. Title fights were broadcast live on the radio, and one of Eddie's favorite memories was the time he heard the radio announcer say, "The American is entering the ring," as Louis climbed through the ropes to take on the pride of Nazi Germany, Max Schmeling. It was the first time he had ever heard a black man referred to as an "American."

For a brief time, Eddie thought he'd become the next Joe Louis instead of the next Julius Kraft. He trained in secret, and once whipped a bully who had insulted Daddy Frank just to get Eddie mad enough to fight. Neither the bully nor Eddie's father knew that Eddie had been learning to box. Eddie studied newsreels of the Brown Bomber's boxing style and won his first few bouts. Convinced he had a future in the ring, he confidently informed Mama Lydia, "I'm going to be your Joe Louis, and I'm going to buy you a house," just the way he'd heard Joe had done for his mama. Lydia didn't like the idea of Eddie taking punches, and, as Eddie told it, replied, "Well, that's all right. But I want you to get one thing clear. If you win, you can continue. If you lose, you're through." By the third round of his next fight, Eddie laughingly recalled in an interview decades later, "I knew I was no Joe Louis. So, I'm a football coach, not a boxer."

Louisiana State University had not yet opened its football games to Negro spectators in 1934, when Eddie and a friend tried to sneak into a game during the hiatus in football at McKinley. Because he had been able to attend games at all-black Southern University in Baton Rouge, it never occurred to Eddie that white LSU didn't sell tickets to Negroes, much less provide seating for them. When Daddy Frank heard Eddie talking afterwards about the unsuccessful foray, off came the belt. The lesson was simple: If you aren't allowed in, don't ask for trouble by breaking the law or ignoring the policy. Never mind whether it was fair or right; that's simply how it was. Determined to see the LSU Tigers play, Eddie found another way. He learned that he could stay for the game if he was in the stadium as a worker, so he got a job helping with various chores on game mornings and in the afternoon before play began.

McKinley's football team resumed play in Eddie's third year of high school after Kraft scraped together enough money to equip twenty-two players. He invited a group of boys to tryouts, activities that were limited to running, blocking and tackling since they had no football. They practiced all season in street clothes. Only after assuring Kraft that he could pass and punt the football did Eddie become the final player awarded a jersey. He played first-string quarterback for two years, passing to his classroom seatmate and best friend since fourth grade, George Mencer, whom he credited with making him a better student as well as a successful football player. "Eddie wasn't much of a runner," said A.C. O'Dell, who played at McKinley years later and watched Kraft's teams as a youngster. "But he could pass that ball, and he could kick. He was smart. He was a general." With Eddie at the controls, McKinley won every game, Kraft's seventh and eighth of what would be thirteen undefeated teams in a row. Already inseparable, Eddie and Mencer did even more together. Some classmates remember seeing them sweeping the halls of the school and putting stuff in the trash bin after the dismissal bell because McKinley didn't have a janitor. Eddie and George even continued on to the same college. "They were like brothers," said O'Dell, who eventually played for Eddie in college.

Eddie's final year at McKinley High School was the first season of Arnett "Ace" Mumford's historic tenure as head football coach at Southern University. One of eight black coaches with more than two hundred career victories, Mumford was inducted into the College Football Hall of Fame in 2001 with a record of two hundred thirty-three games won, eighty-five lost and twenty-three tied in thirty-six seasons. He won more games than any other football coach in Southern's history, compiling a record of

169-57-14 in twenty-five seasons that included a stretch of 36-0-2 from late '47 through early '51. During his quarter-century there, Southern won five black national championships and eleven conference titles, and produced thirty-five All-Americans.

It is one of the great ironies of Eddie's life and career that he challenged Southern from the opposing sideline for parts or all of six decades, including six games while Mumford was still the coach. He envisioned himself playing for Southern after Mumford visited McKinley in person while Eddie was the starting quarterback. He was sure he'd be recruited by the emerging legend, who already had won one black national championship at Texas College. When he wasn't, Eddie decided he'd go to Southern anyway and show the coach what he had overlooked or underestimated. Feeling ignored and rejected after about ten days, however, Eddie left for Leland College, a Baptist school with about 3,000 students located in Baker, a small town twelve miles north of Baton Rouge. Mumford must have been paying more attention than Eddie realized, because he went to Leland to try to persuade Eddie to return to Southern. It was too little, too late.

With Eddie playing quarterback and George Mencer again catching his passes, Leland's football team was competitive despite a shortage of talent. In one stretch during his last year, Eddie completed more than 70 percent of his passes. More important to him than his performance on the field, though, was what Reuben Turner, a Baptist minister who doubled as the football coach, taught him about coaching a team. Most of what Turner knew about coaching football he had learned by attending the clinic held annually at Northwestern University in conjunction with the *Chicago Tribune's* charity game between the College All-Stars and the defending National Football League champions in Chicago each August. He imparted that knowledge to Eddie in sessions at the coach's home, where they drew up plays. Turner relied on Eddie to be an assistant coach as well as the quarterback, and had Eddie run practice whenever he had to miss a workout, usually to recruit a future player. The experience developed in Eddie an understanding of strategy before and during games, the ability to evaluate players, and a knack for choosing plays based on game situations, the opposing team's strengths and vulnerabilities, and player alignment on the field.

5

TEMPLE ROOF Garden was the social hub and center of entertainment for Baton Rouge's black population from the 1930s into the 1950s. Duke Ellington, Cab Calloway, Fats Waller, Count Basie, Louis Armstrong, Ella Fitzgerald – name a famous black musician or band – all played the ballroom on the fourth floor of the Prince Hall Masonic Temple on North Boulevard, a landmark that achieved inclusion in the National Register of Historic Places in June, 1994. Young Eddie Robinson and his girl Doris heard and danced to virtually all of the Roof Garden's headline entertainers. And when they weren't upstairs, there was a good chance they were in the Temple Theater on the first floor of the same building.

The Roof Garden was an elegant room in its prime with globe lights hanging from the ceiling and a reflecting ball suspended above the center of the dance floor. A thick wood railing with ornate spindles bordered an upstairs balcony that followed the exterior walls on three sides. A separate upstairs balcony at one end was used by white city officials whenever they wanted to hear a particular big-name act while keeping their distance from the black crowd. On warm evenings, large windows wound open to bring fresh air into an almost always packed room. That allowed the sounds of the big-name performers to fill the surrounding blocks of neighborhood stores and businesses with dance music and the latest popular songs. The neighborhood had more than forty merchants and businesses, including meat markets, grocers, a hardware store, a dry cleaner, a jeweler, a tailor, a drugstore, a motor car company, a lumber company, a funeral parlor and much more.

Eddie was thirteen years old when he first noticed Doris Mott at a seventh-grade party. If he was too young for love at first sight, the combination of pretty, well-dressed, funny, smart and charming at least made him want to see more of her, a lot more. Demur, or maybe coy, Doris didn't reveal her feelings as quickly, though it wasn't long before they began holding hands and she was "dating" only him. Eddie was a handsome guy heading into high school, with a fun-loving – some would call it boisterous – personality that George Mencer helped keep under control in both high school and college. Soon Eddie and Doris were taking in a movie almost every weekend, at the cost of twenty-five cents apiece. Eddie earned his courting money by cutting hair for the bargain price of twenty cents, and working at a fish market, where he pulled down fifty cents for a half-day's work cleaning and bagging shrimp. Frequent trips to Temple Roof Garden followed once they reached high school. The music started at nine and ended at one in the morning, but it was a short walk home.

Doris's mother Lillian, one of Eddie's teachers at Perkins Row Elementary School, liked him well enough. But she became concerned at one point during high school that her daughter and her boyfriend might be getting too serious, too fast. So she shipped her off to a boarding school. It was outside Baton Rouge but not far enough away to keep Doris and Eddie from seeing each other regularly. Eventually, Mrs. Mott found out that her efforts to keep Doris from seeing so much of Eddie were not working, and accepted that the two really were in love. Mrs. Mott's worries were unnecessary. While Doris and Eddie had known since sometime in high school that they wanted to make a life together, they had promised each other that they would not let their feelings for each other keep them from getting their college degrees.

Doris's mother and father separated as Doris and Eddie were finishing college. That breakup, added to Eddie's parents' divorce, deepened their resolve to build a life together that would endure. In June,1941, not long after they had both finished college, they boarded the Mississippi River ferry to Port Allen – the same ferry some of their McKinley classmates rode to and from school. Choosing to make the moment a private one only they would share, they found a preacher and were married on the spot. On the ferry ride back to Baton Rouge, they talked about having children, taking care of their parents, and pursuing their dreams. "Eddie always had a love for football, and always knew that he would become a coach," Doris recalled. She wanted to teach as much as Eddie wanted to coach. They both knew that segregation meant they would have to find their opportunities at all-black schools. There were no immediate prospects.

The story of Eddie and Doris, or Doris and Eddie, is well told by the people who knew them through the years – coaches, players, colleagues and friends. These acquaintances described a couple totally devoted to each other, driven to achieve and delightful to be around. Doris was stylish, attractive and a touch flamboyant in her speech and manner. Eddie was an athletic-looking 6-foot-2, with a firm handshake, flashing eyes and an electric smile powered by beautiful teeth. They made a dashing couple. As parents they were dedicated to their children and determined to make a good home for them, yet unavoidably challenged by the difficult demands of celebrity and success. In decline, when Eddie was confused and dependent, Doris was there at his side, his constant, loving care-giver to the end.

"Everything with Doris was Eddie, Eddie, Eddie," said John Williams, who played for Coach Robinson in 1952 and made his home in Grambling. "When he would go on football trips, she was always there with him. She was just a nice lady, and everybody respected her because of her support for her husband." Describing Eddie's devotion to Doris, retired Grambling baseball coach Wilbert Ellis said: "He was crazy about his wife. He always said he was blessed by God; he had only one job and one wife." Sports consultant Dave Whinham, whom Eddie befriended before Whinham left coaching, and former Baylor University football coach Grant Teaff, expressed similar feelings. "She was the center of his universe," said Whinham. "She was his heart and soul," said Teaff. "They had a long, beautiful life together."

Ellis, who was four years behind Williams at Grambling, worked with Eddie at the university for almost forty years after graduating. He first knew Doris as his English teacher at Lincoln High in Ruston. "She would save up days so she could go on Fridays with her husband," he said. "She wanted Eddie to be successful. She worked with him. She helped him. She wasn't going to let anything get in the way of Eddie getting to the mountaintop in his profession. When you would see him, you would see her with him." The Robinsons often visited the home of Adolph Byrd and his wife in Baton Rouge. Their daughter Yvonne observed the same thing. "Eddie and Doris were inseparable," she said. "Anywhere you saw him, you saw her. And they were holding hands."

Doris once described Eddie as "a wonderfully committed and spiritual man" who "believes in God, family and fellow human beings," and another time wrote that, "He is a champion of all causes that he considers just." She also called him "the greatest, kindest, most caring and most loving husband and father ever." She spoke of the satisfaction she felt in seeing her husband realize his dreams and being able to support him in his pursuit of them, and referred to their lifetime together as "our career in football." She viewed the football players and other students at Grambling as her "extended family" and said of their partnership, "We are truly a team."

In the early years their teamwork included making sandwiches in their home for Eddie to take on the old Blue Bird bus when Grambling played a road game. Unwelcome in the segregated restaurants along their routes, the players and coaches would eat whatever Doris packed, on the side of the road. After games played at Grambling, her way of helping was to open her home to the combatants and cook for them. "Eddie and Doris would always have the visiting coaches and officials over to their house after the ball game," said Marino Casem, who coached Alcorn from 1964 to 1985. "We were tremendous rivals, and you wanted to beat the other guy. You wanted to win badly. But when the game was over, we were friends. We talked football, how we could help each other."

Every small town has its cliques and rumormongers, and the most privileged residents are easy targets for gossip and petty criticism. While not immune from some unkind whispers, usually among those envious of her status or wardrobe, Doris was widely respected around Grambling for the way she handled her husband's prominence. "Mrs. Robinson was a graceful lady," said former police chief Claude Lamar Aker. "He was the coach of the university, and you would think she'd be so highfalutin she wouldn't have time for you. But that wasn't her. Whoever she met, she was down to earth. She was just like Rob."

Eddie always went out of his way to acknowledge the great woman behind the successful man – "the real coach, my wife Doris." In his early years as a coach, it was Doris who reined him in when she thought he was losing control of himself and behaving badly on the sideline during games. Throughout the years, it was Doris who "adopted" many of the young men playing for Eddie who were homesick or needed a mother figure. And as Eddie's fame grew and invitations to speak became common, it was Doris who insisted that he rehearse before her so she could make sure he didn't ramble or overstay his welcome at the podium. "My wife kept me up just about all night making me wind up with five minutes," he teased during one Pro Football Hall of Fame induction speech. She was continually watchful for material Eddie could use in future talks.

"There's no question in my mind that part of his greatness came from her," said Doug Ireland, who got to know the Robinsons through the Louisiana Sports Hall of Fame. "She knew she married a man whose profile had grown to a point that wherever they went outside their own backyard, people wanted to meet Coach Rob. And she was so graceful in allowing other people access to him, and allowing him to do things that he might have felt he needed to do or he was obligated to do. She always enjoyed being as much a part of the occasion as dictated, but she was willing to step back when it wasn't time for her to be in the spotlight. Doris has always struck me as the extraordinarily gracious, uh, *royalty*, among us. In Eddie's declining years, I can't imagine anybody being better equipped to care for him, and still enjoy him as much as was possible, until the end."

Eddie and Doris started and completed their family quickly. Lillian Rose was their first-born, arriving in February, 1942. Eddie Jr. came along in late October, 1943. Eddie and Doris involved themselves in their children's lives as all good parents do. But as daughter and son grew, they experienced the inevitable burdens that come with having a famous father or mother. They never knew who might be calling when the phone rang – once it was the President of the United States! – or who might be on the front porch when the doorbell sounded. The children couldn't always go to Grambling's games, almost never the ones away from home. And the conventions and speaking engagements further interrupted the normalcy of home life.

For Eddie Jr. there was the additional matter of his father's footsteps. When he played football, he was a quarterback, just like his dad. So he was compared to his dad. And then he went into coaching, just like his dad. And he was measured by the yardstick of his dad's record. The reality is that, in the face of such expectations, the son of a renowned, successful man is rarely his equal, either in fact or in the eyes of those who judge him, no matter what he does. Seeing Eddie Jr. lead Grambling to its first outright South-western Athletic Conference championship as the starting quarterback in 1965 was a proud moment for Eddie. Having Eddie Jr. join him on the side-line in later years meant even more. "That was one of Coach's greatest thrills," said Wilbert Ellis, "having his son coach on his staff."

Eddie Jr. coached the offensive backfield and receivers on his dad's staff for fifteen seasons, but had little time to savor the experience. "At the time, there wasn't much time to think about that," he said in 2005. "When it all boils down, it was like any other situation when you work for a guy. He could be very demanding, and that caused you to be that way." This is not to say, though, that Eddie Jr. would trade those years. "It was quite an experience for me," he said, "because I had grown up around Grambling football. We got to go to a lot of places that I never dreamed I would go. And I got to go there with him."

PART TWO

Mantra

PREVIOUS PAGE:
"The best way to enjoy America," Eddie said, "is to first be an American, and I don't think you have to be white to do so ... America is the greatest country in the world."

6

GRAMBLING DID not exist by name as an institution of higher learning when the newlyweds began their life as Mr. and Mrs. Eddie Robinson in 1941. Possible college coaching opportunities were limited to two private schools, Eddie's alma mater, Leland College, and Dillard University, which was the result of the merger of Straight and New Orleans universities, or two state-supported public schools. One was Southern University, the other Louisiana Negro Normal and Industrial Institute, which then was a two-year teachers college that fielded a football team. All had football coaches in June 1941, leaving Eddie to find employment elsewhere – anywhere. He soon found himself hefting sacks of corn at the Kalmbach-Burckett Feed Mill in the neighborhood where he and Doris lived – in a house without running water. He called it the toughest job he ever had – harder work than lifting blocks of ice or delivering coal, as he had done during high school and college – and admitted hating it, mainly because of the creepy bugs that crawled over his arms and under his shirt every time he hoisted a sack of corn onto his shoulders. But it paid twenty-five cents an hour, and he needed regular wages. With Lillian Rose due the following February, the economic realities were impossible to ignore. The average house rent in America in 1941 was thirty-two dollars a month. A quarter would buy three cans of tomato soup, two cans of baked beans or two loaves of white bread.

A pound of hamburger cost double that, and eggs were almost sixty-five cents a dozen. Gas sold for twelve cents a gallon, which only mattered if you were fortunate enough to have a car.

Relief came unexpectedly in August when the feed mill foreman told Eddie to stop working long enough to take a telephone call. Grace Jackson, Doris's aunt, wanted Eddie to know that the football coach had quit at Louisiana Negro Normal and Industrial Institute. (He later learned that Emory Hines had resigned to become an assistant on Ace Mumford's staff at Southern.) Aunt Grace, who worked at Louisiana Normal, told school president Ralph Waldo Emerson Jones he should consider her niece's new husband, because he knew a lot about football. President Jones was interested; he remembered Eddie as quarterback of Leland's teams from the past couple seasons, the best teams Leland ever had. Eager to pursue the opportunity, Eddie offered to make the 225-mile trip from Baton Rouge to meet with Jones at the school. But the president told him that wouldn't be necessary; he would be visiting the capital for a meeting and would interview Eddie while he was in town. President Jones didn't realize immediately that one of his four sisters was a close friend of Doris and Eddie, and frequently met them at Temple Roof Garden. That became apparent when the lobbying effort on behalf of Eddie Robinson commenced soon thereafter.

Eddie's interview with Dr. Jones didn't go well at first. "He told me I would have to learn how to coach in order to be with his program," Eddie recounted many times. "I told him, 'You give me the job and we'll win.'" When the president of the school responded sharply that he had coached the team himself for seven years and knew what it would take, Eddie became concerned he wouldn't get the job. Baseball actually saved the day. President Jones had been a pretty fair country pitcher, as they said then, who found time to coach Louisiana Normal's baseball team while running the school. Eddie, too, had played baseball and was good at it. He changed subjects and they launched into a discussion of their favorite Negro League ballplayers. After that discussion ran its course, President Jones offered

Eddie the job as Louisiana Negro Normal and Industrial Institute's sixth football coach. Neither man could have imagined that it would be almost sixty years before number seven would be hired.

Louisiana Negro Normal and Industrial Institute began as the Colored Industrial and Agricultural School on November 1, 1901 in a little town named for a white sawmill operator, P.G. Grambling, who donated land for the school. It was founded by the North Louisiana Colored Agriculture Relief Association, an organization of Negro farmers in rural north Louisiana, to provide education for children of the members, who were former slaves, since the state wasn't making much of an effort. The original purpose was to teach students how to farm, build houses and maintain sanitary living conditions. The Association asked Booker T. Washington, pioneering head of Tuskegee Normal and Industrial Institute, for help, and Washington responded by sending Charles P. Adams, the school's first president. The school was renamed Lincoln Parish Training School the year before Eddie was born, and became Louisiana Negro Normal and Industrial Institute, a junior college, in 1928.

Adams served until 1936, when he was succeeded by the man everyone came to know simply as Prez, R.W.E. Jones. The grandson of a slave and son of the first dean of Southern University, Prez joined the faculty at twenty-one and already had put his mark on the developing institution, having started the baseball team, formed the school band and served as dean of men and registrar, in addition to teaching chemistry, physics and mathematics. He was near his thirty-first birthday when he assumed responsibility for the future of what would become Grambling State University. By 1940 Prez had established the first degree program, in elementary education, and by the 1958-59 school year, a full liberal arts curriculum was in place. He persuaded state legislators to change the 17-syllable name of the school to Grambling College in 1947, humorously contending that the change was necessary because, "By the time our fans have finished shouting 'Hold That Line, Louisiana Negro Normal and Industrial Institute,' the other team has already scored."

Eddie was twenty-two when he went to work for Prez, and was expected to be as versatile and energetic as his boss. Besides coaching the football team, Eddie mowed and lined the field before games, directed the drill team at halftime, tended to injured players, drove the team bus and, after the games, wrote and sent stories to newspapers that otherwise would have ignored the small black school's sports competition. He even made the team's first weights by filling coffee cans with cement. Still, there was only one of him; he needed an assistant coach. When he discovered that night watchman Jesse Applewhite had played a little football, Eddie asked if he'd help – strictly on a voluntary basis since there was no money to pay him for the extra duty. Together, they comprised the football "staff." After football season, Eddie coached the basketball team.

For all of this, Eddie was paid about $675 per year – less than $65 a month, and barely a third of the average annual wage in America then. Still, he was about to realize his third grade dream, and he no longer had to endure those awful bugs and beetles that lived in the sacks of corn. "When he took me out of that feed mill," he once said of Prez's decision to offer him his first and only coaching job, "I wanted to kiss him." Instead, he asked if he could start learning how to be a coach by attending the coaching clinic at Northwestern University, as Rev. Turner, his coach and coaching mentor at Leland, did. Prez approved, so Eddie made his first trip to the big city and first visit to the North, riding the train from Grambling by himself. Rev. Turner picked him up at the station in Chicago and drove him out to the Northwestern campus in Evanston where he met and learned from the famous Michigan coach, Fritz Crisler, Northwestern's own "Pappy" Waldorf, Cornell's Carl Snavely and other prominent coaches of the era, who accepted him even though he was black and they all were white. It was then that that Eddie began to believe that coaching and sports could eclipse racial differences. After that, he attended at least one clinic every year, and eventually became one of the featured speakers at many himself.

During his visit to Chicago, Eddie met another historic Robinson – the four-sport wonder from UCLA, Jackie Robinson. In 1941, Jackie's destiny to be the first black major league baseball player was not yet evident. He was better known as a collegiate football and basketball star and likely Olympian in track, than as a baseball player, good though he was at that sport, too. If pro baseball was in his future, surely it would be in the Negro League with Satchel Paige and the other "colored" stars who had no other option. Named to the college football All-America team after the 1940 season, Jackie was chosen to play for the College All-Stars against the fearsome Monsters of the Midway, the nickname attached to the Chicago Bears of George Halas because of their physically punishing style of play. The Bears had won the National Football League championship the previous December by drubbing the Washington Redskins 73-0, still the most lopsided final score in pro football history.

Among Jackie's teammates on the College All-Stars were Charley O'Rourke, quarterback of the undefeated Boston College team coached by Frank Leahy; heralded Michigan star Tom Harmon, winner of the Heisman Trophy; and running back George Franck of Minnesota, who would be named the 1941 College All-Star Game's most valuable player. Jackie wasn't the first Negro player to participate in the College All-Star Game, but there hadn't been many before him, and none who starred as he did. On the night of August 28, the All-Stars lost 37-13. But six of their points came on a 46-yard touchdown pass from O'Rourke to Jackie Robinson that was called by many the most spectacular play of the game, largely because of Jackie's sensational run after catching O'Rourke's throw. More than 98,000 fans filled Soldier Field – Eddie's first exposure to the spectacle of a big game on a big stage. It was a sensation he would relive many times in decades to come.

In addition to attending the clinic at Northwestern, coaches were invited to observe the All-Stars' practices. It was too good to be true for Eddie, who had yet to direct his first workout as a college coach. But nothing topped the opportunity to speak one-on-one with Pappy Waldorf, who in one impromptu meeting helped Eddie develop the long-term foundation of his program. It was the day Eddie was to catch the train back to Louisiana, and he wanted to say goodbye to Waldorf. He couldn't resist posing one more question, in request form, to the future hall of fame coach. "Coach Waldorf," he began, "I just got a job and I want you to tell me something a young coach could do going to his first job." Pondering his answer until Eddie began to wonder uncomfortably if he had made a mistake by admitting he was a rookie, Waldorf said, "The first thing I will tell you to do is to get a system." Eddie admitted he was not familiar with the term as it applied to coaching football, so Waldorf explained the concept. "If you want to use what you played in college," he said, "or you want to use Carl Snavely's plays, or you want to use Fritz Crisler's plays or Northwestern's plays, you diagram them and when you get back, you have them mimeographed and give them to your guys. But when you get there, you've got to have a system before you go to talk to your team."

Throughout his career Eddie called that the most useful knowledge he gained from his first coaching conference. "I think that was the beginning of whatever Eddie Robinson was all about," he said during the inaugural session of the American Football Coaches Association's Master Coach Series in 1995. All the way home on the train he drew plays he had run at Leland and plays he'd heard discussed at the clinic. "I used Michigan's spinning single wing," he said, "some of Waldorf's plays and Carl Snavely's plays." By the time the locomotive stopped at the small wooden shed that served as Grambling station, he was ready. "When I got to them, I said, 'This is the system. This is what we're doing, what we're going to play.'" Twenty years later, after Waldorf had retired from college coaching and was working for the San Francisco 49ers, he visited Eddie at Grambling. He'd always find an excuse to spend an extra day or two, talking football with Eddie.

Looking back, Eddie often marveled at the opportunity awaiting him upon his return from Chicago. The campus consisted of a handful of frame structures. The football field was almost a vacant lot, and had no bleachers. Those who came to watch his early teams had to stand beyond the sidelines or behind the end zones. The practice field was red clay – no grass anywhere, his early players told later generations. "When I got here there wasn't much to look forward to," Eddie would say, "but they hadn't done anything so there wasn't much to look back on." President Jones understood the challenge facing his young coach – better, in fact, than the confident-but-naïve rookie did. "You're gonna coach some of the guys you played against last year," Eddie recalled Prez telling him. "What you're going to have to decide is if it's good for them to be on the team, because you're not going to get anything done until you get rid of some of those boys who played against you. You're gonna say one thing, and they're gonna go do something else."

At thirty-six, the school president was still a young man himself, but he proved wise beyond his years. Some of Eddie's players couldn't accept taking orders from a coach who had been one of the opposing team's players the previous season and was barely older than they. Louisiana Normal lost its first five games under its new head coach. "I wanted to make it without having to drop anybody," he said in an interview, "but two of them got so obnoxious that I had to let them go." Louisiana Normal beat Tillotson handily in the next game, the first of four hundred eight coaching triumphs. Eddie finished his debut season with three victories; more important, he had made a leap forward as a coach by taking charge of his team.

7

"CLOSER TO ninety than to eighty," is the way Adolph Byrd described himself in February 2009. For more than fifty years he was one of Eddie Robinson's closest friends, so close that his daughter Yvonne called the Robinsons "Uncle Eddie" and "Aunt Doris," and didn't find out they weren't really part of her family until she was in her thirties. In addition to confidant and trusted advisor, Adolph also filled another very important role in Eddie Robinson's long and immensely successful coaching career. He was Eddie's eyes and ears – his chief recruiter – "from Baton Rouge to Zachary, Port Allen, Plaquemine, Denham Springs, Bogalusa" and points in between.

"I was at McKinley, coaching football, but I was teaching at the middle school," Adolph recalled. "That was back in 1951. I told him, 'Coach, they've got some boys down here that you need to come and look at.' He said, 'I tell you what, Byrd. You take this envelope and put it in the back of your car. And if you see a boy that you think is Grambling material, take a scholarship form out of it and go to his parents, and tell them he has a scholarship. Tell them I'm going to require him to go to class and to go to church, and if he comes up here and doesn't get an education, we failed. He didn't fail; we will have failed him.' He told me, 'The only thing I want to know about the boy is his name, his age, his weight, his height and his position. If you send him, he's got a four-year scholarship. And, if he wants, a five-year, because I'll red-shirt him.'" Using this simple system, Adolph figures he sent between three and four hundred players to Grambling. Many of them eventually became well-known pros.

Adolph Byrd began attending McKinley when Eddie Robinson was in eleventh grade and leading the football team to another unbeaten season. Byrd looked up to Eddie for the triple-threat player he had become by working hard to develop passing and kicking skills to go with his running ability. Adolph hoped that when he was old enough to play for Julius Kraft, he could become a really good football player, too. And he did. While Eddie was starring at Leland College, Adolph Byrd grew into a starting lineman who helped McKinley extend its string of perfect records. His final season, when McKinley finished unbeaten for the 13th and final year in a row, was Eddie's first as the football coach at Louisiana Negro Normal and Industrial Institute. Adolph wasn't sure what would come next in his life. After high school he joined former classmates hanging out at what became known as Crooks' Corner.

The intersection of South Boulevard and South Thirteenth Street in Baton Rouge had a little of everything in 1942. A barbershop, shoe shop, drugstore, night club, restaurant and pressing shop served the people who lived in the modest homes nearby. The merchants and residents started calling it "Crooks' Corner" because of all the teenagers – mostly boys – who congregated there with no particular purpose other than to talk loudly, laugh at each other and roughhouse some. "We weren't doing anything bad," Adolph Byrd assured. "We weren't really crooks. All of us youngsters had finished high school and didn't have nothing to do, so we were just hangin' out." They were all there on the corner, Adolph recalled, when Eddie Robinson showed up one afternoon looking for football players. Between the ones he'd thrown off the team during his first season as head coach and the ones who had finished school, he had a lot of holes to fill on his second team in the fall of 1942. "He came back from Grambling during the summer, and he wanted to know why were we standing on the corner,"

Adolph said. "We told him we didn't have jobs and were not going to go to school because we didn't have the money. He told us if we could get to Grambling, we wouldn't have to pay for anything but we'd have to work in different areas, like the cafeteria and the gymnasium and other different areas. He said we could get a place to stay, and three meals a day . . . and they'd change the linen on Friday."

Twenty-three congregants of Crooks' Corner, including Adolph Byrd and A.C. O'Dell, found their way to Grambling. "When we got there," recalled Byrd, "all of us had a place to stay, three meals a day, and we went to class. From seven to eight-thirty, we worked. From nine 'til three, we were in class, and from three-thirty until dark, we worked." During football season, of course, they practiced. Not all of the Crooks' Corner crowd played football, and not all of them stayed. But there were enough reinforcements among them, and they were good enough, to make a once-in-a-lifetime difference during the 1942 season. With thirty-three of the school's sixty-seven male students in uniform, the football team opened with a 27-0 shutout of Alcorn A&M. Eight games later, Louisiana Normal had completed its entire season undefeated, untied and unscored-upon, winning by an aggregate 93-0. The final record almost certainly would have been 10-0 if Eddie had not felt compassion for his mentor at Leland, who had beaten him on a last-minute play in his first season. "The next year we were much stronger and had to play Leland in the last game," he said. "Coach Turner wasn't doing well, and I wasn't particularly interested in beating him. So I just canceled the game. He meant more to me than the win." That 1942 team matched a feat accomplished by the 1939 Tennessee Volunteers but unequaled in more than sixty-five years since. *Sports Illustrated* featured the 1939 Vols in a lengthy piece titled **"Absolute Zero"** in 1998, but never mentioned the comparable achievement by the 1942 Louisiana Negro Normal and Industrial Institute team. Eddie always wondered why.

No one will ever know what Coach Rob and his gang from South Boulevard and South Thirteenth could have done for an encore. The Japanese attack on Pearl Harbor occurred December 7, 1941, just after he completed his first season as coach. By the time his perfect second season concluded, the United States of America was immersed in all-out war in both Europe and the Pacific. On November 13, 1942 Congress lowered the draft age – the minimum age when a young man could be ordered into military service – from twenty-one to eighteen. With all of Eddie's players over eighteen, there would be no more intercollegiate football competition at Louisiana Normal for the duration. Many universities suspended play in 1943; the majority resumed in 1944. "Most of us went into the war," Adolph Byrd explained, "and a lot of them didn't come back to school afterwards. Some of them passed in the war, and some just didn't want to go back to school after what they went through."

The clash of Uncle Sam and Jim Crow made the war years doubly difficult for blacks who were asked to fight for freedom abroad even though at home they were required to accept the restrictions on freedom that segregation imposed. The contradiction felt by most black Americans as patriotism quickly became the dominant theme of the collective national effort was powerfully articulated by James G. Thompson, a cafeteria worker from Wichita, Kansas, in a letter he wrote to Robert Vann's *Pittsburgh Courier* in January, 1942:

DEAR EDITOR:

Like all true Americans, my greatest desire at this time, this crucial point of our history, is a desire for complete victory over the forces of evil, which threaten our existence today. Behind that desire is also a desire to serve, this my country, in the most advantageous way. Most of our leaders are suggesting that we sacrifice every other ambition to the paramount one, victory. With this I agree; but I also wonder if another victory could not be achieved at the same time. After all, the things that beset the world now are basically the same things which upset the equilibrium of nations internally, states, coun-

ties, cities, homes and even the individual.

Being an American of dark complexion and some 26 years, these questions flash through my mind:

Should I sacrifice my life to live half American?

Will things be better for the next generation in the peace to follow?

Would it be demanding too much to demand full citizenship rights in exchange for the sacrificing of my life?

Is the kind of America I know worth defending?

Will America be a true and pure democracy after this war?

Will colored Americans suffer still the indignities that have been heaped upon them in the past?

These and other questions need answering; I want to know, and I believe every colored American, who is thinking, wants to know.

This may be the wrong time to broach such subjects, but haven't all good things obtained by men been secured through sacrifice during just such times of strife?

I suggest that while we keep defense and victory in the forefront that we don't lose sight of our fight for true democracy at home.

The "V for Victory" sign is being displayed prominently in all so-called democratic countries which are fighting for victory over aggression, slavery and tyranny. If this V sign means that to those now engaged in this great conflict, then let colored Americans adopt the double VV for a double victory . . . The first V for a victory over our enemies from without, the second V for victory over our enemies within. For surely those who perpetrate these ugly prejudices here are seeking to destroy our democratic form of government just as surely as the Axis forces.

This should not and would not lessen our efforts to bring this conflict to a successful conclusion; but should and would make us stronger to resist these evil forces which threaten us. America could become united as never before and become truly the home of democracy.

In way of an answer to the foregoing questions in a preceding paragraph, I might say that there is no doubt that this country is worth defending; things will be different for the next generation; colored Americans will come into their own, and America will eventually become the true democracy it was designed to be. These things will become a reality in time; but not through any relaxation of the efforts to secure them.

In conclusion let me say that though these questions often permeate my mind, I love America and am willing to die for the America I know will someday become a reality.

The *Courier* turned Thompson's letter into a full-fledged campaign for an end to racial prejudice. Staff artist Wilbert L. Holloway created a "Double V" insignia that promoted **"Democracy – Double Victory, At Home, Abroad."** It was used on placards, shirts and pins, and as the identifying logo for all related material published in the *Courier*. Photographs of people who endorsed the campaign, blacks and whites, were prominently featured in every issue. Double V clubs were formed across the country, and the *Courier* began publishing a Double V column for news from such clubs. A photograph of two attractive young women published with the caption, "Debs (as in debutantes) Support DOUBLE V Drive" evolved into a regular photo feature, the "Double V Girl" with a pretty young woman flashing the Double V sign every time. Unsuccessful Republican presidential candidate Wendell Willkie openly supported "Double V" and was pictured in an edition of the *Courier* wearing a "Double V" insignia pin, which could be purchased by mail for five cents. "Double V" became so widespread that black publishers were investigated for wartime sedition by J. Edgar Hoover's FBI and the U.S. Postal Service, and the *Courier* was banned on U.S. military bases out of concern that the issue of equal treatment would divide the troops and undermine morale.

Adolph Byrd was unaware of the "Double V" campaign while he was a soldier, and is certain that it had no effect on conditions in the Fourth Armored Division commanded by General George S. Patton. Byrd drove trucks for Patton, hauling howitzer shells across Europe. After the Battle of the Bulge, his cargo changed to "displaced" persons, a euphemism for prisoners, and mail. The segregated army greeted him at every American camp. "Everywhere we stopped," Byrd said, "all of the places were white. And all of them had a dog named 'Nigger.' They'd call the dog – 'Here Nigger' – and the dog would come running. All we could do is take our food and our water, and drive off. They had places to stop where the whites could stay, but we could not stay. If we were out overnight, we had to sleep under our trucks – they were high and we could sleep under them – or in the cabs. Or we slept in the bed part where we hauled ammunition, if we had delivered our load and were empty." Black soldiers were a special curiosity to the French, Byrd recalled. "When we were in France, the people there used to question us after dark, because they were told by the white soldiers that all niggers had tails, and they came out after dark."

Pvt. Jackie Robinson, who became 2nd Lt. Jackie Robinson after a contentious trip through Officer Candidate School at Fort Riley, Kansas, was subjected to a similar array of demeaning treatment. He angrily resisted the insults and degradation, and ultimately faced court-martial at Fort Hood, Texas for his confrontational responses (winning acquittal on all charges). Adolph Byrd, meanwhile, was among the majority of black soldiers who resignedly endured more of the only life they'd ever known. "We were used to it," he said. "At home in Baton Rouge, we couldn't walk on the campus of Baton Rouge High School. We could go down and stand on North Boulevard and look through the fence at the football games, but we couldn't go in." It continued after Byrd had married and started a family. "We would go uptown during the holidays, and my kids had to come back home to go to the bathroom. There was a fountain there that had a 'colored' sign, and one that had 'white.' We couldn't drink out of the 'white' fountain." Daughter

Yvonne will always remember the difference: "The white fountain was cool water. The colored fountain was over by the room where they kept the mops and brooms, and the water was as hot as if they boiled it."

On June 8, 1946, the *Chicago Defender* published a complete list of the Army's Negro casualties in World War II. Among the 2,604 names, more than half, 1,432, had been killed in action. The banner headline put the Double V campaign in perspective without ever mentioning it: **"They Died In The Name Of A Democracy We Must Yet Achieve."**

8

"MEN WITH dependents" qualified for deferment from military service at the beginning of World War II. By January, 1943, Eddie and Doris not only were the parents of Lillian Rose but also were awaiting the birth of their second child. So Eddie was spared the danger common to everyone in uniform, as well as the humiliation that accompanied all black soldiers during World War II. When Eddie Jr. arrived in late October, his father was coaching football and girls basketball at Grambling High School. The girls lost the state basketball championship game by one point in 1943, the same year the football team made it to the state finals for all-black schools. "We had gone undefeated," said Luther Ensley, who played on that team with his twin brother Frank, "and we had our last game, to be played in New Orleans, to be declared state champ." That game, however, wasn't the story that became part of the Eddie Robinson legend.

Luther and Frank almost missed playing for the state championship because their father needed them to help harvest a field of cotton. Time-consuming and back-breaking work, it took between twelve hundred and fifteen hundred pounds of hand-picked cotton to make a bale after the seeds were removed, and one good picker could be expected to pick about two hundred fifty pounds in a day. So the Ensley twins figured to be good for less than half of the cotton it would take to produce one bale each day they worked, and the harvest was expected to produce numerous bales. "Aw, we could pick that cotton," Eddie told the twins' daddy, and sent his entire high school team into the field. Luther and Frank's teammates finished the job in record time, and the twins joined them in the title playoff against Gaudet. "We lost by seven points," Luther recalled. A year later – Eddie's last season as interim high school coach – Grambling won it all.

The Robinsons had been living with President Jones and his family since Eddie started coaching Louisiana Normal, a beneficial arrangement on his meager monthly pay though less than ideal for a young couple that already had started a family. The situation, coupled with the wartime suspension of the college's football program, eventually left Eddie unsatisfied and restless. "I was having some tough personal times," he said later in his life. "Coaching the high school guys kept me occupied. But it was one of the toughest periods for me because I knew my college guys were risking their lives every day in the war. I had gotten to the point where I was getting tired of the job."

The principal at McKinley called and asked him to become, in effect, the next Julius Kraft. Eddie sent Doris and Lillian Rose back to Baton Rouge, and informed his boss that he didn't want to stay any longer. Ralph Waldo Emerson Jones, however, was not about to lose the young man he already realized could accomplish an important part of the vision he had for the school still named Louisiana Negro Normal and Industrial Institute. Prez came up with a stuffy little apartment, and convinced Eddie to stay. On their own to find relief from the typical discomfort of continuous heat and humidity spring through fall, Eddie and Doris borrowed a window fan each night from a nearby laundry, while saving up money to buy their own.

Coaching a bunch of returning war veterans would have been daunting enough for a seasoned leader with years of sideline experience. For a 26-year-old about to direct his third collegiate team – after a two-year hiatus, no less – dealing with post-war attitudes and the particular disillusionment that discharged black soldiers felt upon re-entering the still-segregated society in America represented the ultimate test when Eddie resumed his career as a college football coach in 1945.

Adolph Byrd, who returned to Grambling for the 1946 season, expressed the feelings he and many others were experiencing as they came home and tried to pick up civilian life where they had left off. "I had been in the Army forty months and overseas thirty-four months," he said. "When I got back I was mad at everybody. I had been in a combat zone so long that the only thing we knew was, if it was payday, it wasn't Sunday. You lose track of the days. The only thing you know is it's another day. We were treated in the Army just like we were treated here, but you had to stay there. If you left, they'd write you up as AWOL and punish you. I knew two guys who killed themselves."

Making the situation even more difficult for battle-fatigued black soldiers as they came home were the racial stereotypes that permeated the American consciousness from coast to coast. Some examples from the Jim Crow Museum of Racist Memorabilia:

"Maybe Cream of Wheat ain't got no vitamins," a Negro cook named Rastus said in one printed sales pitch for the hot cereal. *"I don't know what them things is. If they's bugs, they ain't none in Cream of Wheat, but she's sho' good to eat, and cheap. Cost 'bout 1 cent fo' a great big dish."*

In a display advertisement in *Life Magazine*, the lady of the house is shown asking herself how she'll ever manage to feed a group of surprise guests. But smiling Aunt Jemima, in her best servant's garb, reassures her: *"Don' yo' fret none, honey, 'cause here's how to fix a reg'lar feast as easy as 1-2-3. Jus' follow dese directions . . . for de world's mos' delicious pancakes."*

Stores routinely sold ash trays, salt and pepper shakers and cookie jars in the forms of Negro caricatures. The Sambo figure was particularly popular. Postcards ridiculing the race were mixed in with those that depicted a vacation spot or famous landmark.

The radio program *Amos 'n' Andy,* heard by forty million listeners at its peak of popularity, had evolved from a nightly 15-minute dramatic serial to a half-hour weekly comedy that depicted Amos Jones, Andy Brown and their entourage (George "The Kingfish" Stevens, leader of the Mystic Knights of the Seas lodge who was always pitching some get-rich-quick scheme, his wife Sapphire, beautician Madame Queen, Amos's wife, Ruby, and a slow-moving hanger-on named "Lightning") in ways that accentuated the characterizations that Daddy Rice had popularized roughly a hundred years before.

"Even when things like these don't register, they shape us," said David Pilgrim, who holds a doctorate in applied sociology and is founder and curator of the Jim Crow Museum of Racist Memorabilia at Ferris State University in Big Rapids, Michigan. "There is tremendous power in something being normal. It's part of life, so it's accepted."

Martin Luther King was sixteen years old and finishing his freshman year at Morehouse College, still years away from proclaiming his trademark message of equality and nonviolence, when these conditions presented Eddie with the first significant opportunity to express his remarkable thinking on the subject of how best to overcome racial prejudice and achieve success in America. In the crucible of the next fifty-plus years, Eddie's beliefs influenced thousands of athletes and students, and set a tone of moderation and self-determination for all who came in contact with him or Grambling football. Eddie's mantra, imparted with consistency and unwavering conviction, can be expressed in a series of statements gleaned from his own words:

America is the greatest country in the world . . .

I learned very early on that despite a lot of obstacles, America gives you opportunity . . .

If you are willing to pay the price, you can be anything you want here, even if it sometimes comes slow. . .

If you work hard enough, dreams can come true . . .

We need to understand the American system and the Constitution . . .

To use the system, we have to understand it; that's what education is all about . . .

If you aren't prepared, you can't take advantage of the free enterprise system and the best judicial system in the world . . .

Everything can change, including the laws, if you're willing to pay the price . . .

You can't expect to change something if you don't understand it . . .

The best way to change attitudes is to prove them wrong by showing you can do it, whatever IT is . . .

The best way to enjoy life in America is to first be an American, and I don't think you have to be white to do so . . .

"Like all great leaders, he refused to be defined by external circumstances, deciding very early in life that he would be a positive human being," wrote Bill Curry, former NFL star, successful college coach and Southerner by birth, in a column for *ESPN.com* when Eddie died. "In this era of many claims and few results in the area of uniting disparate segments of society, Robinson used our sport to do precisely that . . ." Said Melvin Spears, who coached at Grambling after Eddie retired, "Eddie Robinson believed in the American way: If you worked hard, did all the little things, you could be successful. He didn't see black and white. He saw hard work. He broke down barriers." Doug Williams put it another way: "He never told us that life was unfair and that we'd have to be ready for it. He always told us that this was America, and we could be anything we wanted to be." Said Greg Brown, who played for Eddie during the early 1970s, "We never discussed race relations, because it was more about individuals and how each one of us prepared for whatever endeavor we wanted to accomplish."

The message wasn't always immediately well-received, especially by battle-hardened men who had risked their lives "for a democracy we must yet achieve," as the *Defender* put it. A.C. O'Dell, who played for Eddie from 1947 through 1949, recalled, "A lot of the players would call him, under cover, 'Tom'." But nearly all, sooner or later, realized his wisdom, O'Dell added. "He was a smart man. The moves he made were based on knowing what the race problem was, knowing the kind of problems we would run into, and what it would take to change things. He taught us patience." Thelma Smith-Williams, who published *Grambling: A Pictorial History* in 1980, also heard unflattering shots at Eddie from "townfolk" after she moved to Grambling in 1956. "Rob was one of the few that was swimming on both sides of the fence," she said. "They called him a white man's nigger – I'm just telling it like it is. He never answered. He just went on being nice to people, being himself. In the long run, it paid off."

One of Eddie's favorite lines was, "I don't believe anybody can out-American me." Charlie Joiner, an 18-year pro who played for Eddie in the turbulent decade of the 1960s, saw his coach back up that claim daily: "The thing he always wanted to stress," Joiner said, "was to be a good citizen and a good American. He wanted to make sure we adapted to the American way of life." Added James "Shack" Harris, who played with Joiner at Grambling and had a noteworthy National Football League career himself: "We didn't always believe in the American flag at that time, but Coach Rob did."

The resumption of football at Louisiana Normal provided President Jones with the perfect opportunity to implement his blueprint for using football to elevate the profile of his anonymous little college, whose name would be changed to Grambling before the 1947 season. Notre Dame was the model, and Eddie was key. His football team needed to make a national name for itself (and the college) by winning consistently. At the same time, education had to come first; Eddie's players had to earn their degrees so they could be successful in life, not just play football until their eligibility was used up. Prez strongly believed that Eddie needed to progress as a coach until others recognized him as one of the best in his profession nationally, white or black. A natural rivalry had to be developed, and the whole package had to be marketed. Publicity was out of Eddie's direct control, but he would play an integral part in it, too, as the face of the program. Finally, cracking the pro ranks was imperative. Eddie had to develop a player who could show everyone that blacks could excel in head-to-head competition against those who were paid to play. If he could find one, others surely would follow, which would spread recognition of the college.

Some might call it fate. Others, luck. Whatever the explanation, the time Eddie spent at Grambling High School during the war proved instrumental to his expedited execution of Prez's plan. The star player of Eddie's state championship high school team in 1944 was a bruiser named Paul Younger, a prodigy destined to become one of the most significant figures in football history. "Boots" Moore, considered the equal of Grambling's most heralded quarterbacks from later decades, was a three-sport phenom who also excelled as a baseball pitcher and warranted a tryout with the Harlem Globetrotters basketball team. And, of course, there were the Ensley twins, joined by older brother Robert, who was serving in the military when Eddie coached the Grambling High team.

Soon to be nicknamed "Tank," Paul Younger stood taller than six feet and weighed more than two hundred pounds, unusual dimensions for a boy only sixteen years old, a very young age for a college freshman. He played tackle on both offense and defense but possessed the speed of a running back, a rare combination for athletes of that era. Curiously, this exceptional physical specimen went unnoticed, or underestimated, by college football recruiters, quite possibly because he was a black teen living in rural Louisiana. So he decided to stay at home and play for his former high school physical education teacher, who had returned to his regular job coaching the Louisiana Normal football team. From the start Eddie made sure Younger knew he had the potential to be a groundbreaker both for his school and for generations of black football players. "He pulled me aside one day and told me that if Tank Younger failed, Grambling football, Eddie Robinson and black football would also fail," Younger said. "Throughout my career he reminded me that I was representing all of black football." Tank always said he was fine with that burden: "I never really had any doubts about making the pros."

Robinson devised two plays that enabled Younger to carry the ball while remaining a lineman. Tank would line up at tackle, then often shift to end. Running plays named end reverse and end around, he scored twenty-five touchdowns in his first two seasons. As a sophomore he once ran eighty-six yards to set the school record for the longest non-scoring run from scrimmage. These feats were enough to convince Eddie to move his wunderkind to running back full-time for his last two seasons. Immediately Tank was the most dangerous player in college football. In his junior year he ran for more than 1,200 yards, caught eight passes for another two hundred yards, and threw four touchdown passes on fullback option plays. Of course, Tank didn't do it alone, and he was quick to acknowledge the teammates who helped make his gaudy numbers possible, including tackle Adolph Byrd. "A runner is only as good as his blockers," he said, "and I was fortunate to have some good blockers." Tank concluded his college career with sixty touchdowns scored, eleven touchdown passes thrown and 2,631 yards rushing, and was voted black college football player of the year after his senior season. Grambling's won-lost records during his four years were

10-2, 6-6, 9-2 and 8-3, a combined thirty-three victories and thirteen losses. It would be almost twenty years before Grambling enjoyed four consecutive seasons with more combined success.

As prolific as Tank Younger was in college, the game that meant the most to him was one in which he did not directly account for a single point – though he did gain seventy yards rushing. "I got my biggest kick in college the night we beat Southern," Tank told Doc Young of the *Chicago Defender* during an interview at the beginning of his rookie season in the National Football League. Young had asked him to tell about the biggest thrill of his college career. "I played fifty minutes of the game, but I didn't score. I was used mostly as a decoy. I got a big kick out of that game because it was the first time in history we had beaten Southern." Grambling upset Ace Mumford's Jaguars 21-6. It was Younger's junior season. One of only two losses for Southern in 1947, that stunner would be Eddie's only victory in six tries against the coach who had blown the chance to have him become a part of Southern's legacy. But it furthered the realization of the master plan President Jones had laid out for Eddie. That upset sowed a seed for what would become the biggest spectacle in black college athletics years later, the annual Bayou Classic between Grambling and Southern.

Soon after Tank graduated in the spring of 1949, the Los Angeles Rams signed him to a free agent professional contract for $6,000. Eddie and Prez extracted that sum from Rams scout Eddie Kotel by driving him around the Grambling-Ruston area for hours, ostensibly on a sight-seeing tour, until Kotel finally offered the amount they had decided Tank should receive to begin his historic pro career. The National Football League had integrated three years earlier when the Rams signed Kenny Washington and Woody Strode as a condition of being able to play their games at the Los Angeles Coliseum. And groundbreaking coach Paul Brown, leader of his namesake Cleveland Browns, ignored a gentlemen's agreement among members of the All-America Football Conference that barred African American players from that league, and signed two future members of the Pro Football Hall of Fame in Marion Motley and Bill Willis. But Washington and Strode had played at UCLA; Motley was signed off the Great Lakes Naval Training Center team; and Willis was an All-American on Ohio State's 1944 unbeaten national champions, coached by Brown. Younger became the first player from a historically black college to get a chance to play pro football.

"You've been voted the best football player in the country from a black school," Eddie told Tank at the Grambling whistle stop as he climbed aboard the "colored" car of a train bound for Los Angeles. "You are now going to play for the Los Angeles Rams. And if you don't make it, they can always say, 'We took the best you had to offer, and he wasn't good enough.' And in all likelihood, it may be years before another black guy gets an opportunity." Tank Younger looked his coach in the eye and replied, "I can't make it as a basketball player, but if they're playing football, I'll make it."

Make it, he did. In a 10-year career Tank Younger was selected to play in the Pro Bowl, the league all-star game, four times; helped the Rams play for the National Football League championship four times in a seven-year span; scored thirty-five touchdowns; and gained almost 5,000 yards combined as a runner and pass receiver. The Rams' overall record during the Younger Years was 66-37-5, a winning percentage only slightly below the same calculation for his four seasons at Grambling. "He made the most of an opportunity," Eddie said, "and because he did, players from schools such as Grambling saw the chance to become a professional player, too." About two hundred Grambling players would follow in his footsteps, and many more from other black schools across the Jim Crow South. Eddie's words echoed behind them: *If you are willing to pay the price, you can be anything you want here, even if it sometimes comes slow.*

9

BOTH "TANK," as the moniker for Grambling's first recognized football star, and "The Bayou Classic," as the name of the annual national showcase of black college football, originated in the audacious mind of Collie J. Nicholson, a pioneer of Younger-like proportions in the field of public relations. For thirty years "the man with the golden pen" extolled the attributes and accomplishments of Grambling players and their coach, while helping to establish within collegiate athletics the position now routinely called "sports information director." At the same time, he was the marketing genius behind the series of national and international productions – the "Classics" – that put Grambling in the spotlight coast to coast in the 1960s and 1970s, beginning with a game between Grambling and Morgan State at Yankee Stadium in 1968. "All the things Grambling did, Collie was the instigator," said R. L. Stockard, who was the first black sportswriter for a white, general-circulation newspaper in the state of Louisiana. "He didn't hesitate to walk into (Yankees owner) George Steinbrenner's office and say, 'Man, we need some money.'" Howie Evans, sports editor of *The Amsterdam News,* said: "He created a legacy by opening doors previously closed to black colleges. His media efforts and his salesmanship made owners and scouts of professional teams aware of Grambling and other black colleges."

Just as Eddie Robinson knew at an early age he wanted to be a football coach, Collie Nicholson decided he wanted to be a writer while he was a student at Winn Training School in Winnfield, Louisiana. An avid reader, Collie enjoyed what could be done with words used the right way. Seeing his byline on his first story in the local paper was pretty exciting, too. That gave him the confidence to write to the editor of the *Shreveport Sun*, a black weekly published eighty miles from his hometown, to propose writing a weekly column. To his surprise, the editor said he could start right away.

Collie graduated from Winn the same year Adolph Byrd and the Crooks' Corner crowd finished their days at McKinley. He enrolled at Southern but left during his first year, partly because he couldn't afford to stay and partly because he just didn't feel comfortable in the big-school environment. Osiah Johnson, a former Negro League ballplayer who was helping Prez with Louisiana Normal's baseball team, saw Collie play baseball during past summers. After Collie left Southern, Johnson offered Collie the same deal Eddie told the Crooks' Corner guys they could get – a job at the school, three meals a day, a place to stay and an education. The only difference was he wanted Collie to play baseball. Prez himself greeted Collie when he arrived, and placed him in a job in the business office. Within six months Collie went from zero to sixty (words per minute) on the typewriter, a skill he would put to great use the rest of his life.

The opportunity at Louisiana Normal was short-lived, as it was for Eddie's football players. Collie was among the first black recruits in Marine Corps history when he reported for duty in September, 1943. Parlaying his documented newspaper experience with his newfound typing skill, he became the first black correspondent the Marines ever had. He was assigned to the Pacific Theater, but racial prejudice within the Corps denied him the opportunity to cover combat. So he reported extensively on the men and support activities of the all-black 51st Defense Battalion in the Gilbert and Marshall Islands. Collie produced a four-page daily newsletter circulated on the island bases, and filed stories about the troops that were distributed, after review by Marine Corps censors, to black newspapers across America via the Associated Negro Press. America's black press would remember Collie and welcome him enthusiastically after the war as he sent a steady stream of stories about Coach Eddie Robinson and the (soon-to-be-renamed) Grambling College football team.

Discharged from the Marine Corps in March, 1946, Collie was planning to finish college at the University of Wisconsin, his goal a journalism degree. On his way north, he decided he'd stop in Grambling just long enough to say goodbye to friends there, including Prez. That was it. Prez convinced him to finish his degree right there, and arranged for him to have a part-time job and a place to stay. He graduated in 1948 and went right to work fulfilling the public relations and marketing aspect of the master plan Prez had outlined to Eddie when he convinced him not to leave a few years earlier. Not long after that, Paul Younger became "Tank" – the name by which he'd be known for the rest of his life. Collie had only to see him run over would-be tacklers, virtually crushing them with his strength and power. "I'd been in the South Pacific," Collie explained, "and it reminded me of what I saw those tanks doing there."

There is no evidence to suggest that Marshall Hunt and Collie Nicholson ever met. They were born twenty-five years apart, yet their professional similarities seem more than coincidental, even if it was mere happenstance. Hunt was a 24-year-old, one-man sports department at the *New York Daily News* when a certain baseball player came to town and he decided to make a career out of covering the star exclusively. Collie was twenty-five years old when he stopped in north Louisiana on his way to a life elsewhere, and wound up chronicling (and orchestrating) the emergence of a college and a coach on the national stage. Hunt eventually sold his inside stories about George Herman Ruth to a newspaper network he created, making himself the first syndicated writer. Appealing to the same collection of black newspapers that welcomed his wartime dispatches, Collie became, in effect, the Grambling News Service. Undoubtedly, Babe Ruth would have been bigger than life and the most famous baseball player of all time without Marshall Hunt chronicling his every move, and Eddie Robinson would have become a coaching icon and an African American hero even if Collie had not documented his countless accomplishments in papers across the country. But both legends grew to greater proportions because of the writing of their personal scribes, who shared an appreciation for description and an interest in detail that most writers during the early decades of the 1900s lacked.

"Collie is the one who promoted and glamorized Eddie Robinson," said Marino Casem, who became one of Eddie's closest friends. Casem knew first-hand that Eddie was not a self-promoter. "Eddie would not have been as big a name without Collie. The talent was there, but the motivation and the ideas weren't there. It took somebody to proclaim it. Eddie was dedicated to getting his players and Grambling prepared for competition in the world. He was dedicated to getting his players to graduate. He was dedicated to getting his players to be at the top of their game when they played you. That was his world. Eddie was about Grambling; Eddie was about north Louisiana." Collie, said Casem, was the outside influence Eddie needed. "Collie was the bell-ringer. He would say, 'C'mon, let's make that speech over here today.' And Eddie did what Collie told him to do. He could carry it out. Collie would write the speech, and Eddie would embellish it, add the sideline comments."

Hunt and Collie both mastered the art of purple prose, the flamboyant, florid style that dominated newspaper writing until the 1960s. Describing the Bambino testing a new bat in his hotel room in Hot Springs, Arkansas, in March of 1924, Hunt wrote:

> *"He gripped the bludgeon firmly and swung it far back . . . The heavy piece cut downward, severed from a bedpost a large brass ball and propelled it devastatingly against the bureau mirror, which collapsed into a thousand flashing daggers . . ."*

Describing the Babe's mood on February 27, 1925, as he prepared to leave Hot Springs for spring training in St. Petersburg, Florida, Hunt wrote:

"Vast gloom unprettied the features of Herman Ruth today when he gave himself to serious contemplation of the distressing futility of many things and how increasingly tough it's becoming for an honest feller to get along in this wearying world."

Typical of Collie's lavish use of the language, he began an account of Grambling's rigorous practice regimen with:

"Coach Eddie Robinson rolls his Grambling College gridders out of the hay every morning at an hour when most burglars are returning home from a hard night with the crowbar and wedge."

His preview of Eddie's 1949 squad acknowledged the graduation of Tank Younger, *"one of the all-time greats of sepia football,"* yet promised, *"even with the 'Tank' gone, the pre-season prophets, through force of habit no doubt, have labeled Grambling as the team to beat."*

Describing "Buck" Buchanan, one of Eddie's four players eventually inducted into the Pro Football Hall of Fame, Collie wrote:

"Despite his size he is catty afoot and full of competitive zest . . . Buchanan considers it a personal affront to give up a yard and refuses to associate with teammates who can't block and tackle. Truly a remarkable athlete, he is tormented by ineptitude and constantly strives for self improvement."

The greatest beneficiaries of Collie Nicholson's publicity barrage were Grambling's players. Beginning with Tank Younger, Collie made it impossible for professional scouts to ignore the stream of black prospects coming out of the little school in rural northern Louisiana. "Collie's articles opened the road for all black athletes in this part of the country," Eddie often said. "One NFL scout told me that he was glad when Collie left Grambling in the early 1980s because he had written so much about our student-athletes that his team felt they had to draft our players. He said that if they didn't draft a player after all Collie had written, and somebody else drafted him and he did well, that he would lose his job as the team's scout." Collie's impact went beyond exposure for the players, Eddie added. "Collie's writing brought people to our games. Collie helped establish us as more than a school in northern Louisiana. (He) did a whole lot for our program by putting our vision of what we could do in the mind of the public."

Collie began working on Eddie's own image at the start of the 1950 season.

"Eddie Robinson, a mild-mannered pigskin perfectionist, is known as the 'Cinderella coach' of Negro football," he wrote. *"In less than ten years, Robinson has developed football at the North Louisiana Institution to such an extent that football and the Grambling Tigers have almost become synonymous on the national scene . . . Robinson has a combination baseball-football-basketball record of 190 victories, 3 ties and 59 defeats . . . The youthful mentor is a moulder (sic) of championship squads and a builder of character. Four athletes he touted have been signed to professional contracts (including) Paul "Tank" Younger, considered by many the finest football player to come out of a colored college in recent years . . . Robinson's coaching success stems from the fact that he will often work hours to perfect what appears to be only a minor detail. His football teams are noted for their crisp blocking, sharp tackling and wide-open play . . . "*

Despite Grambling's first losing record since Eddie's initial season as coach (3-5-1), Collie in May, 1952, again touted Eddie to readers of black newspapers across America – in a manner Marshall Hunt surely would have admired:

> *"Grambling College can never be expected to stay out of the news as long as resourceful Eddie Robinson is directing its athletic fortunes . . . Though virtually lost in the Louisiana bushes, Grambling, largely because of Robinson's efforts, holds strong claim to sectional mastery in athletics in its neck-of-the-woods. Flippant savants boast proudly that the institution sends more fellows into professional sports each year than any other school its size in the country . . . Robinson is a hard worker, a high-velocity producer and a stickler for facts and figures. A good example of the latter is his up-to-date accumulation of notes and letters of information on over 200 of his boys – all former athletes. This personal file, by his own admission, helps him keep detailed records of what the Grambling graduate does after he leaves school . . . If you are looking for a coach, minister, teacher, postal clerk, principal, carpenter, bricklayer, electrician, mechanic, plumber, baseball, football or basketball player, Robinson knows the fellow for the job – one of his boys . . . Robinson likes to boast occasionally, and takes pride in telling everybody that 'my boys always get jobs'."*

Collie's persuasive writing notwithstanding, neither Eddie nor Grambling football achieved real, lasting fame in his first ten seasons. Tank Younger's career and the unscored-upon, unbeaten team of 1942 represented the first big steps, but five decades lay ahead, years filled with star players, championship teams and showcase games. The journey would lead from north Louisiana through Jackson, Lorman and Itta Bena in Mississippi; Montgomery, Alabama; and Jacksonville and Miami, Florida to New

York, Philadelphia, Chicago, Houston, New Orleans, Los Angeles, Honolulu, and even Tokyo. Off the football field, meanwhile, an even bigger story would unfold along a course that linked Louisiana, Arkansas, Mississippi and Alabama with Tennessee, North Carolina and the nation's capital. The history-making datelines included cities everyone had heard of – Nashville, Montgomery, Little Rock, Birmingham, Washington – and many not so familiar, among them at least a half-dozen small towns in Mississippi and a place called Selma in rural Alabama.

The 1950s would come to be known as the decade of a great awakening in America as an isolationist nation, exposed by war to the world beyond its shores and forced by enemy aggression to recognize and harness its own immense capability, began to modernize, expand and achieve its full potential. With that came the opening events of the modern Civil Rights Movement as black America demanded an end to Jim Crow and the oppressive ripple effects of all that it represented. As much as Eddie wanted to focus on football, he was required by the tragedies and triumphs of the parallel era, with its outrages and acts of courage, to assume a different kind of leadership role. His involvement would be overshadowed by the actions of the more vocal and visible, yet it would be pivotal in the lives of many, particularly the young men who played for him.

"Eddie transcended his time," Marino Casem said in 2009. "Back when Grambling was just a small school, when he first took over, Eddie was bigger than life. Young kids, and young adults – grown people who were young and didn't have any hope or aspirations to be anything – the only thing they looked up to was Eddie Robinson. For all the young people in north Louisiana, the biggest thing to them and the role model for them was Eddie Robinson . . . how he dressed . . . how he spoke . . . the things he cared about. His nonviolent way of getting things done was a guide which they looked to.

"When they would have racial problems in north Louisiana," Casem recalled, "they'd call Eddie. And Eddie would intercede. Eddie would always try to mediate the incident. Times could be tight; kids might want to strike or something. Eddie would always be the intermediary. He'd be the person to go in and say, 'Let's solve it this way. Let me talk with them.' He'd go in and talk to the powers-that-be, and they'd turn it over to him. They'd say, 'Eddie, you handle it. Just don't let this happen.' He'd go back and say, 'We can do this and we can do this, but let's don't do it this way. He'd intercede between white America and black America in north Louisiana."

Eddie's influence was felt not only in times of conflict, Casem added. "Eddie would vouch for kids when they wanted to get a job. Or say a grown guy, who might not have been a student at Grambling but was just somebody who wanted to get a loan to buy a car; they'd come to Eddie and Eddie would go talk to the bank and reference the guy. They didn't have anything to look forward to but an Eddie Robinson. He was the pillar. It wasn't the minister. It wasn't the priest, or it wasn't the undertaker. It wasn't a lawyer. It was Eddie Robinson. He was the biggest, most respected pillar in that area of the country."

PART THREE

Journey

10

HISTORIANS DIFFER in their views of exactly when the Civil Rights Movement began in America. Some say efforts as far back as the 1930s cannot be ignored, and that they represent the beginnings of the activism that gained popularity and attention in Alabama in the mid-1950s under the leadership of the Southern Christian Leadership Conference (SCLC) and blossomed after formation of the Student Nonviolent Coordinating Committee (SNCC) in 1960. Others identify Jackie Robinson taking the field with the Brooklyn Dodgers in 1947 and President Truman's executive order that integrated the armed forces in 1948 as the events that marked the dawn of change in response to public pressure. Still others peg *Brown vs. Board of Education* (actually the consolidation of separate cases filed in four states and the District of Columbia in 1951) as the tipping point. *Brown* represented a strategy frequently referred to as "mass action," while the boycotts, sit-ins and marches that typified the Movement at its height under SNCC and the SCLC are identified as "direct action." Most Americans who lived through "direct action" consider it the most-recognizable face of the Civil Rights Movement. If so, a credible argument can be made that the opening salvo actually occurred in Baton Rouge in June, 1953.

Eddie was out of the state, attending classes at the University of Iowa in pursuit of his master's degree in physical education, as the summer of

1953 heated up. Rev. T. J. Jemison, born the same year as Eddie but in Selma, Alabama, organized a direct action protest after seeing "buses heading into south Baton Rouge, filled with people standing behind rows of empty seats." The pastor of Mount Zion First Baptist Church, who had been in Baton Rouge only four years, was appalled by the bus company's failure to implement a city ordinance adopted four months earlier that established a first-come, first-served basis for seating white and black passengers. The company had not made certain its drivers were informed of this exception to Louisiana's law requiring segregated seating on public transportation, so nothing changed. The inaction and resulting confusion, coupled with an increase in the fare from ten to fifteen cents, brought matters to a head.

Drivers went on strike after two in their ranks were suspended – one for assailing a black woman who sat in what before the new ordinance would have been a seat reserved for a white passenger, and the other for seeking to have a black man arrested for sitting in a seat the driver thought should be saved for a white passenger. The issue, they insisted, was the preservation of segregated seating. Independent black buses had been out-lawed a few years earlier because they threatened to put the city transit system out of business since so few white residents relied on public transportation. As a result, black riders, including Eddie's Mama Lydia, represented more than two-thirds of the city bus system's passengers and revenue. In response to Rev. Jemison's call to action, they refused to ride the city buses.

Crosses were burned outside Mount Zion First Baptist Church and Rev. Jemison's home, and the councilwoman who authored the new seating ordinance began receiving threatening phone calls. Drivers' wives picketed city hall. Undaunted, the United Defense League (UDL), founded by Rev. Jemison to direct the protest, immediately organized a network of car pools called the Free Ride System to provide black residents with alternative transportation. More than a hundred vehicles are said to have been utilized, ranging from an ambulance to a twenty-year-old Dodge sedan. The UDL held mass rallies nightly, the second one occurring at McKinley High to raise money to pay for gasoline sold at cost to Free Ride drivers by a black businessman who owned several filling stations.

The boycott ended after three days with a compromise Rev. Jemison deemed sufficient, even though it did not entirely eliminate segregated seating on the buses or satisfy all of the boycott's participants. His response to those who wanted to broaden the boycott to attack the principle of segregation sounded a lot like something Eddie Robinson would have said. "You cannot change traditions and customs overnight," Rev. Jemison said. Two years later, Dr. Martin Luther King and the Montgomery Improvement Association modeled the more famous Montgomery Bus Boycott after its forerunner in Baton Rouge, adopting many of the tactics Rev. Jemison and the United Defense League had devised. Dr. King in his memoir wrote that Jemison's "painstaking description of the Baton Rouge experience was invaluable."

Willie Davis, one of the greatest Green Bay Packers of all time and a member of the Pro Football Hall of Fame, was one year into his Grambling career when the bus boycott played out in Baton Rouge. Though the action itself had concluded by the time he took the field for summer practice his sophomore year, it remained a topic of conversation, both in Baton Rouge and as far north as Grambling. To Willie and his teammates, the boycott was a shocking departure from the way blacks had always accepted life as they knew it in the South. "Texarkana itself, where I grew up, had every racial thing that you typically encountered anywhere," Willie recalled more than fifty years later. "Blacks had their own special bathrooms, and all that. We traveled by bus to many of the places we went to play, and we'd stop at a place and you just automatically knew that you probably had a special bathroom you were expected to go into. You look at those things today, and you think how interesting it is that it was not a bigger issue. It's almost like everybody had lived with it if they grew up in the South. You just didn't go anywhere expecting anything much different than what you got."

The possibility of altering the "seemingly inevitable" is what made the bus protest in Baton Rouge so intriguing. It provided a glimpse of how blacks might be able to change things for the better if they stood up to Jim Crow. "I didn't know, in many ways, what to think of it," Davis admitted. "You know, college kids always played some role in those events for the most part. But Coach Robinson pulled us together and had a conversation about not doing anything that was going to get you more or less in trouble. In many things like that he would definitely get to you early, and consciously try to explain why you shouldn't get caught up in it. He would say things like, 'The most important thing for you is to stay focused on getting an education, and not get caught up in some of these things.' And really, in many ways they made sense." While Eddie discouraged his players from getting personally involved, "he was dearly concerned," Davis said. "He had shared a big part of his life, growing up in Baton Rouge. He had lived through segregation himself. Many times he would say something like, 'Hey, one of these days this thing is going to change, but I don't know when.' He'd say, 'Right now, we can't get caught up in it. We need you to think about this football team.' Maybe that's where that term 'coachable' first got its meaning. If you were coachable, you pretty much adhered to what the coach said. And that was on, or off, the field."

It is no surprise that Willie Davis took Eddie's words to heart regarding the budding civil rights struggle. Eddie was the father figure in Willie's life from the night he had dinner with Willie and his mother and said the magic words that brought Willie to Grambling. "My mother never wanted me to play football," Willie recalled. "My mom and dad were divorced, and I grew up with the single parent thing with my mother (and a brother and sister who were much younger). I think that's one of the reasons she didn't want me to play. She didn't know how she'd take care of me if I got hurt. I finally convinced her when I was a junior in high school to let me go out for the team. Because down in that part of the country, if you have any chance of being an athlete and you're not involved in football, people would be asking what's wrong with you." Willie didn't miss a game in two seasons at Washington High, and was team captain as a senior.

"When coach Robinson came to Washington High in Texarkana," Willie said, "we had won the state championship and there were four of us he was interested in. I had never gone to Grambling and really had heard very little about Grambling there in Texarkana. Most of the black colleges you heard about there were Arkansas State and the schools in Texas, like Texas Southern, Wiley College, Prairie View and places like that. He came to our school that day and spent the whole day talking to us. Actually, I thought he maybe had convinced a couple of the guys that they might consider Grambling." Willie's mother, Nodie Bell Allen, couldn't leave her job to meet Coach Robinson during the hours he spent at Washington High. So she invited Eddie to come to dinner at her house that evening.

The head chef at Texarkana Country Club, Nodie Bell made one of her menu specialties, roasted chicken. While they ate, it was hard to tell who was recruiting whom. "Oh, your mama's cookin'!" Eddie kept saying. "Nobody makes it better," Willie assured. "We all had a great meal." Nevertheless, Willie remained unconvinced and uncommitted as the time for Eddie to leave drew near. When Eddie wrapped up his recruiting pitch, he shrewdly focused not on Willie but on Willie's mother. As Willie recalled: "Coach got up and said, 'Well, I guess we better head back to Grambling. There's just one thing I must tell you before I leave, because we try to tell a parent everything they should expect. If Willie goes to Grambling, he has to go to church every Sunday.' With that, my mother came up out of her chair and said, 'Oh Willie! You gotta go to Grambling!' Somebody obviously had told him how religious my mother was." It became a running joke between Eddie and Willie in the years ahead. Whenever Eddie saw him, he'd grin and say, "Ah, Big Dave. I knew what to say, huh."

Two historic events during 1951, one involving the University of San Francisco football team and the other centering on Drake University's star runner and passer, Johnny Bright, underscored the reasons why Willie and his Washington High teammates were almost certain to attend and play football for a black college fairly close to home. Although universities outside the South had slowly begun to open their teams to black players, much of the nation was far from ready to embrace them.

The San Francisco Dons won all nine of their games during 1951, a record that certainly was deserving of an invitation to a bowl game. The most likely bowls were the Orange and Gator, both played in Florida, or the Sugar, played in New Orleans. In the age of Jim Crow, however, an invitation to any of those southern bowls was contingent on the Dons leaving behind their two black players, running back Ollie Matson, a future member of the Pro Football Hall of Fame, and linebacker Burl Toler, considered the best player on the team, who became pro football's first black official after injuries cut short his playing career. Members of the San Francisco team were unanimous: Everybody goes, or nobody goes. So nobody went. Baylor (8-2-1) played in the Orange Bowl (and lost to unbeaten Georgia Tech), and the Gator Bowl matched unranked Miami (8-3-0) against twentieth-ranked Clemson (7-3). San Francisco badly needed the extra revenue a bowl appearance would have brought. Without it, intercollegiate football at USF was discontinued after that season, and the 1951 San Francisco team began referring to itself as "undefeated, untied and uninvited," a catchy tag that became an enduring epitaph. At a 50th anniversary reunion and celebration honoring the players from that team, Dan Boggan, senior vice president of the National Collegiate Athletic Association said, "When you think about the time the decision was made by the Dons not to play in the bowl . . . it gives me hope that we as people will continue to learn that standing together, we are stronger."

By the time University of San Francisco players had turned down a bowl game rather than leave Ollie Matson and Burl Toler at home, Johnny Bright was recovering from a broken jaw, his hopes of becoming the first African American to win the Heisman Trophy dashed by a racially-motivated, in-game assault on October 20, 1951. The attacker was Oklahoma

A&M defensive end Wilbanks Smith, who slugged Bright in the jaw on a running play – well after Bright had handed off the ball. The dirty blow was captured in a sequence of six photographs that won a Pulitzer Prize for *Des Moines Register* photographers John Robinson and Don Ultang, and made the cover of *Life Magazine*. What became known as "the Johnny Bright Incident" resulted in rules changes concerning illegal blocks and blows, and mandating the use of improved helmets with face guards. But neither the player nor the coaches who urged him to "get that nigger" – nor the university which allowed the unsportsmanlike behavior – were ever punished by either the Missouri Valley Conference or the NCAA. Drake withdrew from the conference in protest of the incident and the lack of disciplinary action against Smith or A&M. Johnny Bright was drafted by the Philadelphia Eagles of the National Football League in 1952, but chose to play in Canada rather than be Philadelphia's first black player. "I didn't know what kind of treatment I could expect," he said years later. He became a star for the Edmonton Eskimos and was named the Canadian Football League's most outstanding player for the 1959 season. He played thirteen seasons, gained 10,909 yards rushing, and is considered the greatest running back in CFL history.

11

WILLIE DAVIS' arrival at Grambling was made more difficult by his three Washington High teammates, who all chose to attend all-black Arkansas AM&N, later known as Arkansas-Pine Bluff. "I will never forget that first night," he said. "It was the first time I spent a night away from home without it being a relative. You could hear kids coming in from all over the state and from Texas; we had a few guys from Texas. Many of them knew each other or had played against each other. In my case, I was flat-out isolated. I didn't know anybody and had not played against anybody, as far as I knew, that was coming into Grambling at that time. It turned out there were a couple guys I had played against, but I didn't know they were there at that time. That night it was like I never slept. I got up the next day, and I'm still thinking, 'I don't know if I like it here.'"

Two days later Willie flagged down a milk truck and hitched a ride to Shreveport, about seventy miles west of Grambling. He had made the decision to leave, but "when I got to the bus station," Willie recalled, "one of the assistant coaches was there. He said, 'Where you going?' I said, 'I'm just going home.' He said, 'Nah, you gotta come back. Coach Robinson sent me to get you.' I went back, and the whole environment changed. We started practicing and I immediately felt a part of everything. Four years later, I'm graduating and feeling good about the whole thing."

Willie decided to attend Grambling because of Eddie Robinson, and he stayed at Grambling because of Eddie Robinson. "I was always concerned about my mother," Willie said, "whether she was okay. And I would talk to him about it. Many times when I came to his office, he would call her from there. She literally loved coach Robinson from the time he talked about me attending church. When we'd first get on the phone, she'd say, 'Coach, is Willie still going to church?' He'd say, 'Yes, he is.' He was like a father." Eddie also helped Willie cope with the ups and downs of dating the same girl for three years, until she graduated a year ahead of him. "Once we were having a little problem," he said, "and I went to Coach. He could tell something was bothering me, and said, 'What's wrong? What's the problem?' I said, 'Aw coach, I don't know.' He said, 'Is it your girl?' I said, 'Yeah,' and he laid out everything you encounter with a girlfriend. He made you feel like you could go to him with any kind of problem."

The Willie Davis Years were good ones for Eddie and Grambling, better even than the Tank Younger Years in some respects. Twenty-nine victories in four seasons were four less than the Younger teams produced, but Willie's squads posted four straight winning seasons (to Tank's three), lost only eight games (to Tank's thirteen), and had a higher career winning percentage. After returning from the Shreveport bus station and finding his comfort level on the practice field, Willie started every game at linebacker in his freshman season. The team won seven, lost three and tied two. While Rev. Jemison was leading the transit rebellion in Baton Rouge the following summer, a rules change abolished two-platoon football at the collegiate level. That allowed Willie to start at offensive tackle as well as linebacker during his sophomore season. That team won eight and lost two. Graduation left some holes to be filled the next year, and when several other players were declared academically ineligible, "it kinda took the heart out of our team," Willie said, explaining only four wins, two ties and three defeats in 1954. Rebounding spectacularly in his senior year, Willie and his teammates made Grambling history, compiling the only 10-0 record the school ever had and winning Grambling's first black national championship. With Willie leading the defense, the national championship team allowed but fifty-four points all season. Only the unscored-upon Crooks' Corner team of 1942 held opponents to less in Eddie's fifty-seven seasons as head coach.

The 1955 team's success should not have been a surprise to anyone who read Collie Nicholson's preview of the coming season. Presciently, Collie had written:

"The Tigers gave a tip off of '55 expectations late last season when they scored 167 points in the last five games . . . Chief assets are fine all-around line speed, excellent receivers and a surplus of fast and clever runners . . . Co-captains Joe Dixon and Willie Davis, a pair of bear-sized but active tackles, are giving the front wall a handsome look and should cut quite a dido (sic) on both offense and defense . . . Davis and Dixon, along with All-Midwest Conference center Melvin Lee (and seven others) round out a rugged middle line array capable of charging into the campaign for a rousing round of giant killing . . . A capable gridiron craftsman, the coach views the campaign with rosy but not necessarily glowing optimism . . ."

Winning the black national championship elevated the stature of Grambling's football program among the Historically Black Colleges and Universities (HBCUs). The premier programs during that era included Arnett Mumford's Southern Jaguars, Morgan State of Baltimore, Prairie View from Texas, Tennessee State, and Jake Gaither's Florida A&M Rattlers, host of black college football's national showcase, the Orange Blossom Classic. Begun in 1933 as the unofficial but de facto national championship game for black college football, the Orange Blossom Classic was the equivalent of the all-white bowl games at a time when black football was ignored by the white press. Annually, Florida A&M would invite the black team generally considered the best in the nation for a showdown in December. The *Pittsburgh*

Courier selected the black national champion from 1920 through 1980, and while the title was shared by two or more teams several times, most often the winner of the Orange Blossom Classic received the trophy outright.

Grambling won all nine of its games to earn the invitation to the 1955 Orange Blossom Classic, outscoring its opposition 302-33. Florida A&M had won seven and tied one to that point, with a combined 348-66 result. Both defeated Bethune-Cookman that year, Grambling by 26-7 and A&M in a shutout, 32-0. In the only other yardstick game, A&M routed Mumford's Southern team, which went into the game unbeaten in eight games, by a 51-0 score. (Southern and Grambling had not played each other since 1948, the year after Grambling's upset victory.) Previewing the big game, Russ Cowans in the *Chicago Defender* advised the anticipated crowd of 40,000 fans to pay special attention to game-breakers Adolphus Frazier and Willie Gallimore of A&M and Grambling's Edward Murray, a sophomore speedster from Houston whom Willie called "one of the greatest running backs I'd ever seen." After recounting their many long touchdown runs during the season, Cowans wrote, "The big classic will be the power of Grambling against the speed and power Coach Jake Gaither has developed in his T formations . . . and from this distance it looks very much like Florida will emerge the winner."

With Willie dominating on defense and Murray scoring two touchdowns, one on a 75-yard run, Grambling beat A&M 28-21. Willie's memory of the landmark victory remained vivid more than fifty years later. "There was an article in the paper the next day that said Paul Brown came to town to look at Adolphus Frazier and Willie Gallimore, and went away talking about Murray and Davis. They credited me with twenty-eight tackles that night. I don't know how many I had, but I know how well we played." Paul Brown indeed noticed, too. Willie Davis signed with Cleveland in the spring of 1956, though he wound up in the Army before the '56 season began and never played in a regular-season game for the Browns. Military service ultimately landed Willie in Green Bay when the Packers traded for him before the 1959 season, based on the recommendation of another Packer great, Hall of Fame tackle Forrest Gregg. Gregg played with Willie on the Fort Carson Mountaineers, the base team at Fort Carson, Colorado, and upon returning to Green Bay told coach Vince Lombardi that Willie was "the best guy on our team."

Finally out of the Army and looking forward to trying to make something of his interrupted pro football career, Willie was distressed and disillusioned when he learned of the unexpected trade. "I was working as a substitute teacher on the west side of Cleveland, " he said, "and I had signed a contract two weeks before, believing I was going to go to camp as the left tackle for the Browns. I was driving home and I heard on the radio that I had been traded to Green Bay. My first reaction was, 'Oh my god!' Green Bay was considered the Siberia of football. I was ready to go to Canada. Saskatchewan had pursued me more than even the Browns at the time I came out of Grambling. As far as I was concerned, I was headed to Canada. Coach Lombardi himself changed my mind. He said to me, 'You're going to come to Green Bay and you're going to play left end for us, and we're not going to try to put you at any other positions. We believe you can do the job for us.' It was the confidence he showed in me on the phone. I thought, 'Maybe this is the place I should go.' I started every game that next season and played every game the next 10 years."

Playing for Vince Lombardi - on some of the most famous pro football championship teams of all time - afforded Willie a unique opportunity to experience playing for three of football's most historic coaches. To be asked to compare them is only natural. "I can tell you, there's no coach I've ever seen who was better with Xs and Os and how to play the game than Paul Brown," Willie said. "Lombardi had this ability to get you to feel a part of the game, to be engaged. He made you feel you were playing the game out of personal satisfaction. From Coach (Eddie), I learned the basics about the game, but most of all, being able to go to him as a father figure was extremely important. If I had gone to a major school, I'm not sure I would have made it, because I needed that father-counseling that much."

Lombardi succumbed to cancer at the age of fifty-seven, eleven years before Willie became a member of the Pro Football Hall of Fame in 1981. That made Eddie the obvious choice to be Willie's presenter at the induction ceremony in Canton, Ohio. After calling "the honor and privilege of presenting and seeing the enshrinement of Willie Davis . . . one of my most gratifying moments in football," Eddie praised his former player for greatness in football, in business and in life. "To be a captain of the Grambling football team now," he said, "you are judged by the standards of Willie Davis." His remarks, of course, included the retelling of the moment that shaped Willie's life – the turning point in Willie's recruitment thirty years before. With Willie amused by what he knew was coming next, Eddie said:

"It is frightening now as I stand here and think what might have happened if my pride would have overruled me, and I had walked out of Willie's home when he couldn't make up his mind whether he wanted to go to Grambling and, frankly, his mother was not too concerned about him playing football. But before I closed the door I walked back and said, 'There's one thing I forgot to tell you, that if Willie Davis comes to Grambling, he'll be in Sunday School and church every Sunday.'"

As Nodie Bell gazed proudly at her son, Eddie concluded: "I had Willie Davis."

12

UNLIKE TODAY'S college football coaches, Eddie had no time to revel in his first national championship at the end of the 1955 football season, nor even to concentrate solely on recruiting the next wave of runners, passers, blockers and tacklers. He was busy coaching the Grambling basketball team and its Tank Younger-Willie Davis equivalent, six-foot eight-inch Robert Hopkins, an Adolph Byrd referral even though this one didn't play football. Dubbed "Lil' Abner" by the ever-glib Collie Nicholson, Hopkins led Grambling into the National Association of Intercollegiate Athletics (NAIA) playoffs in 1955, and set thirteen collegiate scoring records during his four-year career, including averaging almost thirty points per game; scoring thirty or more points in ninety-one games; and making fifty-one free throws in a row. A feature story by Collie in January 1954 told it all:

> "Basketball fans in North Louisiana are scurrying about in search of an untapped source of superlatives to describe Grambling's sophomore cage star Robert Hopkins. . . . In 46 college games "Lil' Abner" has managed to twist between or around men guarding him for 1,281 points with a variety of hooks, driving layups, overhand, under-hand, backhand and push shots. A spectacular performer since his first college game in December of 1952, he has hastened the aging process of

*at least 25 coaches by a couple dozen years. Players trip each other up
every game, trying to muzzle him, and opposing coaches have tried to
double and triple-team him – all to little avail. (He has been) called a
"wonder in the bucket and a fast breaker without superior. . . ."*

As Hopkins neared the end of his fabulous career at Grambling in
1956, Collie went at it again:

*"In a sudden outburst of candor, Coach Eddie Robinson leaned
back in his office chair and called Robert Hopkins 'the greatest all-
around college basketball player in the game.' For Robinson, a fatal-
ist to the core, this impromptu phrase was long overdue."*

Hopkins attended high school in Jonesboro, a small town about thirty
miles south of Grambling, and attracted the attention of several college
coaches, not only for his outstanding basketball ability but also for his baseball prowess. He once hit five home runs in one game in high school,
though the fifth was disputed because he hit the ball *through* the wooden
fence instead of *over* it. "One school," he recalled, "told me, 'You come on
up here, and, hell, man, you don't have to worry about going to class.' My
intention as a young man finishing high school was to be a coach. How
could I be a coach if I didn't go to class?" When he told one coach he did-
n't think his clothes were nice enough for him to be comfortable on campus, that coach told him, "We'll buy you some clothes."

Eddie, meanwhile, used the same approach whether he was recruiting
standout football players the likes of Willie Davis or a budding basketball
star such as Robert Hopkins. "When he was recruiting me, Coach Rob spoke
at our high school athletic banquet a couple times," Hopkins said, "my junior year and my senior year. He always said, 'Son, you've got to go to school,
and you've got to graduate.' My mother was highly impressed with that.
She told me, 'You need to think about it because he said you've got to go to

class, and you're going to have to go to church.'" That's how it was, too. "He would be over in the dormitory on Sundays, Hopkins recalled, "making sure all of the athletes got up and went to church. Coach Rob looked at you as more than just a piece of property out there playing ball for him. That's one of the things many former athletes at Grambling, and many of the parents of the kids he recruited, can appreciate. He always stressed moral values and getting an education. You had to go to class, and then if you needed tutoring, he would have somebody to help you. I was weak in math, and he had someone to come and help me in math."

Eddie served as head basketball coach at Louisiana Normal-Grambling (in addition to head football coach) for thirteen seasons, a particularly demanding combination during the six to eight weeks from mid-October to early December when the sports overlapped. "We practiced mainly in the evenings Hopkins said. "He'd leave the football field and come straight to basketball practice. He didn't turn it over to anyone else; he did it. He always made time to do both." Conditioning and repetition were hallmarks in basketball, just as in football. "Coach was a fanatic when it came to conditioning," Hopkins said. "He had this drill called the Flying Three. We'd run baseline to baseline, shooting layups. We'd run it for an hour. You were going to work hard, and you were going to be in superb shape. You were going to be ready. There were times when Coach would get us up in the morning, like three-thirty or four o'clock, and we'd go practice if he didn't like the way we were running or we didn't score a hundred points."

Although his passion was football, Eddie Robinson was a very good basketball coach, too. When he resigned as basketball coach in October 1956 – not coincidentally the fall after Hopkins graduated – Eddie had won two hundred eighty-eight games and lost one hundred twenty, a success rate just over 70 percent. Over that same time, his football teams won eighty-nine, lost thirty-seven and tied seven – a winning percentage roughly equal to the basketball team. Hopkins became a three-time All-American, and probably will forever reign as Louisiana's all-time career scoring leader with 3,759 points – ninety-two ahead of Louisiana State's Pete Maravich. (Hopkins played four varsity seasons, while Maravich played only three because freshmen were ineligible for varsity action during his college career. Maravich holds the record for the highest collegiate career scoring average at 44.2 points per game.)

It was Eddie's personal coaching, Hopkins said a half-century later, that elevated "Lil' Abner" to record-setting heights and enabled him to succeed as one of pro basketball's early black players. "He would go out and work with me individually," Hopkins said. "He would get out there sometimes for over an hour, working on individual skills with me. I was a little surprised, knowing he was a football coach, that he would take that much time to teach individual skills." Eventually, Hopkins realized that Eddie's emphasis on basketball technique simply matched the attention to the fundamentals of blocking and tackling that left such a lasting impression on so many of his football players. "Coach was a teacher," Hopkins said. "It didn't make any difference what sport it was. He was an excellent teacher. He would put a chair on the floor and a cone, and have me practice my footwork and crossovers, and teach me how to do reverses and fake reverses. Coach would teach 'clock pivoting' – from three o'clock to six o'clock, or three to nine; front turn, rear turn. He helped me tremendously. It added to my game from the standpoint of being able to do so many of the things that smaller people did, the ball-handling and things like that. Before I got to Grambling, my high school coach didn't want a big guy to take a dribble. He wanted you to get as close as you could to the basket."

Partly because Eddie could use Younger's pioneering experiences in pro football to prepare Grambling athletes who came after him, and partly because black players already were playing for five of the eight National Basketball Association teams by the mid-1950s, it was not quite as much of a landmark moment when Hopkins was drafted after his senior season. Hopkins signed with the Syracuse Nationals, and played four seasons as a teammate of the first black player to participate in an NBA game – Earl Lloyd of

West Virginia State. Still, racially hateful behavior made it unpleasant in some league cities, particularly St. Louis, Minneapolis and Fort Wayne. "We couldn't eat in the hotel restaurants in those places; you had to use room service," Hopkins recalled. "We had to wear towels on our heads coming onto or leaving the floor because people would spit on us. I'm not sure I could have made the transition as well as I did without Earl; Earl taught me the ropes. I couldn't have had a better teacher."

Hopkins wasn't the prolific star as a pro that he was in college, but he was a solid contributor, usually coming off the bench. Syracuse, which won the 1954 NBA championship, made four straight trips to the playoffs while Hopkins was part of the team. A knee injury ended his career in 1960. That year, Grambling won the National Association of Intercollegiate Athletics (NAIA) national championship behind sophomore center Willis Reed, who would later become an NBA star. Adopting much of what he learned about coaching while playing for Eddie – but tempering the fanatical emphasis on physical conditioning – Hopkins became a successful college coach. In sixteen seasons at Prairie View, Alcorn State, Xavier of New Orleans, Southern and Grambling, he developed players who went on to successful NBA careers, coached one unbeaten team, won conference championships and qualified for the NCAA tournament. He also coached the Seattle Supersonics for twenty-two games during the 1977-78 season, and was the principal architect of the Seattle team that beat the Washington Bullets in five games to win the 1979 NBA championship. His eye for talent led the Sonics to draft center Jack Skima from Illinois Wesleyan eighth in the first round and to steal guard Dennis Johnson from Pepperdine with the twenty-ninth selection in the second round. Sikma became a seven-time NBA all-star, and Johnson was most valuable player in the NBA Finals when Seattle won the title and a five-time NBA All-Star who also won two NBA titles with the Boston Celtics later in his career.

In 1999, the Louisiana Association of Basketball Coaches selected a 15-man "All-Louisiana College Basketball Team of the Century." Maravich was voted "player of the century." Among those joining him on the all-century team were three players from the decade of the fifties: Bob Pettit, a member of the Pro Basketball Hall of Fame who played at Louisiana State; Jackie Moreland, an All-American at Louisiana Tech; and Grambling's "wonder in the bucket," Bob Hopkins.

13

DISNEYLAND OPENED near Los Angeles in July 1955 – unquestionably the most fantastic playground in the history of American amusement parks upon its debut. Negroes were welcome to come and enjoy the fun and excitement of this fabulous make-believe world the same as whites and other minority groups. Walt Disney stressed tolerance and diversity, even then. His visionary creation was roughly 1,800 miles from the heart of Jim Crow Country, but it could have been located on another planet. Blacks and whites ate, drank and used the bathroom alongside each other without incident in Frontierland, Adventureland, Tomorrowland and Fantasyland. At the same time, life was becoming uglier, more contentious and more violent by the minute in Mississippi, Louisiana, Alabama and Arkansas.

On August 28, barely a month after Disneyland opened to the integrated public, 14-year-old Emmett Till disappeared near Money, Mississippi, a cotton mill town of four hundred residents in the northwest part of the state. Till had come from Chicago to visit relatives; it was only his second visit to the South. Accounts differ, but all versions support the conclusion that he violated Jim Crow social tenets either by whistling at, making suggestive remarks to, or possibly touching Carolyn Bryant, the attractive young wife of white store owner Roy Bryant, as she worked in the store. The boy's ravaged body, bound by barbed wire to a 150-pound cotton gin fan, was found a few days later in the Tallahatchie River. He had been beaten with an ax and shot in the head. An Illinois Central train brought him home to his horrified mother, Mamie Bradley, on September 9. Angered by the brutality of Emmett's murder, she insisted that her son's casket remain open during his funeral at Church of God in Christ so that the sight of his disfigured body and mutilated face could make a lasting impression on all who saw it. Many civil rights historians believe the accounts of Emmett Till's murder and the graphic photographs published in many northern newspapers after the funeral provided impetus for the Civil Rights Movement by calling national attention to the extreme nature of racial injustice in the South.

On Saturday, September 17, Eddie Robinson, Willie Davis and the rest of the Grambling football team began their march to the 1955 national championship by drubbing Paul Quinn College 39-0 in the season opener. That same day, the *Defender* published full pages of photos of Till's funeral, which had been attended by thousands in Chicago the day before. "For me, personally," recalled Willie, "that stuck with me as much as anything. I'm sure if I had been asked, or if I was part of an organized group, I would have been prepared to do anything to go and bring about change or just redeem that situation itself. But when you're in a situation like that, with a bunch of football players, you just don't go much further than what the team asks you to do." And even at that early stage of his career, Eddie discouraged any type of involvement or response. His foremost concern, throughout the emerging struggle, would always be the safety and well-being of the student-athletes entrusted to his direction.

Roy Bryant, 24, and his half-brother, J.W. Milam, 36, were charged with Till's murder a few days after the boy's body was found. Their speedy trial began two days after the funeral and lasted two weeks. The all-white jury in Sumner, Mississippi, deliberated just one hour and seven minutes before finding both men not guilty of Emmett Till's homicide. Blacks held mass rallies in Detroit, Baltimore, New York City and Chicago to voice their outrage. "It is getting to be a strange thing," said one Negro leader at the rally in Baltimore, "that the FBI can never seem to work out who is responsible for killing Negroes in the South." Four months later in a national magazine interview, Bryant and Milam admitted to killing Till. In a quote attributed to Milam included in the Till display at the National Civil Rights Museum in Memphis, he says: "What could I do? He thought he was as good as any white man."

Louisiana didn't make indelible headlines the way its more reactionary neighbors in the Deep South did with their sensational murders and blind white juries or defiant segregationist governors, fire hoses, police dogs, and National Guard troops. That does not mean, however, that Louisiana embraced or welcomed integration, nor that Louisiana's African American residents passively accepted their enforced second-class citizenship while their brothers and sisters in nearby states resisted. Events involving Louisiana's black residents and the actions of its state legislators were significant. And they are worth recounting here, not only because some have been forgotten and news coverage of others paled in comparison to the media attention given developments in other states, but also because collectively they paint the backdrop against which Eddie Robinson built Grambling football into a nationally recognized powerhouse that accentuated black accomplishment yet transcended race.

The white supremacist organization called the White Citizens' Council did not originate in Louisiana, nor did the states' rights theory of interposition – the twentieth century's version of the nullification doctrine espoused by John C. Calhoun in South Carolina. But both flourished there under the leadership of William Monroe Rainach Sr. Willie Rainach served twenty years as a state representative and senator from Claiborne Parish, which shares a border with Lincoln Parish, where Grambling is located. He was in the second of his three terms as a state senator when he became the first (and only) chairman of the Louisiana Joint Legislative Committee on Segregation in 1954. As such he was the face of segregation in the state, and his hand could be seen in dozens of actions – legislative and otherwise – aimed at reinforcing Jim Crow in Louisiana. This included the purge of more than half of all black voters in the city of Monroe (forty miles east of Grambling), the formation of Louisiana's first White Citizens' Council in the town of Homer (thirty-five miles northwest of Grambling), and landslide approval of a segregation enforcement measure known as Amendment Number 16, which authorized the use of state police powers to preserve segregated public schools in the interest of "public health, morals, better education, peace and good order." The amendment passed throughout Louisiana, but nowhere did it receive greater acceptance than in Rainach's home parish, where it recorded 99 percent voter approval even though more than half of the parish's residents were black.

The first White Citizens' Council was formed about thirty miles from the Louisiana border in Indianola, Mississippi on July 11, 1954 – a direct response to the U.S. Supreme Court's landmark *Brown v. Board of Education* decision of May 17, 1954 that struck down "separate but equal" as the basis for racial segregation. The stated purpose of Citizens' Councils was "to spell out expressly that the states have the sovereign right to regulate education, health, morals and general welfare in fields not specifically related to the federal government." A firm believer in that philosophy, Rainach established Louisiana's first White Citizens' Council in April 1955, and soon thereafter founded the Louisiana Association of Citizens' Councils. Within a year Councils existed in nearly half of the state's sixty-four parishes.

Interposition, meanwhile, was promoted for the first time in November 1954 on the editorial page of the *Richmond (Va.) News-Leader* by its young editor, James J. Kilpatrick, who hammered home the principle of "standing between federal encroachment on the rights of a sovereign state" almost daily for six weeks. A staunch segregationist and states' rights advocate at the time, Kilpatrick became a nationally syndicated conservative columnist who much later renounced his segregationist views (though not his belief in states' rights). Kilpatrick's message was enthusiastically embraced in Louisiana. Over the next ten years the Louisiana State Legislature, which actually passed a resolution censuring the U.S. Supreme Court for "unwarranted and unprecedented abuse of power" just three days after the *Brown* decision, passed more than one hundred thirty acts and resolutions based on the theory of interposition – more than double the total enacted by any other state. All were designed to block desegregation in the public schools.

An event with far-reaching consequences for Louisiana occurred in 1955, just days before Grambling's showdown with Florida A&M in the Orange Blossom Classic. On Friday, December 2, Georgia Governor Marvin Griffin attempted to prevent the University of Pittsburgh from playing Georgia Tech in the upcoming Sugar Bowl on January 2, 1956 because Pitt's team included a black player, fullback/linebacker Bobby Grier. Adopting the position taken by the University of San Francisco four years earlier, Pittsburgh officials said their team would play the Sugar Bowl game only if Bobby Grier were allowed to play. (The Rose Bowl that year matched UCLA, with six black players, against Michigan State, which had seven.) Pittsburgh also insisted that seating for its fans not be racially segregated.

Georgia Tech's president refused to break the school's bowl game commitment, and Tech students protested Griffin's actions at the governor's mansion and marched to the State Capitol, burning Griffin in effigy. How ironic that Georgia Tech would find itself again in this type of situation, only four years after it played Baylor instead of USF in the Orange Bowl. Grier became the first black player to participate in a bowl game in the Deep South, though not without a price. His team lost 7-0 – the lone score of the game significantly influenced by a dubious pass interference penalty called against him in the first quarter. And, determined to prevent any such embarrassment in the future, Sen. Willie Rainach and his colleagues in the Louisiana State Legislature – urged on by influential constituents who were members of White Citizens' Councils – banned all interracial athletic contests in the state henceforth.

Passed unanimously by both the House and Senate in mid-July 1956,

Louisiana's so-called "race-mixing" bill outlawed "mixing of the races at dances, social functions, entertainments, athletic training, games, sports or contests, or such other activities involving personal and social contacts." An amendment to the bill just before its passage delayed the effective date of the new law to October 15 to allow Shreveport's Texas League baseball team to finish the season then in progress. Texas League teams including Shreveport, it was noted, had Negro players. Newspaper reports summarized the adverse impact of the legislative action: "Under the proposed measure, Louisiana State University could not carry out its plans to play schools in the Big Ten, many of which use Negro players. Nor could teams with Negro players engage in the post-season Sugar Bowl event. Major league baseball teams, which have been playing exhibition games in Louisiana each spring, would be forced to bypass the state. Presumably, Shreveport would have no Texas League opponents next year since most of the other teams in the league have Negro players." Grambling was playing only HBCU teams, and thus was not directly affected. But the legislation – and the attitude it reflected – definitely explains why it was 1970 before Eddie and his team faced a team with white players in a regular-season game, and 1971 before a team with white players came to Grambling to play (in both cases, Cal State Fullerton). "I was told who I could play, where I could play and when I could play," Eddie often said.

Less than a week after the race-mixing bill was approved by those elected to vote the wishes of the citizens of Louisiana, Sugar Bowl officials publicly urged Governor Earl Long to veto it "in order to preserve the ideals of American sportsmanship." Unmoved, Governor Long signed the ban into law in late October. Predictable chaos followed. The University of Wisconsin, with several black players including Sidney Williams, the first black starting quarterback in Big Ten Conference history, immediately cancelled a two-game series with Louisiana State scheduled for Madison in 1957 and Baton Rouge in 1958. A game between the Air Force Academy and Louisiana Tech, to be played in November of 1956 in Shreveport, was cancelled by

Tech because of a clause in the contract submitted by the Academy stating that no "player of the U. S. Air Force Academy be barred from participating in this game because of creed or race." (Tech never played Grambling during Eddie's fifty-seven years, even though the two campuses are minutes apart.) Tulane's scheduled game against Army in 1957 was moved from New Orleans to West Point, at Army's insistence, because of the Louisiana law's requirement for segregated seating as well as the prohibition on interracial competition. And Orange Bowl officials were quick to declare that the race-mixing ban would surely enable them to arrange more attractive games than the rival bowl game played in New Orleans. Sugar Bowl officials, despite the concerns implicit in their request for a veto by the governor, dismissed the claim. Two seasons later they were forced to face the Orange Bowl prophecy in the most painful way imaginable.

The home state team, Paul Dietzel's Louisiana State Bayou Bengals, won the 1958 national championship with a perfect 11-0 record, and quickly accepted an invitation to play in the 1959 Sugar Bowl. (Wisconsin, which would have been a regular season obstacle to that perfect season, won seven, lost one and tied one.) Army, Oklahoma, Air Force and Syracuse (along with Wisconsin) all were ranked in the top ten, and any one would have provided a marquee match-up for the game. State law, though, effectively limited LSU's prospective opponent on January 1 in New Orleans to only those schools with all-white teams. The choice came down to 12th-ranked Clemson, with eight wins and two losses, or Southern Methodist, ranked 18th but with only six wins in ten games. U.S. District Court in New Orleans ruled the law banning interracial sports activities unconstitutional in early December of 1958, but by then the New Year's Day bowl games were set. Okalahoma and Syracuse were paired in the Orange Bowl, and Air Force was going to the Cotton Bowl in Dallas. Army stayed home despite an unbeaten season of eight wins and a tie, and a lineup that featured Heisman Trophy winner Pete Dawkins. Clemson became LSU's opposition in the Sugar Bowl; LSU eked out a surprisingly tight 7-0 victory.

Boxing, one of Eddie's keen sporting interests, did not escape the effects of the race-mixing law, and Ralph Dupas, one of Louisiana's most acclaimed boxers, was particularly plagued. The second of eleven children born to Evelyn Foto Dupas, Ralph Dupas was the reigning light middleweight champion of the world at one point in his 16-year career, and also had title fights in both the lightweight and welterweight divisions. He trained under Angelo Dundee, whose most famous fighter was Muhammad Ali, and in boxing circles was in a league with Joey Giardello, Emile Griffith, Carmen Basilio and Sugar Ray Robinson, all titleholders or legitimate contenders. Between April 1957 and May 1958, Dupas ran a gauntlet more exhausting than any series of bouts as he attempted to prove he was not a black man.

In March 1957, 74-year -old Lucretia Gravolet wrote to Sen. Rainach and the Joint Legislative Committee on Segregation, claiming that she could prove that Dupas was a Negro. If proven, her allegation would have prevented Dupas from participating in a bout against Vince Martinez scheduled for April 8 in New Orleans. The Louisiana State Athletic Commission investigated, then rejected, Gravolet's claim, and allowed Dupas to meet Martinez. "I knew it would end this way," Dupas was quoted saying, "but it has been an embarrassing experience." His mother is said to have added, "Maybe all of Ralph's troubles are over now." A few weeks after that fight, though, the Louisiana State Boxing Commission intervened in response to political pressure, ordering Dupas to produce a "white" birth certificate before he could fight again in Louisiana. The fourth-ranked lightweight in the world by that time, Dupas filed suit seeking to have himself declared a white man. (No birth certificate had ever been issued for him, even though birth certificates existed for all of his siblings.)

His mother's family history became the subject of intense scrutiny in the court proceeding, which played out intermittently over almost five months. Her parents were white, she testified, but she was reared by a black family named Duplessis after being orphaned. She gave birth to all eleven of her children before claiming Peter Dupas as their father and her husband. She could neither read nor write. Along the way it was revealed that the birth certificates of Ralph Dupas' ten brothers and sisters had been revised by the city health department's director of vital statistics to show them to be Negro rather than white, as originally issued. No explanation was given for the change. In response, Dupas testified that he had lived his whole life as a white man, including attending white schools. A Roman Catholic nun provided an affidavit declaring her knowledge that Dupas was a white man to corroborate his testimony.

The trial, like six of his one hundred thirty-five boxing matches, ended in a draw: the judge could not decide if Ralph Dupas was white or Negro. After a one-month continuance, the court ordered the City of New Orleans to issue a white birth certificate to Dupas – without ever deciding the fundamental question of his race – on the conclusion that the state had failed to prove Dupas to be Negro (rather than deciding that Dupas had proven he was white). The ruling was successfully appealed by the state attorney general, a newspaper headline at the end of March 1958 heralding the continuing absurdity: **"Rule Dupas Negro Again."** Even that decision, however, was submitted for further review. Finally, in late June 1958, the Louisiana Supreme Court saw the facts, or lack of them, the way Civil District Court had nearly nine months before. Its arguments exhausted, the attorney general's office gave up the fight: Ralph Dupas could have a white birth certificate if he wanted one. Of course, he couldn't fight a black opponent in his home state until the race-mixing law was repealed. An upcoming bout with Joe Brown for the lightweight championship of the world would be held in Houston, instead of New Orleans. Brown won the title.

There was no similar race-mixing prohibition in Florida law in 1958, but the same principle caused the University of Buffalo Bulls to decline to play in the Tangerine Bowl in Orlando at the end of that season. The Bulls won the Lambert Trophy as the East's best college football team, winning eight and losing once, and were the top choice for a Tangerine Bowl invitation. The Orlando High School Athletic Association, which operated the Tangerine Bowl stadium, however, had a clause in its standard rental agreement that prohibited mixing races in sports contests held there. Two of Buffalo's players, including star running back Willie Evans, were black. Without hesitation or debate, the team unanimously chose to pass up the Tangerine Bowl rather than leave its black players behind. It would be fifty years before the University of Buffalo football team received another bowl bid. Members of the 1958 team, who reunited every year during Buffalo's homecoming, were honored guests when the Bulls played Connecticut in the International Bowl January 3, 2009.

While Negro players were not yet allowed on the Tangerine Bowl field in Florida nor on any field in Louisiana, the only National Football League championship game to be decided in overtime was played December 28, 1958, when the Baltimore Colts beat the New York Giants in what many consider the greatest game in pro football history. Both teams had African American stars who later were inducted into the Pro Football Hall of Fame – Lenny Moore of Penn State and Jim Parker of Ohio State for Baltimore, and Emlen Tunnell of Iowa and Roosevelt Brown of Morgan State for New York. It was a sign of the times that all had played their college football outside the Deep South.

Much was happening on the larger stage of the Civil Rights Movement in the South, as events in Louisiana unfolded. On December 1, 1955, a 42-year-old seamstress named Rosa Parks, the volunteer secretary of the local NAACP chapter, refused to relinquish her seat on a city bus to a white rider in Montgomery, Alabama. Her historic resistance triggered the Montgomery Bus Boycott that was patterned after Rev. T. J. Jemison's Baton Rouge bus protest. The boycott, in turn, launched a reluctant young Baptist minister, Martin Luther King, into a leadership role in the unfolding quest for an end to segregation and racial discrimination. By the time the U. S. Supreme Court affirmed, three hundred eighty-one days later, that the city's segregation of public buses was unconstitutional, King had been arrested for the first of many times and his home had been bombed. In Eddie's view, the historic victory achieved by Montgomery's black residents proved what he had been telling his players: *If you learn the law, use and trust the American justice system, and are willing to pay the price, you can change things in America.*

In February, 1957, at a meeting in New Orleans, the Southern Leadership Conference elected Rev. Martin Luther King Jr. as its president and Rev. T.J. Jemison of Baton Rouge its secretary; in August it became the SCLC. "We advocate nonviolence in words, thought and deed," the group declared. "We believe this spirit, and this spirit alone, can overcome the decades of mutual fear and suspicion that have infested and poisoned our southern culture." At the National Civil Rights Museum, the explanation attributed to Dr. King for the emphasis on nonviolence sounded a lot like something Eddie would have said: "If you use the law 'an eye for an eye, a tooth for a tooth,' you wind up with everyone blind and toothless."

Also that summer, segregationist Senator Strom Thurmond – from John C. Calhoun's South Carolina – set the record for the longest filibuster in the history of the U.S. Congress when he spoke continuously for twenty-four hours and twenty-seven minutes to obstruct pending civil rights legislation. The next week, Arkansas Governor Orval Faubus, in defiance of the Supreme Court's *Brown vs. Board of Education* decision, denied nine black students access to Little Rock Central High School. As tension mounted, President Dwight Eisenhower sent federal troops to protect those students and restore order. Eventually Central High would shut down for a year in an effort to calm the situation.

14

HE WAS a classic black preacher with charisma, who could express, with practiced pulpit presence and carefully measured cadence, what the masses of oppressed blacks would have said if only they'd had the power and gift to do so. Because of that, the Rev. Martin Luther King captured the imagination of the public and the media in a way no other civil rights figure did from 1956 through 1965. Early on he was featured in *LOOK* and *Time* magazines, in *The New York Times* and on *Meet The Press* – only the second African American to be interviewed on the network television public affairs program. He received honorary degrees from Howard, Morehouse and the Chicago Theological Seminary, and the NAACP"s Spingarn Medal, presented to "American negroes who perform acts of distinguished merit and achievement." Later he was named *Time's* Man of the Year and was awarded the Nobel Peace Prize, among literally hundreds of honors. *The Amsterdam News* proclaimed him "the number one leader of sixteen million Negroes in the United States."

Yet, while Martin Luther King was the face and the voice of the Civil Rights Movement in the South and is revered today for his unforgettable words and visible leadership, the Movement's heart and soul during those years was John Lewis and a dozen or so other members of the group with the acronym SNCC, pronounced "snick." It was they, the founders and leaders of the Student Nonviolent Coordinating Committee, who took their places on the firing line of virtually every major confrontation across the South; they who were hauled off to jail repeatedly; they who risked life and limb in the face of tear gas, billy clubs, angry mobs and marauding police-men – and they who refused ever to strike back, no matter what the brutal members of law enforcement and enraged white citizens did to them.

For the first five years of its existence, SNCC taught the passive, non-violent principles of Gandhi, and its followers lived, risked injury and some-times died in the name of that restraint. Dr. King espoused Gandhian nonviolent protest, too, of course, and faced arrest and experienced assault himself. But it was the courageous men and women of SNCC who boarded the Freedom Ride buses, expecting to travel from Washington, DC to New Orleans to make a statement about nondiscrimination in interstate trans-portation, only to have the first bus firebombed and its passengers assaulted shortly after crossing the Alabama state line. It was SNCC's vol-unteer activists – mostly students – who endured cigar smoke in their faces, cigarette ashes in their hair, and coffee in their laps when they sat down at lunch counters in Greensboro, North Carolina; Nashville, Tennessee; and other cities including Baton Rouge, and refused to leave after they were denied service. They were hunted, abused, jailed, prosecuted – and mur-dered – in Mississippi because they tried to help black Americans register to vote and exercise their individual rights, and were mauled by troopers on horseback as they attempted to peacefully march fifty-four miles from Selma to Montgomery in the name of full citizenship. Lewis himself, later to become a highly respected member of the U.S. House of Representatives, was arrested more than forty times, beaten and seriously injured. Not until the late 1960s did SNCC acquire a very different image, one of militancy and radicalism, after Stokely Carmichael, with his strident "black power" philosophy, and "Rap" Brown, the McKinley High grad who would wind up in prison, took over the organization. By then, the hard-earned break-throughs had all been achieved.

It is only natural to question Eddie's reluctance to join the fray in any public way and his decision to discourage his players from participating in the ongoing activism. He wrestled with these choices himself. On the one hand, he felt a clear responsibility to steer his players away from potentially dangerous encounters; their parents counted on him for that, especially those mothers who trusted him to be a father figure and role model. But at the same time, people like John Lewis were absorbing unthinkable punishment and risking their lives for a principle Eddie certainly supported; he admired them and appreciated their tremendous sacrifices. He heard criticism and felt its sting. Yet, in the final analysis, Eddie remained convinced that his greatest contribution as a leader would be to develop his players into young men who were prepared for the opportunities a desegregated society would offer once it had been realized; to show them that they were capable of achieving success the same as white citizens if they got an education and worked hard; and to foster a love for the America that he considered "the greatest country in the world."

"His philosophy was, if you're going to beat the white people, beat them at their own game," said Charlie Joiner. "Outperform them in the classroom, outperform them on the football field, and outperform them in life as a citizen. Then you'll get everything you want. If you want equality, that's the way to get it. Those were his principles. He didn't believe in going out in the street and throwing bricks and breaking out windows and all that. Beat them at what they do. Beat them as citizens, by being a better citizen. He believed in being a good citizen, because he was one. "

Marino Casem was close enough to Eddie to understand and explain Eddie's reasoning. "Eddie was very hurt by incidents that happened to him," Casem said. "But he understood the times. It wasn't that he didn't get upset about it. But he knew that him taking a beating, or him being arrested, wasn't going to do the situation any good. Somebody had to be there to keep the program running. And that was Eddie."

Doug Porter, another College Football Hall of Fame coach, who was an assistant for Eddie from 1966 through 1973 and knew him well added: "Even though he realized that the injustices were there, and inequality was there, he did not feel the football players should be using their position as football players as a platform to fight against it. He was certainly in favor of change. But he just did not want to use the football team as a platform to create some statements about the injustices. In the State of Louisiana, segregation was so stringent and so outwardly flagrant that to have had a lot of Grambling players involved in that type of thing perhaps would have resulted in repercussions for the university through the legislature. Rob didn't want to do anything that would hinder the growth that was possible for Grambling."

Without realizing it, Eddie was in harmony with the fundamentals of SNCC as John Lewis explained them in his memoir, *Walking with the Wind*. Referring to Jim Lawson, the minister and future civil rights leader who conducted workshops in Gandhi's philosophy for the Nashville students who formed the nucleus of SNCC, Lewis wrote: "We learned during our early days with Lawson – and he imbued us with this idea – that there were roles for everyone to play in this movement, and not everyone's role was the same. If a person felt that he or she could go only to a certain point in terms of active demonstration, that was okay. That went for the med students over at Meharry and the football players at Fisk. And it went for Martin Luther King Jr. as well."

Author and educator Kenneth Shropshire, a recognized expert and popular speaker in the areas of diversity and race in sports, made a similar point when interviewed for the NBC television documentary *Every Man A Tiger*, produced as a tribute to Eddie before the 2007 Bayou Classic. "I think too often we think of civil rights leadership as being the fiery, motivational leadership speeches of Martin Luther King," Shropshire said, "or we think of the more radical movements. But there's a whole core of men who had to make these decisions about how to lead black America in this changing time."

Two months before he was assassinated in 1968, Dr. King preached a sermon at Ebenezer Baptist Church in Atlanta titled, *The Drum Major*

Instinct. Based on the tenth chapter of Saint Mark's Gospel, the lengthy homily equated the request by James and John – to sit at the right and left hand of Jesus Christ in Eternity – to the desire of all human beings to be recognized, to be praised, to be first. What he called "The Drum Major Instinct" was every individual's sense of personal ambition, that irrepressible drive for attention and importance. Dr. King preached that "The Drum Major Instinct" could be a good instinct if it is used to benefit mankind. He urged his congregation to heed Christ's teaching that those who wanted to be first must be willing to serve others, and to realize that all could achieve greatness by serving. If members of the congregation wanted to speak of him after The Lord had taken him, Dr. King told them in conclusion, "say that I was a drum major for justice . . . say that I was a drum major for peace . . . say that I was a drum major for righteousness."

Wilbert Ellis, a close friend for almost fifty years, was a student in Doris Robinson's English class at Lincoln High in Ruston in 1955. He enrolled at Grambling the next year, and after finishing college became one of Eddie's Grambling colleagues. He portrayed Eddie's example of restraint and preparedness in Dr. King's context of service to others. "Coach Robinson was a drum major for a way of life, for people getting through different periods, as he did," Ellis said. "He was a great football coach, as we know. But he was an individual who cared about the human being, the total person. He prepared you not only on the field in football as players, but he prepared them for life, getting them ready to go out into the world to meet people, into the work world and how to handle yourself. He always told his players, if you're given the opportunity to work, do a good job. He didn't get into the race thing. He said, show people what you have to offer if given the opportunity. He was just a great individual who wanted to get the most out of an individual. He was a drum major for freedom."

Ellis's longevity exposed him to generations of Grambling football players, and gave him an appreciation for Eddie's contribution to their lives. "Coach Robinson was working with young men who came from homes where there was only one parent in the home, maybe the mother," Ellis said. "He taught that individual that no matter where you came from, or who your parent was, or how hard the struggle was, you still can be somebody; there's a way through it, a way out. He planted the seed and laid a foundation to make you want to be somebody. He was that kind of individual who touched your life, and once he touched your life, you were motivated to want to be the best in whatever area you went into."

In an interview during his 12th term in Congress, Rep. John Lewis said the Movement never approached Eddie about assuming a prominent role, not even after celebrities such as Sidney Poitier, Lena Horne, Charlton Heston, Sammy Davis Jr. and Harry Belafonte became involved. And no one ever voiced dissatisfaction with Eddie for remaining in the background or "not doing enough" to support their efforts. "I never had that feeling, and I never heard of anyone having that feeling," Lewis said. "We always felt there were roles for people to play. Some were going to be president of a college, or a principal of a school, or a coach. Just do your job and do it well. Be successful."

In fact, Eddie's emphasis on being a good American and debunking stereotypes by excelling on the field, in the classroom and in society are exactly what SNCC and the Movement stood for. "He must be looked upon as one individual who made a major contribution to the cause of racial equality in America," Rep. Lewis said. "He had a real impact on the lives and directions of the young men that he coached, but not only on the people he coached. His impact was on students and others at Grambling, too, and all the people he came in contact with. You have to be consistent. You have to be persistent. And you never give up or give in. You pace yourself for the long haul, for the long struggle. That's what the Coach was able to do. And people around him saw him, and they tried to live by the standards that he established for himself. And I think he influenced many other people to follow his example." The Congressman recalled an encounter with Eddie in an airport years ago, and the lasting impression he made. "He was a patriot. He believed in America; he never gave up on America. He had this idea that somehow and some way, if you get out there and you do your best, things will get better."

As a SNCC leader, Lewis always wore a suit and tie when he led marches and other forms of protest. Everyone in the Movement did. He sees a valid parallel to Eddie wearing a white shirt and tie on the sideline and his insistence that Grambling football players don white shirts and neckties whenever they traveled. "We had this whole idea that image was part of the projection, part of the message. What type of image are you projecting? So you put on a suit and tie. That was important, sitting-in at a lunch counter, in a restaurant, or standing-in at a theater, or when you were going on a march. We saw, and I'm sure that Coach saw, that it was not just good to be on the field and play well. When you left the field, you'd go out and you'd dress a certain way; you'd act like a gentleman and you'd look like a gentleman."

As the seeds of SNCC were being cultivated in Nashville in 1959, Grambling football under Eddie Robinson was entering its next phase: competing in the Southwestern Athletic Conference (SWAC). Junious "Buck" Buchanan, an imposing 6-foot 6-inch, 225-pound young man from Gainesville, Alabama, enrolled in January, after Eddie acted quickly on a letter from Buchanan's uncle, Glennen Threat, insisting that Eddie visit with Buck and convince him to play for him. And Willie Brown of Yazoo City, Mississippi, smaller at six-two and two fifteen but just as much an athlete, came to Grambling to stay that summer, right after graduating from N.D. Taylor High School in Yazoo City.

Destined to be best friends who attended each other's induction into the Pro Football Hall of Fame many years later, Buchanan and Brown would become Eddie's team leaders as Grambling began play in the SWAC. With Grambling's other Hall of Famers, Willie Davis and Charlie Joiner, Buchanan and Brown became part of a storied SWAC football history that includes the greatest running back of all-time, Walter Payton of Jackson State; the greatest receiver of all-time, Jerry Rice, from Mississippi Valley

State; former NFL Most Valuable Player Steve McNair of Alcorn State; two-time NFL Defensive Player of the Year Michael Strahan of Texas Southern; and Mel Blount, a six-time all-pro defensive back for Pittsburgh's four-time Super Bowl champions.

Grambling had been a member of the Midwest Conference since 1950, which was better than not being part of a collegiate league at all yet not enough to satisfy the ambitions outlined by President Ralph Waldo Emerson Jones. Midwest Conference schools such as Tennessee State, Kentucky State and Wilberforce were recognized for fielding competitive teams in several sports, including football. But the prominence Prez envisioned required a larger stage, and, in particular, one rooted in the Deep South where Eddie recruited almost all of his players and Grambling attracted most of its students. The emerging, expanding SWAC offered exactly the kind of exposure and stature Grambling's football program needed to continue to gain more recognition. And so, in January, 1956, Collie Nicholson began one of his trademark publicity campaigns, cranking out year-end summaries of the school's overall athletic accomplishments to make sure everyone in the SWAC knew just what Grambling had to offer as a prospective new member.

Collie's 1955 recap, written in early 1956, began:

"When the buzzer rasped to signal the end of the Xavier Holiday basketball tournament last Wednesday night in New Orleans, it marked the end of Grambling College's most successful athletic year. The Tigers won the tournament with a victory over Tennessee State, 72-61, to run their composite basketball, baseball, football record to 56 victories in 64 athletic events. For a school where prospects were regarded as "extremely dubious" last New Year's Day, Grambling cleaned up national honors in football and won Midwest Conference titles in baseball and basketball. Playing against the best teams in the country, the extraordinary record was compiled in this fashion: basketball, 27-5; baseball, 19-3; football, 10-0. All three teams played

like veteran units and solved each problem as the opposition presented it. This was especially true of the football squad which defeated Florida A & M 28-21 in the Orange Blossom Classic last December after some writers said the team couldn't finish at the top of the heap . . . Robinson was named "Coach-of-the-Year" with the enthusiastic endorsement of the nation's top writers and fellow coaches . . ."

In January 1957, Collie summarized the preceding year's performance with:

"In future years Grambling rooters are going to look at the school's composite football-basketball-baseball record for 1956 with a dreamy expression of rapture. Grambling hit the jackpot in national prestige during the 12-month period by winning 52 of 63 athletic events to raise its two-year total to 108 victories in 127 games. The extraordinary record was compiled in this manner: basketball, 25-7; baseball, 19-3; football, 8-1 . . . Athletic director Eddie Robinson, whose guile is apparent in the over-all picture, attributes the success to "capable, shrewd, resourceful boys with competitive spirit you seldom see." The Tigers won only one championship during the year – the Mid-West loop baseball title – but they scandalously manhandled foes from the four major Negro conferences in football and basketball . . ."

The SWAC was founded in 1920 by representatives of six all-black Texas colleges: Bishop, Paul Quinn, Prairie View A&M, Sam Houston, Texas College and Wiley. Langston College – the only all-black college in Oklahoma, Southern University and Arkansas AM&N were added during the 1930s, and Texas Southern was included in 1954. Conference membership is not permanent, though, and by the mid-1950s, Paul Quinn College was long gone, and Bishop and Langston were about to withdraw. That attrition would reduce conference membership to seven institutions.

Sam Houston's departure after the 1958-59 season would reduce the conference to six members, including only three remaining charter members: Texas College, Prairie View and Wiley. Clearly there was room – and a need – to expand. The conference announced the acceptance of Grambling and Jackson State on May 31, 1958, their entry effective with the start of the '58-'59 basketball schedule. (It was too late to start with the upcoming football season.) The news story reporting the vote to expand – not attributed to Collie though it sounded a bit like him – declared:

> "The addition of Grambling and Jackson to the Southwest body is certain to add zest to the already torrid competition in this section due to the fact that annually both schools rank high in the national setup in both football and basketball. Already there is much talk about the coming cage race that will feature Texas Southern, Grambling and Jackson State. Louisiana grid fans are looking forward to the Grambling-Southern football game in the fall of 1959. These two Pelican State powers quit playing football ten years ago due to the intense rivalry. Outside of the Sugar Bowl and LSU Stadium in Baton Rouge, it is doubtful if there is any place in Louisiana that can comfortably accommodate the large gathering that will be on hand."

Adjusting to a new offense, the wing-T, Grambling won the first two games of the Brown-Buchanan Era in 1959, then lost the resumption of competition with Southern by a 12-6 score. The narrow defeat was a sign of bad things to come that season. A week later, on October 10, Eddie took his team to Nashville to play Tennessee State, which would finish with a 9-1 record and win the Midwest Conference. As Grambling lost another close one, 26-21, nearby, Jim Lawson taught Gandhi's principles and tactics of peaceful civil disobedience to those students who would be the foundation of SNCC, including John Lewis. Neither Lawson and his pupils nor Eddie and his players were at all aware of each other.

Grambling lost three straight games, each by a point, later in the season, and finished with a mere four wins and six losses – only the second losing record for Eddie's teams since 1941 when his first team won three and lost five. The disappointing season ended encouragingly, however, when Grambling drubbed Mississippi Valley State 93-0 on November 21. One week later a group of well-dressed black students – the men wearing coats and ties, the women in skirts and blouses – sat down at the lunch counter in a downtown Nashville department store called Harvey's, and waited to be told, "I'm sorry. We can't serve you here." After asking to see the manager and hearing that it was against store policy to "serve colored people," the group departed, respectfully and without incident.

Grambling's final football game and that trip to the lunch counter were unrelated, except that both were previews of what was to come in 1960.

15

WILLIE BROWN'S first encounter with Eddie Robinson remained a vivid memory fifty years later. A Grambling assistant coach, Tom Williams, had brought Willie from Yazoo City shortly after graduation to check things out, figuring Willie would go home a couple days later and then decide whether or not the small north Louisiana college was right for him. When they arrived in Grambling, Williams drove straight to the Robinsons' house. "This is my first time to meet Coach Robinson," Willie recalled, "and Coach Robinson is out there cutting his lawn with a push mower. I was just amazed that this guy would be doing something like that. Here's the head coach at Grambling, and he's cutting his own grass and stuff like that!"

Tom Williams had told Willie, "You don't have to pack too many clothes. You'll just stay a couple days." But Willie packed a whole trunk, "because I pretty much knew what I wanted to do." Standing in his front yard, sweating in the June heat, Eddie greeted Willie Brown enthusiastically. "We'd love to have you come to Grambling," he said. "We want you at Grambling. We'll take care of you." The remainder of Willie's introduction to Coach Robinson served only to ratify the decision he had made before leaving home. "He listened to me, and I listened to him," Willie said. "He told me about Grambling, what a great school it is. He talked about winning, and how much he was dedicated to Grambling, and what Grambling had done for him. He introduced me to the president of Grambling. And he told me they had some good-looking girls there. Coach Robinson said, 'We'll get you a little job, and you'll like it here.' I didn't go back home until Christmas."

Willie actually worked two jobs that summer at Grambling. First, he drove a water truck and sprayed the dirt roads around the campus to keep the dust down. While trying to impress some girls one day, he managed to flip the truck. Uninjured (through luck or Providence), he was relieved of dust control duties. But, as evidence of the influence Willie's coach wielded at the school, Eddie – despite the previous vehicular mishap – succeeded in having Willie reassigned to transporting students who were in need of medical treatment to and from the hospital in Ruston or a nearer clinic. Everyone made it without incident.

Willie lived on the edge another way, too, during his first couple of months on campus. "Coach had a good-looking daughter," he said of Lillian Rose. "I looked at her two or three times, and she was nice. So I started halfway dating her. But I always got nervous when I had to go to the house to see her, because Coach might come in anytime. A couple times I was there and Coach said, 'Boy, what are you doing over here?' And I'd say, 'Well, coach, I'm just visiting.' Of course, he really knew why I was there. The thing I had going for me is that Mrs. Robinson really took to me and had me come over for dinner."

Willie also worked out faithfully throughout the summer, which meant he was more than ready for Eddie's rigorous workouts when training camp started. Eddie had everyone begin each practice by running ten to twelve 100-yard sprints – hundreds, not forties – as was his conditioning custom. Bob Hopkins, the basketball player, was right when he said: "You were never going to BS Coach Rob about being in shape." Describing the start with a made-up word that sounded like something between 'Shew' and 'Whoosh,' Willie said: "Every time we'd line up, it was . . .! I'm gone. I was in front of everybody. Coach would say, 'Hell, that Brown boy – he ain't read nobody's clippings. He don't know how good you are.'" It wasn't the best way for a freshman to break the ice with new teammates. "But I was just running," Willie said, "doing what I do best." Willie laid low for a while, letting his play speak for itself. Soon enough it was obvious that he could hold his own with the best players. He would become a Hall of Fame defensive back as a pro, but at Grambling he started at tight end and linebacker for four years – even though "we had a quarterback and a halfback who were bigger than I was."

By 1959 Eddie already had begun attracting an exceptional talent pool, the only positive to the insistence on all-white teams at Alabama, Ole Miss, Texas and the rest of the schools in the Southeastern and Southwest Conferences. "When you look at the players we had," said Willie when he was a coach with the Oakland Raiders, "Grambling could have competed with any pro team, with the size and the talent we had. You talk about college; we could have beaten any college team in America. We had just as much talent as Notre Dame or USC or Michigan or LSU – any of the big-time schools." Such depth translated to spirited competition for playing time. "At Grambling," Brown said, "you didn't get hurt. Because if you got hurt, you never got your job back; they had guys four or five deep. We had tryouts pretty much every Monday. After we played the game on Saturday, we'd come back Monday and have a tryout." Eddie called those intrasquad square-offs "Grumblers Scrimmages," named for all the guys who thought they should be playing and complained because they weren't. Play well in a Grumblers Scrimmage, and you might get a chance to play in the next game. "Every week was like the traveling squad," Brown recalled. "They'd put up a list. One week you might be on it, and the next week you might not. So you had to go and read the list."

There was little doubt, though, that Buck Buchanan would find his name in the starting lineup every week. He was, in Brown's words, "one of the biggest and toughest men I ever saw or played with." For Collie Nicholson, Buchanan was the perfect subject for his extravagant prose.

"Junious is a man's man – a six-foot seven-inch, 272-pound giant big enough to play the whole line by himself, fast enough to play halfback and smart enough to be named to the All-American Academic team . . . He has a mind like a computer. He remembers everything he has seen and heard about the sport . . . An immensely likeable fellow, Junious looks like the 'after' advertisement in one of those body-building contests with biceps popping from his T-shirt . . . (Coaches) claim that, 'He looks and acts like Superman.'"

Eddie simply called him, "the best football player in the country." He could have made that the best *athlete*. Buck also played basketball and ran the 440-yard dash in track, qualifying him as one of the biggest sprinters in history.

Eddie's 1960 Grambling football team was one of his best, and included a dozen players who went on to have professional careers. In its second season in the SWAC, Grambling finished in a three-way tie for the conference championship, and Eddie was named SWAC coach of the year. The new wing-T that clicked for ninety-three points in the last game of 1959 produced four hundred seventeen points in ten games, the most that any of Eddie's first eighteen teams had ever scored. His defense, meanwhile, allowed only seventy-eight. The team won nine games and lost only once, 16-6 to rival Southern, which hurt more than any single defeat should in such a dominant season.

That game was played on the first day of October in Baton Rouge, and the victory was a convincing indication that Ace Mumford kept his players focused on football every bit as much as Eddie did at Grambling. Events six months earlier had caused controversy on the Southern campus, tension in Baton Rouge and unrest across the South. It would have been understandable if Southern's team had stumbled through a distracted season. Instead, Southern finished with a 9-1 record, shared the SWAC championship with Grambling and Prairie View, and was declared black national champion.

The incident that triggered turmoil at Southern occurred on February 1 in Greensboro, North Carolina when four students from North Carolina A&T staged the first official lunch counter-sit-in, at a Woolworth's store. The soon-to-be-members of SNCC in Nashville were caught a little off-guard by the protest in North Carolina. It was unrelated to anything they had been training for with Jim Lawson's classes in nonviolent protest and their practice visits to Harvey's Department Store in late 1959, and it forced them to act more quickly than they had planned. Lest they become followers instead of leaders, they began sitting-in at several lunch counters in downtown Nashville in mid-February, ahead of schedule. At first their requests for service were simply ignored and the counters closed early. By early March, though, arrests and abuse commenced. As peaceful protest was treated with aggression, the conviction that the time for change had arrived began to spread, especially among college students. In the last week of March, it reached Baton Rouge.

Seven Southern University students occupied lunch counter seats at the R.H. Kress store on March 28, 1960. They were arrested and charged with disturbing the peace. They had been assured by Rev. T.J. Jemison that the black community would raise their bail, which was set at $1,500 apiece – an excessive amount for a misdemeanor charge, equivalent to about $10,000 fifty years later. (SNCC would not be formally organized or named for a few more weeks, so it was not involved in this effort in any way.)

On March 29 two more students sat-in at Sitman's Drugstore, and another seven went to the Greyhound Bus Terminal. They, too, were arrested and similarly charged. Chaos quickly ensued. Rev. Jemison hosted an overflow crowd at the Mount Zion Baptist Church where he was pastor, and suggested that black residents boycott downtown stores as Easter approached. Shortly thereafter, all sixteen Southern students were "suspended indefinitely" by the university. The sixteen considered "suspension" nothing more than a euphemism for expulsion, and urged fellow students to boycott classes until they were readmitted. Classrooms were empty for a day and several thousand students marched in support of their "suspended" classmates before Southern President Felton Clark moved swiftly to quash the campus rebellion.

In typical fashion, the Louisiana State Legislature responded to the Southern University sit-ins with revisions to statutes intended to stifle such dissent. One change read, in relevant part: "No person shall without authority of laws go into or upon . . . any structure . . . which belongs to another . . . after having been forbidden to do so . . . by any owner, lessee or custodian of the property or by any other authorized person . . ." Another redefined disturbing the peace to include any type of activity that disturbed or alarmed the public, or could be anticipated to have that effect. Yet another stiffened the penalties for such generalized charges as disorderly conduct, criminal mischief and criminal trespass. Outgoing Governor Earl Long was quoted as saying, "I would suggest those who are not satisfied, like the seven at the lunch counter, return to their native Africa." The charges against the group that came to be known as "The Southern 16" were upheld at all levels of Louisiana's state court system, but in December 1961, the U.S. Supreme Court ruled that their convictions violated the due process guarantees of the Fourteenth Amendment to the U.S. Constitution. From a distance, Eddie's faith in America had been vindicated: *We need to understand the American system and the Constitution. If you aren't prepared, you can't take advantage of . . . the best judicial system in the world.*

It was only a matter of time before sit-in fervor extended to northern Louisiana. Once it did, it hit close to home for Eddie. A female student was living with the Robinsons, helping with household chores, cooking and supervising Eddie Jr. and Lillian Rose when they got home from school, because Doris was teaching over in Monroe, thirty-five miles away. In return, the co-ed had a residence and regular meals while she attended Grambling; today she might be called a nanny. When Grambling students began participating in demonstrations in Ruston and Shreveport later in 1960, Eddie discussed the young woman's options in the same way he tried to guide his football players. "One day coach came home," Jean Freeling related, fifty years after her talk with Eddie. "I guess they'd had a meeting about students going to Ruston for a sit-in. He said, 'Jean, I understand the sit-ins are going on. There's something I need to tell you, though. You know, you're going to be graduating soon. You know you could get kicked out of school for participating in those activities, don't you?' I said yes," she continued. "He said, 'Well, I'm not going to tell you what to do. I just want you to be aware of what you might do to yourself. You make up your mind if it's worth it to you.'

"It was worth it to me," Mrs. Freeling said. "I sat-in . . . in Ruston, and in Shreveport, too." But she also took Eddie's caution to heart. "When we were doing the sit-ins in Shreveport, I told those kids, 'I'll sit-in, but when the police start coming to put people in jail, I'm going to the other side of the street because I can't afford to go to jail." Mrs. Freeling graduated in 1961, became a health and fitness consultant, and was the first African American woman hired as a professional counselor for the Texas Rehabilitation Commission. She sounded a lot like Eddie's football players when she reflected on the guidance he provided her. "We talked about what was happening at that time," she said, "Emmett Till, Little Rock and things like that. He had an understanding that very few people have, especially about things like that. Even with the hideous things that were happening in civil rights, he said the main thing that we all needed to concentrate on was getting our education. He stressed that daily: Get your education. 'We're in the midst of changing times,' he said. 'But you get your education so that whenever you get out of college, you will have something to rely on when times change.' And he was right."

16

THE TRIP back home had two parts for Willie Brown, the first covering one hundred fifty-nine miles east to Jackson, the second another forty-four northwest to Yazoo City. Before Interstate 20 was built, it was a five-hour ride by bus. A United States Supreme Court ruling in 1946 and a 1955 decision by the Interstate Commerce Commission together had clearly established that segregation on interstate buses was illegal. Another decision issued that December of 1960 extended the desegregation order to interstate bus *terminals*. So Willie and Isaiah Coleman, a teammate since high school who joined him at Grambling, didn't expect to have a problem when they decided to spend Christmas with their families back in Mississippi after the stellar 1960 football season. However, as resistance to the six-year-old *Brown vs. Board of Education* ruling was showing, it was one thing to win in court and quite another to enforce the law in the Jim Crow South. That's why the Congress of Racial Equality (CORE) was planning the Freedom Ride for spring of 1961, and why SNCC members eagerly responded to the call for volunteers to take part in the ride. They wanted to test the implementation and acceptance of the prohibitions on continued segregation, and call attention to places where the law was still being ignored.

It was on the ride back to Grambling that Willie and Isaiah had their own "Freedom Ride" experience, albeit nothing approaching the violence to unfold during the spring and summer ahead. "We caught a bus to go back to school," Willie recalled in 2009, "and we had to transfer in Jackson. We were sitting in the waiting area of the bus station, waiting for the bus to take us to Grambling. The bus came up and everybody got their stuff and started getting on the bus. We stopped to talk with a couple of guys who were coming back to Jackson State and were getting off the bus."

What happened next would not have surprised the activists from SNCC or CORE. "The bus began to fill up, and pretty much all the way in the back was full," Willie said. "At that time, white folks had the front, and black folks had the back (even though federal law prohibited the practice by then). We got on the bus, and there weren't any seats in the back. But three rows from the front there were two empty seats. So Isaiah and I sat there. The bus driver got on and said, 'You boys have to move to the back.' We said, 'Where in the back? There's no more seats back there.' He said, 'I don't care. You all have got to move anyway.'" Willie was adamant but calm. "I had paid for a ticket," he said, "and I knew I had the right to use that ticket. If they had tried to take us off that bus or called the police, I knew I hadn't done anything wrong." So he said, "I'm not moving. No way. I am not going back there. I'm not moving." Isaiah, a six-foot-five, two hundred eighty-pound defensive tackle, said, "Neither am I."

"The bus driver got off the bus, went back in the station, and came back with a supervisor," Willie continued. "He said, 'Where are you boys going?' I said, 'We're going to school; we're going back to Grambling.' He said, 'All right. If you're going to Grambling, I guess you can sit there.' The bus driver got back on, and we drove off."

Thinking about it years later, Willie was certain that "Grambling mystique" had no bearing on the outcome of that confrontation; it didn't exist yet, at least not the way it eventually came to. "I think it was that we were leaving Mississippi and going back to Louisiana," he said. "They knew if they made us get off the bus, something would have happened. They didn't want any trouble. I don't think anybody wanted to mess with Isaiah anyway." The ride was uneventful, and Willie never even mentioned the incident to Eddie. "It was over," he said. "There was nothing for Coach to do."

New Orleans was the intended termination point of the first Freedom Ride of 1961. Seven black and six white riders left Washington, D.C. on May 4, some aboard a Trailways bus, the others riding Greyhound. Their itinerary called for stops in Virginia, North Carolina, South Carolina, Georgia, Alabama, Mississippi and elsewhere in Louisiana before arrival at their destination on May 17, the seventh anniversary of the Supreme Court decision in *Brown v. Board of Education*. Police-sanctioned mob violence and brutality in Alabama prevented the successful completion of the original trip and led to events throughout the summer in Mississippi. The real trouble started in Anniston, just across the Georgia-Alabama line, on Mother's Day.

Situated at the southern tip of Blue Ridge in the Appalachian Mountains, blue-collar Anniston at that time was reaching its population peak, more than 33,000 according to the 1960 census. Anniston owed its existence to The Confederate States of America, which built and operated an iron furnace there during the Civil War to take advantage of nearby mineral deposits. Rebel sentiments prevailed still, a hundred years later. As the Greyhound bus carrying the Freedom Riders pulled into the terminal there, it was surrounded by an irrational mob swinging baseball bats and pieces of pipe. Its back tires slashed, the bus eventually was firebombed, and the murderous crowd attempted to keep the doors of the flaming bus from opening so the passengers would burn to death. Those trapped inside eventually escaped the inferno, then endured beatings as they lay in the grass, gasping for life-saving fresh air. The Trailways bus arrived in Anniston an hour later to a similar reception, but escaped and headed for Birmingham. The carnage there was worse than in Anniston, except that there was no firebombing. Birmingham Public Safety Commissioner Eugene "Bull" Connor had conspired with the Klan-led mob to allow a vicious attack that left one Freedom Rider with permanent brain damage.

Unfolding history would confirm for Willie Brown and his buddy that timing really is everything. Five months after they held their ground and rode from Jackson to Grambling without dire consequence, and after violence cut short the first Freedom Ride attempt in Alabama, waves of Freedom Riders began arriving at the same Jackson bus station and attempted to do essentially the same things Willie and Isaiah Coleman had done. The significant difference was that the Freedom Riders were out to establish the principle that people like Willie and Isaiah – everyone, regardless of race – should be able to travel through the South on interstate buses without being challenged, harassed, intimidated or attacked. Their goal was to compel enforcement of existing law. In response to such a blatant attempt to undermine Jim Crow, Freedom Riders were routinely arrested – more than three hundred by the end of the summer. Many eventually were sent to Mississippi's notorious Parchman Penitentiary, where they were isolated on Death Row and denied such basic privileges as clothing beyond underwear, regular exercise, and interaction with anyone but guards and their cellmates. When these "prisoners" refused to stop singing their freedom songs, authorities confiscated their mattresses and subjected them to a variety of abuses.

More than sixty Freedom Rides occurred during 1961, and in the end, the sacrifices succeeded. On September 23 – the same day Grambling opened its 1961 football season with a 59-0 rout of Texas College – the Interstate Commerce Commission issued new rules that would end discrimination in interstate travel. Effective November 1, all interstate buses were required to display a certificate reading: "Seating aboard this vehicle is without regard to race, color, creed or national origin, by order of the Interstate Commerce Commission." Eddie may not have had anything as extreme as the Freedom Ride ordeal in mind, but his words rang true nonetheless: *Everything can change, including the laws, if you are willing to pay the price.*

The 1961 team won eight games and lost twice during the Freedom Ride season. In 1962, after starting Willie and Buck's senior year with five straight victories in which the defense they led allowed only thirty points,

Grambling experienced a mysterious slump. Jackson State scored forty-five and won, then Texas Southern put up forty-two in another Grambling defeat. Two ties followed, the second a scoreless game with Wylie College, which had given up 170 points to Grambling in the three previous years combined. A 46-7 victory over Alcorn State made the final record 6-2-2 and concluded the Brown-Buchanan era with twenty-seven victories, eleven losses and two ties, which compared favorably with teams that featured Tank Younger or Willie Davis. All of those four-year records were greater achievements than they might seem today, in Willie Brown's view. "We traveled on a bus; we didn't have a nice plane to fly on," he said. "When we traveled over a long distance, we knew we wouldn't be able to stop at a restaurant, so they'd pack a lunch in the cafeteria for us and we'd stop alongside the road. We didn't have nice facilities like other schools. We had some of the worst fields and played under some of the worst conditions, because we were from a black school. The uniforms weren't as good. Coach Robinson got us through all that because that's the way his life had been."

Despite the disappointing second half of his final collegiate season, Buck Buchanan would soon make more Grambling history. Back in the summer of 1959, as Buck and Willie were embarking on their college careers and Grambling was moving up to the SWAC, Texas oilman Lamar Hunt and several other wealthy businessmen were organizing a new professional football league. It was formally named the American Football League. By the end of Buck and Willie's final college season, the AFL had begun to establish its legitimacy. It had a national television contract and had succeeded in signing some of the nation's top college stars, including 1959 Heisman Trophy winner Billy Cannon of Louisiana State. At least some football fans had begun to debate whether or not the best AFL teams could hold their own against National Football League teams. In the 1963 AFL draft, conducted on December 1, 1962, Hunt's Dallas Texans, who would move to Kansas City the following May, made Buck Buchanan the first player from an HBCU team to be chosen first overall in a professional football league draft. It was another milestone in Eddie Robinson's never-ending campaign to open eyes and doors. *The best way to change attitudes is to prove them wrong by showing you can do it, whatever IT is.*

"I saw Buck Buchanan for the very first time, and I was stunned; he was a giant among men," said the late Hank Stram, who coached Buck for twelve of his thirteen pro seasons with the Kansas City Chiefs and was his presenter when Buchanan was enshrined at Canton. "Don Klosterman, our talent scout, brought Buck to our training facility in Dallas, and he made an indelible impression. Buck had it all. He had style. He had speed. He had quickness. And he had strength combined with the ability to lead with example. He was a consummate team player who was infused with a great, great attitude. His college coach, Eddie Robinson, characterized Buck as the finest tackle he had ever seen. Little wonder that Buck was the first player taken in the 1963 AFL draft."

Buck and Willie were roommates for two years at Grambling, and Buck was best man in Willie's wedding. So it wasn't a surprise that they carpooled to the AFL All-Star Game when both were chosen to play for the West team after the 1964 season. (Amazingly, Willie went undrafted but later was signed as a free agent by the Denver Broncos.) The game was to be played at Tulane Stadium in New Orleans, which made it almost a homecoming of sorts. Little did they know this homecoming would be anything but hospitable. The All-Stars, twenty-one who were African American, began arriving on January 9; the game was to be played January 17. "When Buck and I got to New Orleans," Willie recalled, "a lot of the black players were talking about how they had been treated. They couldn't use the front elevators at the hotel; they had to use back elevators to go up to their rooms. Cab drivers wouldn't pick them up or drop them off at the hotel; you had to get a cab down the street. If you were going somewhere, they wouldn't take you all the way. They'd drop you off early. There were restaurants where we couldn't eat." With Cookie Gilchrist, the bruising fullback from Buffalo, and his Bills teammates leading a unified front, the players announced that they would refuse to play the game.

"The American Football League is progressing in great strides," the players' prepared statement began, "and the Negro football players feel they are playing a vital role in the league's progression and have been treated fairly in all cities throughout the league. However, because of adverse conditions and discriminatory practices experienced by the Negro players while here in New Orleans, the players feel they cannot perform 100% as expected in the All-Star Game and be treated differently outside." New Orleans was hosting the AFL as part of a bid to land an expansion franchise in one of the pro leagues; a boycott generated by racial division was the last thing the city wanted. Mayor Victor H. Shiro's condescending response, however, was hardly ameliorating. "If these men would play football only in cities where everybody loved them," he began, "they would all be out of a job today. Their reaction would only aggravate the very condition they are seeking, in time, to eliminate. The players who walked out should have rolled with the punch. Almost all of them are educated college men, who must be aware that you cannot change human nature overnight. They have done themselves and their race a disservice by precipitous action."

Buck and Willie had left New Orleans and were on the road when they learned that the All-Star Game would be played after all – in Houston. "Buck and I were driving back home," Willie said, "and we had the radio on. They kept announcing that the game was being moved and asking any of the players who were boycotting the game to please report to Houston. They gave out phone numbers to call and addresses where to go. They had it on every radio station." The West All-Stars pounded the East 38-14, and Willie Brown was voted the outstanding defensive player. That honor should have pleased the downtrodden Denver Broncos organization, which often had difficulty meeting payroll in those days. But the head coach, Lou Saban, didn't like it that Willie supported the boycott. "They had me labeled as a troublemaker," Willie said. It was only a matter of time until they traded the future Hall of Fame defensive back – later ranked Number 50 on *The*

Sporting News' list of 100 Greatest Football Players – to Oakland. In return, Denver received a player and a draft choice. Neither achieved distinction on the field in any way.

Denver's reaction validated one of the concerns that shaped the way Eddie advised his players regarding their possible involvement in civil rights demonstrations: namely, that some pro football clubs might look unfavorably upon someone who got involved in a racially-oriented protest. Yet being traded to Oakland was a blessing for Willie. At the age of sixty-nine he remained an active member of the Raiders organization and had been associated with the Oakland franchise for almost forty years. Reflecting on Eddie's impact after he was gone, Willie clearly felt his coach had made the difference in his life by preparing him well for all that he encountered from his early days in college, during his years as a professional football player, and through adulthood. "He taught you values," Willie said. "He taught you leadership skills. He taught you to be a gentleman. And then he taught you football. He taught you about going to church and being on the religious side, and taught you about going to school – just taking care of yourself. All of those things impacted my life, on the field, off the field; all those kinds of things."

17

VIRTUALLY EVERY one of Eddie's former players spoke of him with appreciation and admiration in the years that followed their college careers. For the majority he was the most influential male figure in their lives, a combination surrogate father, role model and teacher who shaped them in ways they will never forget. Nemiah Wilson was among those who felt that way, but unlike most, it took a while for him to reach that point. At first, Eddie's demanding coaching style, his discipline, and the wealth of talent on the team all conspired to frustrate the young man from Baton Rouge. "I didn't appreciate him at first," Nemiah said. "But I became his son." In one of life's little oddities, Eddie's stepmother, Daddy Frank's second wife Ann, was Nemiah's English teacher at Eddie's alma mater, McKinley High. By then Julius Kraft had left coaching for private business, but McKinley was still formidable in football. And everyone knew that Eddie had come from McKinley. "From the time I was old enough to understand," Nemiah said, "Eddie was the man."

McKinley High had relocated in 1950 to a new building at the corner of Louise and McCalop Streets. The Louisiana State University campus was minutes away, toward the far end of University Lake. Under coach Paul Dietzel, LSU won the college football national championship with an all-white team in 1958, and star halfback Billy Cannon won the Heisman Trophy the next year. At the same time, McKinley's football team had gone to the black high school state championship game two years in a row. Louisiana's race-mixing ban, the one that altered football schedules and disrupted boxer Ralph Dupas' schedule of bouts, still reflected the prevailing attitude in Baton Rouge and most of Louisiana. Despite segregation's barriers, though, the young athletes from McKinley and the nearly adult athletes from LSU liked to gather in nearby City Park on weekends once their seasons were over, and play pick-up football games.

"Dietzel and Charlie McLendon (who would succeed Dietzel as head coach in 1962) would tell the guys from LSU not to play with us," Nemiah recalled, "and our coaches would tell us, 'Look. You play with those guys and hurt one of them, and you'll go to jail.' It was that kind of thing. But we would still meet in the park and play. One of those days, Coach Dietzel was driving through the park, and he stopped to watch. After the game was all over, a friend of mine and I were walking home, and we passed his car. He said, 'You know, fellas, I'd love to recruit you. But I'd lose my job.' To me that was victory enough, for him to say that to the two of us. To show you how fate is, Billy Cannon and I ended up being teammates in Oakland. We became really good friends."

An Adolph Byrd recruit, Nemiah arrived at Grambling for the 1961 season, when Willie Brown and Buck Buchanan were juniors. His reaction to the depth of talent that greeted him was a lot like Willie's two years before: reporting for the start of practice was akin to joining an all-star team. "With no integration, Eddie had the whole South to recruit from, " Nemiah said, "and we had twenty-one or twenty-two running backs. It was just a matter of who did what in practice the week before as to who played on Saturday." In those days and for more than another decade, Eddie actually had more really good players than he could keep happy and, in some cases, keep at Grambling. "Eddie told us that Bobby Mitchell was here, in the dorm," Nemiah said, "and the University of Illinois came here and took him out to Illinois. He said, 'It happens all the time. I have to worry about major colleges coming on campus and stealing my players.'" Mitchell went on to earn All-Big Ten Conference honors, then won the Most Valuable Player Award in the 1958 College All-Star Game, scoring two touchdowns in a 35-19 upset of the reigning NFL champion, Detroit. He played eleven seasons with Cleveland and Washington, and was inducted into the Pro Football Hall of Fame in 1983. Honored by the Shack Harris & Doug Williams Foundation at a banquet in Washington in 2009, Mitchell acknowledged leaving Grambling for Illinois. "The story came up that Bobby was at Grambling," Doug Williams related. "He said he looked around and said, 'Shoot, Grambling's got a lot of Bobby Mitchells.' So he left and went to Illinois."

Another player defected during Nemiah's years at Grambling, went on to stardom at a Big Ten Conference university, and then played pro football. This one, however, shall remain nameless because of the dubious circumstances of his departure. "He came to practice one day," Nemiah began, "and he said to Coach Robinson, 'Coach, I have a problem. My mother's about to die, and I need to go home and take care of her.' He didn't have a lot of money, so Coach Robinson told us, 'You guys heard what he's saying. He has a problem. He needs to get home. Why don't you guys all pitch in and get him a ticket to go home and see his momma.' So Eddie took two dollars out of the monthly stipend we all got as part of our scholarships – there were like a hundred guys – and gave it to this guy to get a ticket to go home and see his mom. The guy took the money and, next thing we knew, he was at another school, and he was projected to be an All-American! We were upset because one of our own guys betrayed us. But Eddie told us we were brothers, and we were to watch each other's backs. He said we did the right thing, helping one of our own through a family crisis, even if it turned out not to be a family crisis. He was always teaching."

Nemiah tried to leave once, too. The issue, as usual, was playing time. "When I got there, we had an All-American in the same position I played, by the name of Jerry Robinson. They called him the Grey Ghost. One week I might be the first player to go in and take Jerry's place. The next week I might have done something in practice Eddie didn't like, and somebody else was in there. Eddie had all of the outstanding athletes in Louisiana, Mississippi, Texas and Arkansas, all the African American players. His thing was, 'If you get the big head, I've got somebody to take your place.' My attitude always was, 'I should play.' I knew Jerry Robinson was an All-American, and we were friends. But I figured I should be playing. Make no mistake, Jerry was an outstanding athlete. But I'm not going to accept a role that I'm not as good as somebody else." Never one to hide his true feelings, Nemiah frequently engaged Eddie in debates about playing time. "It was a love-hate relationship," he said. "I just felt there wasn't anybody better than me. That's just me. If I did well in practice, I should play. I didn't care if other guys did well, too. If I did well, I figured I should play."

"You're going to get your chance to play," Eddie would tell him, "but how do you figure you can beat out an All-American?" Nemiah would answer, "By becoming one myself." In one such exchange during his sophomore season, Nemiah announced: "Coach, I'm thinking about going home." Eddie asked why. "I think I should be playing, and I'm not playing." Eddie, of course, had heard this many times before. "Everybody here thinks they should be playing," he said. "If I didn't think they could play, and they didn't think they could play, I wouldn't want them here. But you have to show that to me in the game." Nemiah shot back: "How in the hell am I going to show you in the game when I don't get to play that much?" Conceding Nemiah's point, Eddie said, "I'm going to put you in there, and if you don't play, I don't want to hear any more grumbling out of you."

"I played the next week," Nemiah recalled, "and scored two touchdowns and was the leading rusher for the game. So I'm looking to play some the next week. But the next week, I don't play. So I called a couple of friends in Baton Rouge and told them, 'I'm coming home. I'll be there in three hours. Don't tell anybody I'm coming.' I packed my duffle bag and got on the bus. I got home about five o'clock that evening."

The first question Nemiah's mother asked when she saw him was, "What happened?"

"Coach don't like me," he answered.

"That's not what coach told me. Matter of fact, he said he's got plans for you. What you're saying doesn't make any sense."

"Mom, I'm just telling you, he don't like me."

The next day, after his mother had gone to work, Nemiah was home by himself – "nineteen, figuring out what I'm going to do" – when he heard a knock on the door. It was Adolph Byrd, who had coached Nemiah at McKinley in addition to signing him for Grambling.

"Your momma called me," he said, "after Coach Rob called me. They told me you left school."

"Yeah."

"May I ask why?"

"Coach don't like me."

"That's not what I heard."

"Well, I'm not playing, and I think I should play."

"Nemiah, EVERYBODY thinks they should play."

"Yeah, but I proved I can play."

"Coach said you were doing well. But you're not going to beat out an All-American. Jerry's scoring thirty touchdowns a year."

"That's all right. I'm not going back."

"I want to ask you a few questions," Byrd said. "Did you have three meals a day?

"Yes sir."

"Did you have a place to stay?"

"Yes sir."

"Did they change the linen on Fridays?"

"Yes sir."

"Then WHAT are you doing back here?"

At this point, Byrd changed the tenor of the discussion. "Next thing I know," said Nemiah, "he's telling me he has a board in his hand."

"I want you to grab that duffle bag, and I want you to get in my car."

"No. I'm not doing that."

"I'm going to knock hell out of you with this stick."

"My momma isn't going to like that."

"Your momma told me it's okay to bust you across your butt. Now, you get in this car. We're going to the bus station, and you're going back to Grambling. Coach Rob is saying that by the time you get past Alexandria, he'll have a Highway Patrolman pick you up and bring you on to the campus."

Nemiah reluctantly got into Byrd's car, and they drove to the Greyhound station on North Boulevard. Byrd had six dollars and fifty cents in his pocket, and the fare was five dollars. "I bought him a ticket, and gave him a dollar," Byrd recalled, "and told him to get on the bus." As promised, when Nemiah reached Alexandria, a trooper approached him and asked, "Are you Nemiah Wilson? Coach Robinson told us to pick you up and bring you back to the campus." Eddie met Nemiah as soon as he got back. "Don't you ever do that again," he told him. "Nobody's going to leave here unless I want them to leave here."

During the autumn of Nemiah's discontent another drama attracted national attention in neighboring Mississippi. A black Air Force veteran named James Meredith had applied to the University of Mississippi on January 20, 1961 – the day of John F. Kennedy's inauguration as the 35th President of the United States – but was denied admission. With the support of the National Association for the Advancement of Colored People Legal Defense Fund, Meredith sued the university, claiming he had been denied admission solely on the basis of his race. A year later the U.S. Supreme

Court upheld Meredith's right to attend classes at Ole Miss, but Mississippi Governor Ross Barnett, invoking the doctrine of interposition, publicly vowed that he would prevent Meredith's enrollment.

In an incendiary speech broadcast across the state on radio and television on September 13, 1962, Barnett declared: "In the absence of constitutional authority and without legislative action, an ambitious federal government, employing naked and arbitrary power, has decided to deny us the right of self-determination in the conduct of the affairs of our sovereign state." Accusing "professional agitators, the unfriendly liberal press . . . other troublemakers" and "paid propagandists" of "pouring across our borders intent on instigating strife among our people," Barnett told Mississippians that "we must either submit to the unlawful dictates of the federal government or stand up like men and tell them no. The day of reckoning has been delayed as long as possible." Barnett promised that ". . . no school in our state will be integrated while I am your Governor," and that "I shall do everything in my power to prevent integration in our schools." Borrowing a page from Louisiana lawmakers, the Mississippi legislature quickly passed a law prohibiting anyone convicted of a state crime from being admitted to a state university. Meredith had been convicted of false voter registration in October 1962.

On the afternoon of September 29, 1962, Nemiah and the rest of the Grambling Tigers, including Willie Brown, Buck Buchanan and the Grey Ghost, played arch-rival Southern on Southern's home field in Baton Rouge. That evening Ole Miss took the field against the University of Kentucky at Mississippi Veterans Memorial Stadium in Jackson, where only all-white teams were allowed to play. Ace Mumford had retired after the 1961 season, and Southern had lost its opener under new coach Robert H. Lee, 20-6 to Texas Southern. Grambling, which had lost three straight to Southern since entering the SWAC and resuming the rivalry in 1959, had won eighteen of its past twenty-one games – two of its three losses to Southern. Ignored by the mainstream white press, which was not yet covering the games played by black colleges, Grambling beat Southern 14-3. In Jackson, meanwhile, Ole Miss beat Kentucky 14-0 in a game totally overshadowed by a speech delivered by Barnett on the field at halftime.

With an all-white crowd of 41,000 waving Confederate flags of many sizes, Barnett whipped all those present into a frenzy with a few short sentences. "I love Mississippi," he began. "I love her people . . . I love her customs . . ." Just hours before the game, during one of several telephone conversations with Attorney General Robert Kennedy, Barnett had retreated from the defiance of his broadcast speech two weeks earlier and agreed to allow Meredith to be enrolled. Such wild acceptance by the throng in Jackson, however, convinced Barnett, on the spot, to renege on his deal with the Kennedy Administration. ". . . I love and respect her heritage," he concluded.

During the Civil War, precisely a century before, all but a handful of students dropped out of the University of Mississippi and formed a unit of the Eleventh Mississippi Infantry. They became known as The University Greys. The unit was at Gettysburg and participated in Pickett's Charge, the fateful attempt to overrun the Union force with a frontal rush. Every member of the University Greys was killed or injured in that failed assault, and the sports teams at Ole Miss eventually were nicknamed the Rebels, in their honor. It was the latent passion of this heritage that Ross Barnett's infamous remarks inflamed. A mob of more than two thousand – mostly students and some outsiders – gathered on the Ole Miss campus in Oxford the night after the football game. It was the night before Meredith was scheduled to start classes. U.S. Marshals and federal troops were there, too. Thus, the recipe for a riot was complete. Bricks, bottles, pipes, firebombs, tear gas and bullets began flying a short time later. Before order was restored the next day, twenty-eight marshals were wounded, almost fifty soldiers and two hundred fifty civilians were injured, and two people were killed, one a French journalist. Tension and occasional small confrontations continued through the rest of the football season, which ended with the Ole Miss Rebels undefeated and ranked third in the nation.

18

JAMES MEREDITH graduated with a degree in political science on August 18 the following year, but his success under the duress of a hostile learning environment was little more than a footnote in the history of 1963, given the explosive events that occurred from April through November that year. In those eight months: Martin Luther King wrote his eight and a half-page "Letter from Birmingham Jail," in which he made a compelling, reasoned case for nonviolent civil disobedience in the face of unjust laws. Birmingham Public Safety Commissioner "Bull" Connor approved the use of police dogs and fire hoses against peaceful black civil rights demonstrators, many of them children, producing news photos and film clips that appalled the public nationally and spurred support for civil rights legislation. Thirty-seven year old Medgar Evers, Mississippi's NAACP field secretary, was murdered by a sniper as he arrived at his home in Jackson shortly after midnight on June 12 – only hours after President Kennedy, in a nationally televised speech, announced that he was sending sweeping civil rights legislation to Congress. In late August an estimated quarter-million people participated in the March On Washington, which culminated with Dr. King's famous *I Have a Dream* oration. Less than three weeks later, on September 15, four young girls attending Sunday School were killed in a bombing at the Sixteenth Street Baptist Church in Birmingham. And on November 22, President Kennedy was assassinated in Dallas.

I Have A Dream was ranked the top American speech of the 20th century in a 1999 survey of scholars of public address, and has been recalled, analyzed, quoted in part and, with permission of the King estate, replayed in its entirety on various occasions, including the 2009 inauguration of the first African American president in U.S. history, Barack Obama. Certainly, Dr. King's memorable metaphors, biblical parallels and artful employment of the technique called anaphora (in this case repeatedly using "I have a dream" to introduce and connect related themes) combined to produce a speech for the ages. Delivered two months earlier, President Kennedy's call for change in America – now referred to as JFK's Civil Rights Address of June 11, 1963 – should not be forgotten or overlooked, either. Though this address is rarely ever quoted or cited, and never mentioned in the same breath with Dr. King's extraordinary exhortation, portions deserve to be recalled and repeated because they express the pending imperative in such explicit terms. Never before had the President of the United States spoken so bluntly about the unacceptability of the racial climate in America. Anyone familiar with the Double-V Campaign and James G. Thompson's 1942 letter to the *Pittsburgh Courier* couldn't help but notice similarities in substantive points as Kennedy spoke, even though he used different words.

"This nation was founded . . . on the principle that all men are created equal, and that the rights of every man are diminished when the rights of one man are threatened . . ." the President told America. He was uncomfortable with the growing activism of CORE, SNCC and the SCLC, and had been slow to respond to the outrageous acts of racists and segregationists. Yet he had come to recognize and accept that his administration could no longer ignore the urgent need to correct the deplorable situation he faced.

"It ought to be possible for American students of any color to attend any public institution they select without having to be backed up by troops," President Kennedy said.

"It ought to be possible for American consumers of any color to receive equal service in places of public accommodation, such as hotels and restaurants and theaters and retail stores, without being forced to resort to demonstrations in the street, and it ought to be possible for American citizens of any color to register and to vote in a free election without interference or fear of reprisal.

"It ought to be possible, in short, for every American to enjoy the privileges of being American without regard to his race or his color."

Anticipating the factions that would surely battle over what he was proposing, JFK called for collaboration and cooperation in all quarters. Although violence throughout the South, particularly in Birmingham and across Mississippi, obviously forced the issue, he emphasized that discrimination existed throughout America, though usually less overt and less violent outside the South.

"This is not a sectional issue," he said. "Nor is this a partisan issue . . . This is not even a legal or legislative issue alone . . . We are confronted primarily with a moral issue. It is as old as the Scriptures and is as clear as the American Constitution.

"The heart of the question is whether all Americans are to be afforded equal rights and equal opportunities, whether we are going to treat our fellow Americans as we want to be treated.

"If an American, because his skin is dark, cannot eat lunch in a restaurant open to the public, if he cannot send his children to the best public school available, if he cannot vote for the public officials who will represent him, if, in short, he cannot enjoy the full and free life which all of us want, then who among us would be content to have the color of his skin changed and stand in his place?

"Who among us would then be content with the counsels of patience and delay?"

Declaring that "this Nation, for all its hopes and all its boasts, will not be fully free until all its citizens are free," the President unveiled how he hoped to accomplish that freedom. "Next week I shall ask the Congress of the United States to act, to make a commitment it has not fully made in this century to the proposition that race has no place in American life or law . . . I am . . . asking the Congress to enact legislation giving all Americans the right to be served in facilities which are open to the public – hotels, restaurants, theaters, retail stores, and similar establishments. This seems to me to be an elementary right. Its denial is an arbitrary indignity that no American in 1963 should have to endure, but many do.

"I'm also asking the Congress to authorize the Federal Government to participate more fully in lawsuits designed to end segregation in public education . . . Other features will be also requested, including greater protection for the right to vote. But legislation, I repeat, cannot solve this problem alone. It must be solved in the homes of every American in every community across our country."

His closing thoughts made eminent sense, though scores of Americans were not yet ready to agree with him.

"This is one country," he said. "It has become one country because all of us and all the people who came here had an equal chance to develop their talents. We cannot say to 10 percent of the population that you can't have that right; that your children cannot have the chance to develop whatever talents they have; that the only way that they are going to get their rights is to go in the street and demonstrate. I think we owe them and we owe ourselves a better country than that . . ."

Football may seem inconsequential in such a nation-altering time, but helping his players become the best they could be and preparing them for greater opportunities in the future remained Eddie's focus while the Jim Crow South quaked and erupted, just as John Lewis endorsed decades later: "Just do your job, and do it well. Be successful." Rebuilding after Buck Buchanan, Willie Brown and a dozen other key players graduated, most to opportunities in the NFL and AFL, Eddie did his job quite well as Grambling managed to win five, lose three and tie one. (A one-point loss to Southern and a 7-7 tie with Arkansas AM&N prevented the record from being a much better 7-2.) It was the fourth of what would be twenty-seven straight winning seasons for Eddie, and arguably one of Eddie's finest coaching jobs, as Collie Nicholson's uncharacteristically pessimistic report just before the 1963 opener suggests:

> "... Robinson has predicted his own demise in the Southwestern Athletic Conference, and his prospectus is receiving overwhelming unanimity from league observers. Grambling expects its most excruciating season since 1957..."

The season began six days after the Birmingham church bombing, with Grambling prevailing over Alcorn State 40-23. It ended, with a 34-8 victory over Wiley College, six days before shots from the Texas Book Depository Building killed Jack Kennedy and thrust Lyndon Johnson into a new, politically perilous role: champion of sweeping societal change in America.

It was reported prior to his assassination that President Kennedy already had lined up enough votes in the House of Representatives to ensure passage of his proposed civil rights legislation. But it became Lyndon Johnson's task to deliver the actual "yeas" in both the House and Senate. His forceful leadership and trademark arm-twisting ability made him a formidable advocate, but his open support of civil rights reform also made him an easy target for the rabidly pro-Jim Crow white population of the Deep South – even though he was from Texas and a Southerner himself. One representative postcard in the collection at the Jim Crow Museum of Racist Memorabilia features a tortured takeoff on the Twenty-Third Psalm that ridicules the President and incorporates nearly every insulting racial stereotype of the era:

Lyndon is my Shepherd;
I shall not work.

He maketh me to lie down in front of theaters;
He leadeth me into white universities.

He restoreth my welfare check;
He leadeth me to sit-ins for Communists' sake.

He prepareth the table for me in the presence of White folks;
My Cadillac gas tank runneth over.

Surely the Supreme Court shall follow me all the days of my life, and
I shall dwell in the Federal Housing Project forever.

President Johnson ignored such crass expressions of public disap-
proval, overcame almost three months of procedural delays in the House
of Representatives, outlasted a 57-day filibuster in the Senate and maneu-
vered around other parliamentary technicalities that had the potential to
further stall proceedings (if not kill the legislation entirely). Ultimately,
House and Senate Democrats from the eleven Confederate states voted 107-
8 against the civil rights legislation, and all eleven Republicans from those
same states rejected it unanimously. Nonetheless, the Civil Rights Act of
1964 became a reality with about 70 percent overall approval on July 2. Just
before signing it into law that same day, President Johnson spoke to the
nation from the East Room of the White House at 6:45 p.m. Broadcast on
radio and television, his remarks, along with those of King and Kennedy,
comprise what could be called The Civil Rights Trilogy – three speeches
that together articulated the injustice of segregation and the unacceptability of racial discrimination, and challenged Americans to make America
"the greatest country in the world" (as Eddie Robinson believed it to be).

Noting that the United States of America was about to celebrate its
188th birthday, LBJ began by recalling the "small band of valiant men" who
signed the Declaration of Independence and wrote the Bill of Rights. "They
pledged their lives, their fortunes, and their sacred honor not only to found a

nation," he said, "but to forge an ideal of freedom – not only for political independence, but for personal liberty – not only to eliminate foreign rule, but to establish the rule of justice in the affairs of men."

He acknowledged the perpetual struggle to achieve and preserve justice and freedom around the world, then added, "Now our generation of Americans has been called on to continue the unending search for justice within our own borders.

"We believe that all men are created equal," he continued. "Yet many are denied equal treatment.

"We believe that all men have certain unalienable rights. Yet many Americans do not enjoy those rights.

"We believe that all men are entitled to the blessings of liberty. Yet millions are being deprived of those blessings – not because of their own failures, but because of the color of their skin.

"The reasons are deeply imbedded in history and tradition and the nature of man. We can understand – without rancor or hatred – how this all happened.

"But it cannot continue. Our Constitution, the foundation of our Republic, forbids it. The principles of our freedom forbid it. Morality forbids it. And the law I will sign tonight forbids it."

After briefly summarizing the process that produced Public Law 88-352 (78 Stat. 241) – without mentioning the political obstructionism – President Johnson attempted to answer dissenters before they could speak.

"The purpose of the law is simple," he began.

"It does not restrict the freedom of any American, so long as he respects the rights of others.

"It does not give special treatment to any citizen.

"It does say the only limit to a man's hope for happiness, and for the future of his children, shall be his own ability.

"It does say that those who are equal before God shall now also be equal in the polling booths, in the classrooms, in the factories, and in hotels, restaurants, movie theaters, and other places that provide service to the public.

"We must not approach the observance and enforcement of this law in a vengeful spirit. Its purpose is not to punish. Its purpose is not to divide, but to end divisions – divisions which have all lasted too long. Its purpose is national, not regional.

"Its purpose is to promote a more abiding commitment to freedom, a more constant pursuit of justice, and a deeper respect for human dignity."

The President closed with an appeal to "every public official, every religious leader, every business and professional man, every workingman, every housewife . . . every American" to embrace the spirit of equality for all citizens. "Let us close the springs of racial poison," he said. "Let us pray for wise and understanding hearts. Let us lay aside irrelevant differences and make our Nation whole."

Passage of the Civil Rights Act of 1964 was vindication of a sort for Eddie Robinson. *One of these days this thing is going to change . . . Everything can change, including the laws, if you're willing to pay the price . . .* Of course, neither the new law nor anything the President of the United States could say immediately changed the reality of daily life in the South, particularly in Alabama and Mississippi.

19

FREEDOM SUMMER is one name given to SNCC's 1964 black voter reg-istration campaign in Mississippi. Another is Mississippi Summer, or the Mississippi Summer Project. By any name it was one of the most violent periods in the history of the most racially violent state in the Jim Crow South. The Freedom Summer plan involved establishing a new, additional political party, called the Mississippi Freedom Democratic Party, in defiance of the all-white Democratic Party of Mississippi, and sending elected dele-gates to the Democratic National Convention in Atlantic City that August. The MFDP delegates would represent Mississippi's black citizens, and would demand seats and a voice at the convention where Lyndon Johnson would formally become the Democratic Party's candidate for President of the United Sates. Mississippi's black population was the largest of any state in the nation in 1964 – more than a third of all residents – and remained so almost fifty years later. Yet because of literacy tests, poll taxes and other means of obstructing black registration, including threats and violence, only five percent of voting-age blacks were registered to vote in 1963.

Fannie Lou Hamer, a sharecropper from Ruleville, Mississippi, who became vice-chair of the MFDP, dramatized the plight of Mississippi's dis-enfranchised black voters in testimony before the Credentials Committee at the 1964 Democratic Convention. She told of riding a bus to Indianola in

1962 with seventeen other black Mississippians who wanted to register to vote. At the end of their 26-mile trip, only two of the eighteen were allowed to take the literacy test. On the return home, their bus was stopped by the State Highway Patrol and the driver charged with driving a bus the wrong color. When she finally arrived home, the owner of the plantation where she lived with her husband and two adopted children was so angry with her for trying to register to vote that he told her she and her family would have to leave unless she withdrew her registration. She refused to back down, and was sent packing. A year later, after attending a voter registration workshop, she was jailed in Winona, Mississippi, and endured a vicious beating in her cell. "All of this," she concluded, "is on account of us wanting to register, to become first-class citizens . . ."

Hamer's story, which attracted nationwide television coverage, was a major factor in passage of the Voting Rights Act of 1965. But so were events related to the creation of the Mississippi Freedom Democratic Party during Freedom Summer (and, ultimately, the Selma march in 1965). Bringing the MFDP to life required mobilizing black voters throughout Mississippi. Such a statewide organizing effort would have been a daunting logistical challenge under the best of conditions, but white hostility multiplied the degree of difficulty by an incalculable percentage. Indeed, from mid-June to mid-September, SNCC recorded almost two hundred bombings, church burnings, beatings and shootings related to Freedom Summer efforts. CORE was committed to actively participating, but SNCC still needed hundreds of volunteers to establish a presence in all of the state's eighty-two counties simultaneously.

Colleges and universities were the primary source of those volunteers, and recruitment began on campuses across the country in late April – at the same time the two-month attempt to block the Civil Rights Bill dragged on in the U.S. Senate. Formal training for the first three hundred volunteers began June 13, 1964, on the campus of Western College for Women in Oxford, Ohio, an hour's drive from Cincinnati. Mickey Schwerner and

James Chaney, CORE operatives in Mississippi, conducted some of the training that week. While there, they made friends with Andrew Goodman, one of the many students who were inspired by campus speakers, in Goodman's case, future New York Congressman Allard Lowenstein. As the program in Oxford was wrapping up on June 19, the U.S. Senate passed its version of the Civil Rights Bill. The next day Schwerner and Chaney returned to Mississippi, accompanied by Goodman.

Mickey Schwerner, a twenty-four year old New Yorker and graduate of Cornell University, moved to Meridian, Mississippi with his wife Rita in January, 1964 to operate the CORE field office there. Upon his arrival he became the first white civil rights worker in the state permanently based outside of Jackson, the capital. James Chaney, a twenty-one year old native Mississippian, began as a CORE volunteer in October 1963 when he could no longer find work as a plasterer. Schwerner made Chaney a paid CORE staffer in April 1964. Wary black residents, particularly in rural areas, trusted Chaney because he was black. Goodman, who grew up in a privileged home on the Upper West Side of Manhattan, was a twenty-year old student at Queens College. He thought Freedom Summer would be educational and useful, an experience that would expand his sheltered life.

On June 21, the three Freedom Summer workers went missing in Neshoba County (east central Mississippi) after making the forty-mile drive from Meridian to the small town of Philadelphia. They went there to look into a fire that destroyed a black church mere hours after the Ku Klux Klan assaulted black residents as they left a political forum at the church. Murdered that night, the trio's disappearance made headlines nationally. The subsequent federal investigation and search for their bodies became the basis for the movie *Mississippi Burning,* which received several awards and was nominated for many others, including both the Oscar and Golden Globe for "best picture," but also drew significant criticism for its controversial fictionalization of the historic event. The bodies of the three were found in an earthen dam on August 4. It was about six weeks after they dis-

EDDIE ROBINSON

appeared and barely a month after the Civil Rights Act of 1964 was passed and signed into law the same day by LBJ. But it would be three years – 1967 – before anyone was brought to justice for their killings.

Grambling was seeking its third straight SWAC championship when the football season of 1967 began, but Eddie's team was not expected to repeat. Jackson State – with sixteen players who would sign with National Football League teams the next year – was the pre-season favorite to win the conference title. Close games against Alcorn State, Prairie View and Tennessee State – won by Grambling by a total of eleven points – and a 68-0 rout of Mississippi Valley State put the team's record at 4-0 heading into the mid-season showdown with its foremost SWAC challenger. Jackson State, meanwhile, had stumbled badly in its third game of the season, losing 38-6 to Arkansas AM&N, but had bounced back from that upset with a 3-0 victory over Southern to stand 3-1. *The 1967 Southwestern Athletic Conference football championship may be decided on Saturday when unbeaten Grambling takes on Jackson State in Mississippi Memorial Stadium,"* began a story in the *Jackson Daily News* on Monday, October 16. Advance tickets were on sale at twelve locations around the city, mostly banks and savings & loans, through Thursday afternoon at a cost of $3 apiece. Ticket windows at the stadium were to open at 9 a.m. that Saturday, October 21, for a 1 p.m. kickoff. It was Jackson State's homecoming weekend.

The high-stakes nature of the game and the exalted standing of the two teams, as defender and pretender, were enough to make their meeting a major event. But the site of the game and its timing combined to make this an historic occasion. Mississippi Veterans Memorial Stadium – site of the game that preceded the James Meredith riot on the Ole Miss campus – was a state-owned facility built in 1941, the year Eddie began coaching at Grambling. For decades it was the largest football stadium in the state. And because the limitations of Mississippi's highway system made it harder for football fans to travel to Oxford, Starkville or Hattiesburg than to Jackson, it was the site of virtually every "big game" played by or between Ole Miss, Mississippi State and Southern Mississippi. Until October 21, 1967, however, Mississippi Veterans Memorial Stadium had never been the site of a game involving a black team, or even a team with a black player. Omitting the racial significance of the venue, the *Daily News* preview story continued: *"The 46,000 seat stadium is usually reserved for the likes of Mississippi and Mississippi State. The SWAC opponents will be making their first appearance in it."*

All advance stories about the game appeared on the sports pages, and gave no hint of the developing drama that was dominating Page One. Coverage of the final days of the two-week federal trial of eighteen defendants charged with various crimes related to the deaths of Schwerner, Chaney and Goodman three years earlier overshadowed everything else. *"An all-white jury is deliberating its verdict in the trial of 18 men charged with conspiracy in the murders of three civil rights workers in 1964, following closing arguments,"* read the opening paragraph of the front page lead story the Thursday before the game. The full report left the impression that, unlike so many previous trials in Mississippi and other Jim Crow states, when white juries acquitted white defendants of crimes against blacks no matter how much evidence supported conviction, the day of reckoning was fast approaching for at least some of the men who were responsible for the deaths in this celebrated case.

The irony of the lead headline on the front page of the *Daily News* the next day cannot be overstated. On the day before the first football game between two black teams in the history of Mississippi's showcase stadium, the front page of the *Jackson Daily News* announced: **"Seven Men Found Guilty In Three Neshoba Deaths."** It was the first time in Mississippi's one hundred fifty years as a state that convictions were achieved in a civil rights murder trial.

The convergence of "firsts" presented a most unusual coaching challenge, particularly for Jackson State head coach Rod Paige and his assistants. As he struggled to properly balance the significance of the approaching game and the importance of the unfolding trial, Paige was thirty-four years old and halfway through his fourth season as head football coach at his alma mater. There was no hint that he would become a nationally recognized educational leader in years to come. "We were walking around with quite a burden on our shoulders," he said in a 2009 interview. "These guys came down to make life better for those of us who lived in Mississippi, and they paid the ultimate price for that. There's no way you could live in Mississippi and not have that weigh heavily on your mind."

At the same time, Paige added, "we had a football game to play. The first game in Memorial Stadium was a BIG DEAL." The decision was made to focus on that, rather than the trial itself or justice for the three victims. "Some might say we should have made that a rallying cry," Paige acknowledged. "That was discussed. I don't remember discussing it at all with the team as a group. I remember discussing it with the coaching staff. But we decided we would not mix those two things like that. We weren't sure it was a good thing to make it a rallying cry for the football game. We saw those who lost their lives as much bigger than the game."

No one in the Jackson State locker room could relate more directly to the trial and what it represented than assistant coach W.C. Gorden, who had joined Paige's staff that season. Gorden had coached high school football for nine years in Magnolia, Mississippi, just north of the Louisiana border. He had tried to register to vote in 1960 but failed the test on the U.S. Constitution – even though he taught history and what was then called civics, a class about American government. "The county tax collector administered the test," he said. "It was a subjective test, not an objective test. He'd give you a passage from the Constitution to read, and then you'd give your interpretation of it. Of course, the interpretation you gave was incorrect." Gorden tried again in 1961 and passed, but his wife Vivian, also a teacher, flunked. "It took a lot of courage," Gorden said. "She could have lost her job for trying to register. Mississippians have a love for football, and I think the football coach was treated a little more congenially than the average African American citizen. She's a brave girl. There was no hesitation." Both finally passed – and voted – in 1962. As a reminder of those days, Gorden kept the original receipts issued to him and Vivian for the two-dollar poll tax each one had to pay.

At Grambling, meanwhile, the emphasis remained on football, according to Doug Porter, who, after working alongside Eddie for eight years, was a head coach himself at Fort Valley State in Georgia for twenty-six seasons. "We were so focused on Jackson State and trying to win the football game that, at the time, the significance of that verdict probably didn't register with us the way it should have. That was Coach Robinson. His focus was to take care of the business of winning football games."

Charlie Joiner provided the players' perspective. "We followed all the happenings that were going on with the black community in those days. But we were kind of in a . . . I don't want to say Coach Robinson sheltered us from doing a whole lot of things. We knew what was going on, but we knew we had a great leader who would provide us with great insight on what to do and how to react to all the civil rights things that were happening in the United States at that time. I don't think anybody on that team would have made a move without asking Coach Robinson, or asking if it was right. If you wanted to join a movement, a player would go to him and ask him first. And most of the time he would tell them, 'It's more important for you to stay here,' and 'The best way to beat these things is to be educated, be prepared and be ready to fight for what you believe in.' In other words, do it, but do it the right way." And so, "I just got on the bus and went to Jackson, and played a football game," Joiner said. "I just got off the bus, got dressed and played. I don't remember the significance of it."

The game actually was one to remember in its own right. Grambling scored in four plays on the opening series, the last a 41-yard run by future pro Essex Johnson. Jackson State trailed 14-13 from halftime until a freshman quarterback named Robert Kelly led a drive that produced the winning score with two minutes left to play. Grambling mounted a frantic attempt at a comeback that reached the Jackson State 38-yard line before quarterback James Harris, who would make pro football history after his college career was completed, fumbled as he was buried by a heavy pass rush. The 20-14 victory remained a high point in Paige's coaching career more than forty years later. "We beat Grambling," he said. "You didn't do that too many times."

In typical fashion, Eddie still had a great season. Grambling didn't lose another game; won the SWAC championship outright; beat Florida A&M 28-25 in the Orange Blossom Classic; and shared the black national championship with Morgan State. Jackson State lost two of its remaining four games to finish 6-3. Paige left Jackson State after the next season to pursue graduate studies at Indiana University; Gorden remained on the staff and was named head coach with two games remaining in the 1976 season. The right to vote and the price many paid to secure it remained important to him, and in 1980 he took the entire Jackson State football team to the courthouse to register. "After that," he said, "we commissioned players who were registered to encourage the freshmen and other players coming in to register. Black politicians knew the Jackson State football players were registered voters. They would come to our football meetings and make speeches. Many of our kids worked in their campaigns."

In recognition of the landmark event that it was, the first black football game in Mississippi Veterans Memorial Stadium was commemorated in 2007 when Jackson State hosted a 40th anniversary reunion for the participants from both schools. Eddie had died the previous February, but Doris Robinson came and spent time visiting with Paige and Gorden. Her presence was a telling indication of how much the momentous occasion meant to her late husband, especially coming at a time when his faith in the American system of courts and laws was so sorely tested and so spectacularly vindicated.

20

THE LAST major history-making events of the Civil Rights Movement in the Deep South occurred in the small, south central Alabama town of Selma in March, 1965. Selma was the largest town in Dallas County, which had a voting-age population of 30,000 residents. Barely half of them were could actually vote, however, because only three hundred thirty-five of the approximately 15,000 possible black voters had successfully registered. What became known as "Bloody Sunday" – the March 7 attempt to walk fifty-four miles from Selma east to the state capital of Montgomery to dramatize the need for open voter registration of black citizens in Alabama – ended in a brutal rout. State troopers on foot and a sheriff's posse on horseback clubbed, whipped and trampled the peaceful marchers who were being led by John Lewis and Martin Luther King's stand-in, Hosea Williams. Two Sundays later, this time with Dr. King in the lead, more than 3,200 people, white supporters as well as blacks, began a five-day hike along Jefferson Davis Highway to the city known as the Cradle of the Confederacy. Their ranks swelled to more than 30,000 on the final, triumphant day, which culminated with Dr. King passing Dexter Avenue Baptist Church, site of his first pastorate and the base from which he led the Montgomery Bus Boycott, on his way to the seat of the government led by the staunch segregationist, Alabama Governor George Wallace.

As the flag of the Confederacy, a symbol of Jim Crow to Southerners of both races, waved in the breeze at the capitol, Dr. King addressed the largest civil rights rally ever held anywhere in the South – right before Governor Wallace's very eyes. "Segregation is on its deathbed," King intoned to *"Amens"* from the crowd. He foresaw "the day of man as man," when race or color no longer mattered. Three lives were sacrificed in less than a month in Selma, but not in vain. Those deaths and other violence focused the nation's attention on disenfranchisement as nothing had before. Following so closely the sensational events of Freedom Summer in Mississippi, they were enough to move President Johnson to forcefully correct the glaring omission in the Civil Rights Act of 1964. The Voting Rights Act passed Congress and became law in early August, ending forever the taxes and tests that impeded W.C. Gorden and his wife, as well as countless other would-be black voters, for decades.

Integration as required by law often took years, of course, as in the case of major college football teams across the South from Texas to Florida. But the dawning of "the day of man as man" inevitably meant the sun eventually would set on the black football talent monopoly that Eddie and others had enjoyed for decades in the South. Major college programs had an ever-increasing economic incentive to field winning teams, and the best black players would help them achieve that success. Black athletes also wanted to compete against the best talent – white as well as black – to enhance their professional prospects. It was only a matter of time until there would be no more stories such as Jim Parker's or Bubba Smith's.

Jim Parker went to Ohio State – a long way from his hometown of Macon, Georgia – even though the University of Georgia, Georgia Tech, the University of Alabama, and even Ole Miss were closer. He anchored the offensive line on the first national championship team Woody Hayes coached in 1954, and opened the holes that enabled Howard "Hopalong" Cassady to win the Heisman Trophy the next year. After an eleven-year career with the Baltimore Colts, he would become the first offensive lineman enshrined in the Pro Football Hall of Fame. Hayes knew what an exceptional football player he had anchoring his offensive line. But in 1956, instead of asking Parker if he could help recruit more players as good as he was, Woody told him: "The powers that be tell me I can have no more than two black players, and can only start one. Someday, goddammit, I'm going to change that."

Bubba Smith played high school football for his father at Charlton-Pollard, the black high school in Beaumont, Texas, near the Louisiana state line. An all-state player who was being pursued by numerous college recruiters – all from outside the South – Bubba told University of Texas head coach Darrell Royal that his dream was to play for the Longhorns. But that was in 1963, and although the university publicly lifted its ban on black athletes in varsity sports that year, Royal was aware of an unspoken desire among university regents to delay acting on it. Forty-five years later, in an interview that was part of a cable television documentary of the integration of college football, Smith still remembered Royal's answer. "He said, 'Bubba, I can probably get you a scholarship, but I don't know when the football program is going to integrate.'" It would be 1970 before the first black player, offensive lineman Julius Whittier, took the field for Royal. The year before, Texas became the last university to win the college football national championship with an all-white team.

So Bubba Smith, one of the biggest defensive linemen of his era, a future member of the College Football Hall of Fame, and 10-year pro, went almost 1,300 miles north to Michigan State. He hadn't really been around white people before, and there were about 47,000 of them on campus. He'd never seen snow, and that part of Michigan averaged almost fifty inches a year. And grits, his favorite breakfast food, weren't on the dining hall menu. In that same television interview, he said: "I didn't have no anger. All I wanted to know was, 'Why is it you don't like me, and you don't even know me?'"

Jerry LeVias, a spectacular pass receiver and kick returner, broke the color barrier in the old Southwest Conference when he took the field for Southern Methodist in 1965. LeVias led SMU to the Southwest Conference championship and a Cotton Bowl berth in 1966 – the year that Michigan State, with Bubba, played Notre Dame to a 10-10 tie in one of the most famous college football games of all time. Despite leading SMU to its first Southwest Conference football title in almost two decades, LeVias was anything but the campus hero. Instead, he endured nastiness that left him embittered for much of his adult life. His coach, Hayden Fry, described the ordeal during remarks at a University of Iowa program in his honor in 2009, eleven years after he retired from coaching there, and more than forty years after the fact.

"I would say 95 percent of you present would not believe what Jerry LeVias went through, what I went through, and what our coaching staff went through with the threats (and being on edge all the time)," Fry said, according to a transcript published by the *Iowa City Press-Citizen*. "From examining our locker room, out of town trips, checking airplanes that we flew on to see if there was a bomb on them, or whatever. We even had a sniper in the stands at one of the games that was going to kill Jerry. Anyway, the real bad things I can't ... we screened all of his mail, his telephone calls. He had real problems on campus, some of his own teammates, some of the faculty members. They just weren't used to dealing with African Americans. It was bad, and to this day, it's still bad. A lot of it is (better left unsaid)."

The Southeastern Conference was the last major conference to integrate. The University of Kentucky – a border state that declared neutrality in the American Civil War – went first in 1966, the year LeVias changed the Southwest Conference. Tragically, one of the two original scholarship players, defensive end Greg Page, died from injuries suffered during a contact drill in practice at the start of their sophomore year, and the other, receiver Nat Northington, was so distraught that he left the university shortly after becoming the first black to play in an SEC football game. Wilbur Hackett, a heralded recruit from Louisville, was one of two black freshmen in the next class. Hackett endured abuse throughout the conference but stayed and became a two-time defensive captain. There was no evidence that Page's fatal injuries were racially motivated. In fact, a white player on the same team was left a quadriplegic from injuries he suffered during another practice.

It would take five more years for Georgia, Louisiana State and, last of all, Ole Miss, to give up their all-white teams and complete integration of the SEC. Twenty years later, more than half of all football players on SEC teams were African American, and in 1992, Alabama won the national championship with a starting defensive unit that was 100 percent black.

Conversion in the SEC produced numerous colorful stories, including one involving Eddie. Charlie McLendon succeeded Paul Dietzel at LSU in 1962, and remained head football coach for eighteen years. Sometime after recruiting his first black player, a quarterback named Lora Hinton from Chesapeake, Virginia, in 1971, McLendon approached Eddie at the coaches association's annual convention. As black sportswriter R.L. Stockard recalled, the exchange went as follows:

McLENDON: "Coach, how do you reach black football players? Say I'm behind at halftime, and I want to get through to the players who are African American. I don't know how to get them emotional."

ROBINSON: "Coach Mac, if I had some players who look just like you, I'd tell them the same thing I tell my black ball players. Because, if you want to play football and you've got the ability, and you're behind, you want to win. There's no secret formula. You incite them the same way you do any other football player."

Bear Bryant, Alabama's head coach for twenty-five years, is at the center of another oft-repeated, and hotly debated, account of the integration of major southern college football programs. Bryant scheduled a game with

Southern California, coached by his good friend John McKay, to open the 1970 season at Legion Field in Birmingham. USC featured an offensive backfield with three African Americans: quarterback Jimmy Jones, tailback Clarence Davis – who was born right there in Birmingham – and sophomore fullback Sam Cunningham. Only half of McKay's squad was white. The Bear had no black players in uniform. Cunningham gained one hundred thirty-five yards on only twelve running plays, and scored two touchdowns. Southern Cal piled up almost five hundred yards rushing, to Alabama's thirty-two, and Alabama lost, 42-21.

This game became the subject of books, panel discussions, video documentaries and magazine articles. The popular belief was that Bryant scheduled the game knowing his all-white team would be no match for a team that had the advantage of so many talented black athletes. This view held that The Bear was willing to absorb a rout in order to convince the university's administration and fans to allow him to recruit African American players. In the stands at Legion Field that night, however, was Wilbur Jackson, a black freshman running back who would become eligible the following season under NCAA rules. His presence established that Alabama had already begun to integrate its football team before playing USC. Nevertheless, that game served a purpose, one which Bryant probably intended. It demonstrated to Crimson Tide fans, some of whom had resisted integration up to then, that the time had come. When the coaches met at midfield for the post-game handshake, Bryant reportedly said to McKay: "I can't thank y'all enough for what you did for me tonight."

Ben Williams, a 6-foot-3, 260-pound defensive tackle, and James Reed, a speedy tailback, were the University of Mississippi's first black football recruits in 1972. Their historic arrival was carefully monitored news, according to a young, white sportswriter from Memphis who covered Ole Miss football in those years. He said the press was allowed to interview Williams and Reed, but only in the presence of a chaperone from the sports information department, to ensure against loaded questions and incendiary answers. Williams came from Yazoo City – Willie Brown's hometown – and was accepted by his white teammates and the almost totally-white student body in ways that seemed impossible just ten years earlier, when James Meredith's attempt to become the first black student at the University of Mississippi touched off the all-night riot that killed two and injured about three hundred.

Colonel Reb was the name of the mascot for Mississippi's sports teams for more than a half-century. In the 1940s, it became tradition for Ole Miss students to elect a male student "Colonel Reb" and a co-ed "Miss Ole Miss." Being elected Colonel Reb was the highest honor on campus, and Ben Williams – Gentle Ben as he became known – was accorded it in 1975, his senior year. Of at least equal significance within the locker room that year, Williams – the first black football player in Mississippi's history – also was chosen to be one of the team's three captains. He was a four-year letterman, and was the first black all-SEC player and first black All-American in Ole Miss history. He was chosen by Buffalo in the third round of the NFL draft. Reed, a three-year letterman, was a ninth-round pick by Cleveland.

With the first black players in the SEC, the future of college football had been mapped out. And Florida A&M's Jake Gaither, who won 83.5 percent of his games (203-36-4) while HBCUs enjoyed a corner on the black player market, saw a cataclysm approaching. He retired after the 1969 season, his twenty-fifth at Florida A&M, at the age of sixty-six. "You know integration is going to be a good thing," he said, "but the ones that are going to be hurt are the black schools." Gaither was correct, though the impact wasn't felt as quickly as even he may have feared. The Grambling teams of the 1970s were the most talented Eddie ever had. In a one-decade school record, forty-five players were taken in the NFL draft, including fifteen in the first three rounds. Numerous others signed as free agents and had successful pro careers. Integration's effects weren't really felt until the 1980s, when the number of draftees dropped to eighteen, none going higher than two third-round picks. Between 1995, the last season any of Eddie's players were drafted, and 2008, only three Grambling players were selected.

"You knew that eventually they were going to begin to use kids that they had been overlooking all those years," said Doug Porter, "because the kids were such great athletes. They're now, you might say, almost controlling where the black kids in the South go. The difference is that their pockets are so deep. They're going to beat you with facilities. They're going to beat you with academic support. They're going to push the fact that you're going to be on television a lot. When I first came to Grambling in 1966, we never would have imagined that LSU would have the look it has today when it lines up to play football."

In a column written by Gene Wojciechowski for *ESPN.com* when Eddie died, Florida State's Bobby Bowden, the coach with the most major college victories in history, said: "There's no doubt in my mind that in the late 1960s, when they started integrating Southern college football, nobody played a bigger role than Eddie Robinson and Jake Gaither. At the time, their schools had it made. Their schools were all African American. Even though they were about to lose a lot of their kids, they helped it be successful, telling people how to act and what to say, and to be patient. They made it a wholesome process."

PART FOUR

Icon

21

FOR W.C. GORDEN, being part of the first football game between black universities in the history of Mississippi Veterans Memorial Stadium, combined with the experience of coaching against the legendary Eddie Robinson, made the Jackson-Grambling game of 1967 one of the most memorable moments of his life. It was that way for countless coaches, players, students, businessmen and average citizens who came in contact with Eddie and experienced some combination of his determination, humility, compassion, commitment to excellence, strength of character, core values, passion, enthusiasm, faith and restraint. Eddie's tremendous coaching success and love for the game of football, his amazing concern for others, his unwavering patriotism, and the unique example he set of patience and self-control in the face of racial injustice and resistance to change made him a legend in their eyes, a true American icon.

"During the week before the game," Gorden recalled, "I was inundated by the media for comments on Eddie Robinson and his coaching philosophy, and why he was such a great coach. That was great for me. I'm thinking, 'I'm in high cotton now. I'm coaching in college and I'm being interviewed every day about this great ball game coming up Saturday against coach Eddie Robinson.' Coming from high school, I was wanting to get a little more media attention and be able to express my football knowledge and experiences to the general public. You didn't get a chance to do that a lot in Mississippi on a high school level at that time. I thought my career had arrived because of this great man."

The scene that Saturday afternoon was etched into Gorden's memory. "I didn't see him until game time. But when he walked out on the field, he lived up to his reputation as the 'black pope.' He came out with a briefcase. He had on a suit and a beautiful necktie. He was well-groomed. He was very sophisticated. That caught my attention and just stuck with me. It really took my mind off the game to some extent. I hadn't seen that sophistication on the football field before. When we would make our game plan, as defensive coaches, we'd have one page, front and back; offense the same way. Eddie had a briefcase! I couldn't imagine. I wondered, 'What's in this briefcase that he can thumb through to help him make adjustments during this ball game?' I thought he possibly had our coaching history – how we coached and how we thought, and that sort of thing."

More than a decade passed before Gorden got to know Eddie personally. By then, W.C. was Jackson State's head coach and squaring off with him every season. Gorden coached Jackson State to more victories in sixteen seasons than any other coach in the university's history, and because of that was inducted into the College Football Hall of Fame in 2008. He lost his first six games against Eddie, but still recorded the best winning percentage among coaches who faced Eddie on a regular basis, winning seven and losing nine (.4375). When Jackson State beat Grambling 24-17 in 1988, it was Gorden's fourth straight win against Eddie, and Eddie demonstrated the sportsmanship he was so widely known for. "After the game he came out to the middle of the field," Gorden recalled, "and said, 'Coach, you are doing a fantastic job. I admire the way you guys are preparing your team. You're a great coach.' I said, 'Eddie, you don't have to humble yourself to tell me this. I know what a great coach you are. You beat me five consecutive years. You don't have to tell me this.' He said, 'But coach, I've never had a coach in my lifetime beat me four consecutive years like you have.' That's the kind of person he was. The years when you'd beat him, he'd meet you in the middle of the field and was always the kind, complimentary person."

W.C. and Eddie shared a keen interest in jazz, and over the years often discussed the similarities they found between the music and their sport. "Eddie wasn't so much an inventor of football technique and schemes and formations," Gorden said. "He was like the great jazz musicians, like Illinois Jacquet and all the other good ones." A master of the tenor saxophone, Jean-Baptiste Illinois Jacquet established himself in the world of jazz in the early 1940s. Jacquet (his given middle name was Illinois, even though he was born in Louisiana) was only nineteen when he recorded the groundbreaking solo improvisation, *Flying Home,* while playing with Lionel Hampton's orchestra. He later performed with Count Basie and Cab Calloway, and became a featured soloist for Jazz at the Philharmonic.

"Illinois Jacquet could take a note and bend the note and get a sound that was different than all the other tenor saxophone players," Gorden explained. "Eddie said football was the same way. If we give the ball off to the running back and he's supposed to run to the 'three' hole, he's got to do that. But once he does that, through film study, defensive team speed and the defensive coverage, he may break left, he may break right, or he may go straight ahead. Even I don't know. That's what makes the game so interesting; it's a mystery, just like jazz music. Eddie always said that in football, you had to be innovative; you had to be creative; and you had to be democratic. He would allow his players to come to him and suggest a play or explain what they thought would work that was different than the game plan."

Nemiah Wilson knew exactly what Gorden was saying about Eddie's democratic football. "Eddie wanted to show other coaches they could accomplish what they wanted with players by communicating with them," Nemiah said. "His thing was, most coaches are intense and they get upset and pick on their players or get mad with other coaches. His philosophy was, 'If you're doing something that I don't like, and I'm not getting my point across to you, it's something I'm not doing right. Because, as a coach, I have to figure out a way to get to you, to get you to hear what I'm saying.' He would take it hard if he couldn't get through to a player. Eddie had the personality that people made him. He didn't make himself; people made him."

By 1980, Eddie and Grambling were famous, and the Southwestern Athletic Conference was legitimately competing for media attention with the Southeastern Conference and other major college football organizations, even though SWAC teams had not yet begun to regularly play predominantly white teams. To attract more coverage and promote its star players, the SWAC developed a press tour, a bus trip to the big cities of the teams that played in the SWAC. The stops included Jackson, Mississippi; Montgomery, Alabama; Houston, Texas; and Monroe, Shreveport, Baton Rouge, and New Orleans in Louisiana. Two players from each school – prospective All-Americans and likely future pros – went along and were available for interviews. The players sat in the back of the bus; the coaches were in the front.

"As a coach," Gorden explained, "you sat in a seat on the basis of how well you were able to tell a story. The one who told the best story sat in the front seat. Eddie sat behind the bus driver in the first seat in the bus. Archie Cooley (Mississippi Valley State), who was a very good storyteller, sat across from Eddie. Marino Casem from Alcorn sat in the second seat behind Eddie, and I sat across from him. We were the four storytellers. We would go to a hotel, and we would have a press conference, and we'd have alumni, fans and media. The media would follow us from town to town because we told such a good story. We got more publicity than Ole Miss or Mississippi State because Eddie could spin a story. Casem could spin a story, and I thought I was pretty good. People would judge a coach's ability to communicate the way they'd judge them on their ability to win football games. You had to be able to talk and tell stories. This is how I got to know Eddie Robinson. The beautiful thing about Eddie is, some people have to use profanity to get their punch line across, but Eddie didn't do that. He never used profanity. He was always clean in his storytelling.

"One of his best stories was about Marino, his close friend," Gorden continued. "Coaches would change roommates each night during the SWAC tour. This particular night Eddie had Marino as his roommate. Casem was known as a snorer. I mean, he could SNORE. They talked until about midnight, then they went to sleep. Casem was snoring at two in the morning, and Eddie was still awake. Eddie said 'I couldn't figure out what I was going to do to get this guy to stop snoring because I can't get any sleep.' He said about two o'clock it came to him. He pulled the cover back, got out of bed, walked over to Casem and woke him up. And kissed him on the cheek! Casem looked at him with amazement. What is this man kissing me for? I've known him for years, and I never knew he had female tendencies. Eddie went over and got back into bed and went to sleep. Casem stayed up the rest of the night, watching Eddie. These are kinds of stories these guys would tell, and the same kinds of gimmicks they'd pull on the football field to get themselves a victory."

Gorden himself experienced one of those "gimmicks" when Jackson State played at Grambling during Walter Payton's career. "Our philosophy was speed and quickness," he said. "Grambling had big guys." Jackson was leading at halftime, and had Walter receive the kickoff beginning the second half. "Walter caught the ball about a yard deep in the end zone," Gorden recounted. Shifting to his best imitation of a dramatic radio call, he said: "He brought it out to the five . . . the ten . . . the twenty . . . the thirty . . . the forty . . . the fifty . . . the forty . . .

"Then Walter hit a mud puddle and went up in the air!" Gorden said. "Nobody was near him. He was breaking for a touchdown. Eddie came all the way across the field and told our head coach, Bob Hill, 'I'm sorry, Bob. I'm sorry this field is muddy and wet. I told the grounds crew to turn the water off last night at six o'clock, but they forgot and let it run all night.' You gotta remember," Gorden pointed out with a knowing grin, "Eddie used to manicure his own field and cut his grass when he first started coaching. So he knew all about how to prepare a field. This was AT Grambling. He did that to neutralize our speed." Grambling came back to win, 26-13. "For him to come all the way across the field to apologize," Gorden said, "that's what made Eddie different from everybody else."

Otis Washington, who coached Southern from 1981 through 1986, recalled Eddie's love for ice cream. When it was Washington's turn to room with Eddie on the SWAC tour, he knew they'd have a big bowl of it, then sit up half the night talking football. Eddie would throw in a few jokes – clean, of course – and, in a rare departure, reflect on his life. He reminisced about the early days at Grambling, when he did everything, and growing up in Baton Rouge. But while Eddie would mention some of the more difficult times of his youth, Washington said, the emphasis was always positive, about being an American and the opportunities America afforded anyone who was willing to put forth the effort required to be successful.

Eddie was more than just a good storyteller with his coaching colleagues in the SWAC. He was also their leader. "Eddie moved the SWAC into the modern age," said Casem. "Back in the days of segregation, Eddie was always talking about how we had to glamorize our programs. He talked about television, and how we had to get a game on TV some kind of way. He recognized that we had to sell our own programs. Our dressing rooms had to be clean. He even talked about marking off the field. He'd talk about that to all of us. I'm at Alcorn, and he says, 'Cat, your lines are crooked. Who marks off your field?' When teams came to Grambling, he had an old television in the locker room. You couldn't get but one channel. But he had that TV in there so that, when your team didn't have any other place to go because you didn't have a hotel to go to, he wanted to make it convenient for your team to lounge around. You'd eat in the dining hall, and then the kids could lay around and watch that one station. A little thing like that was big in that day."

The camaraderie among SWAC football coaches was a lot like what you'd find in a fraternity. "Eddie had coaches he really wanted to beat," said Nemiah Wilson, "and those were the coaches that were closest to him." At the same time, Eddie held fast to some unwritten rules. "You never wanted to do anything to embarrass anyone and cost them their job," said Wilson. And you helped whenever you could. "All the other coaches in the conference would call him if they were having problems," Nemiah said. "I don't know any coaches who would help a coach they were playing in two weeks. But Eddie would be there. It was kind of amazing."

The sense of community within the SWAC was never greater than on game days. "Schools like Grambling, Alcorn, Prairie View – they're out there in the woods, isolated," Casem explained. "There's no place for you to go. There weren't any good places for blacks to eat. So you got to the campus in time so the visiting team could eat in the dining hall. And it would be a big thing. The cheerleaders would come in there; the band would be in there. The band would play, and our cheerleading squad and their cheerleading squad would get together, and one would cheer, the other would cheer." After the game, while the visitor's players were eating again in the dining hall and getting ready to get back on the bus to go home, the coaches and game officials would go over to the Robinson's house to enjoy the fixin's Doris had waiting.

Casem, who was inducted into the College Football Hall of Fame in 2003, five years before Gorden and six years after Eddie, coached twenty-two seasons at Alcorn State and three more at Southern. In twenty-five tries he won more games against Eddie – ten – than any other coach (a .400 winning percentage). He did it by beating Eddie at his own game. "I ran the same system," he said years later. "It was like Eddie was playing himself. I studied Eddie. Whenever he would go somewhere and speak – a clinic, a lecture, the American Football Coaches Association, a banquet – I would always go, sit down in front, and take notes. I got to know his people, his assistant coaches. We talked the system. I knew his system as well as he did.

"To the layman, the fan in the stands, and to the unknowing, it looked like he was just running the same thing all the time," he said, "just knocking the other team off the line of scrimmage. But it was actually a complicated front. His system was rule blocking. You thought it was simple, but really it was pretty complicated. Whatever you put up against it, the rules of the system told the offensive line what to do. If a man was on your head, you blocked down; if no man was on your head, you blocked away; that kind of thing. So it looked like he was running the same thing, but you had to really know his system. Everybody thought he only had four plays: the gut play, the off-tackle play, the counter and the sweep. If you could stop them, you could stop Eddie. But the blocking on all of them changed according to what you did. If you put up a six-man front against him, the rules dictated you blocked one way. You put a five-man front up against him, they blocked it another way. You put a three front, and they blocked another way. Players had to know the system; really understand it. They had to recognize and react."

It was as Eddie often told his players, particularly his linemen: "You've got to be intelligent to play our kind of ball."

22

EDDIE ATTENDED his first American Football Coaches Association convention in January 1956, following the only 10-0 season in Grambling history, the one that featured Willie Davis on offense and defense. AFCA was an overwhelmingly white organization then, but that didn't keep Eddie from wondering to himself how long it would take to become the president of the organization – not IF he could, but HOW LONG it would take. Before going to work on the answer to the question he posed to himself, though, he first had to get everyone to know and remember the name of his school. Back then, with a much smaller membership, it was custom at the AFCA convention for each coach to introduce himself and name his university at the beginning of each clinic program. "When it came my time," Eddie often said, "I'd stand up and say, 'I'm Eddie Robinson, from Grambling College.' And, boy, you could hear them laughing. They would say 'GAMBLING College' or 'GRUMBLING College' or 'what college was that?' and ask me to repeat. This went on a number of years, and I would say to myself, 'Well, one day, you're going to know where Grambling is.'"

Becoming president of the Coaches Association required getting elected to the AFCA Board of Directors as a first step. Leadership skills were a key consideration, but an equally pivotal factor was something the coaches call "stick-ability." Board slots were associated with conferences, which meant that once a coach was elected a director, he had to somehow remain in the same conference, if not the same university, if he was to remain on the board, advance up the ladder and have a chance at becoming president of the organization. Even if a head coach moved to a similar position at another school, he was disqualified if that job was in a new conference. This, of course, was not an issue for Eddie; he would remain at Grambling for another thirty years after he began working his way toward the AFCA presidency. Eddie realized this goal in 1976, succeeding Darrell Royal of the University of Texas. In January 1977, as he wrapped up his year as the first black president in the history of the American Football Coaches Association and prepared to pass the gavel to Ben Martin of the Air Force Academy, he told approximately six hundred coaches who attended the annual meeting luncheon of the 54th annual convention just what the achievement meant to him.

"As the late Booker T. Washington said, 'In the economy of God, all persons must succeed by the same standards.' In America, all persons must be judged by the same standards. I am saying here today that this organization has given Eddie Robinson and the other members a chance to be judged by the American standards."

Grant Teaff was in his fifth season as head coach at Baylor during Eddie's year as president. Over the next twenty years, their bond would grow stronger and Teaff's admiration for Eddie would soar. When Teaff was named head coach of the West All-Stars in the East-West Shrine Game in the late 1970s, he asked Eddie to be one of his assistant coaches. It was the first time in his adult life, Eddie later said, that he had ever gone onto a football field and wasn't in charge. "He had never been in a situation where he had a lot of coaches," Teaff recalled. "The organizational part of it fascinated him, how you broke down the schedule and how you used different time periods for drills and so forth. He was constantly taking note, saying he could take it back and make his team better – as if it needed to be better. He also was very hands-on, in the sense that he talked to the individuals a lot. These are all-stars who have been coached through high school and college, some of the best of the best. But his approach was that everybody can be better tomorrow than they were today. He was always individually coaching."

In the late 1980s, Eddie intervened with black coaches who were organizing a spinoff organization. He invited Teaff to join him. "We were in a board meeting," Teaff recalled, "and it came up that a group of black coaches was going to form an association of black coaches, the Black Coaches Association – BCA. Eddie said, 'I'm going to go down there. Come with me.' So I said, 'Sure.' His reputation was such that, when he walked in that room, he got the floor. He made a powerful, spontaneous talk to everybody, saying, 'Remember. It's important that we all remember that we're members of the American Football Coaches Association. He was just so eloquent in that, and it touched me. He was amazing, yet so very humble. He wasn't trying to talk them out of it. He just wanted to make sure that everybody understood that, white or black, we were all members of the *American* Football Coaches Association. It was very interesting and very perceptive to me that he said to them, 'Remember, we're all *members*.' It was like he was saying, 'Remember, we're all Americans.' He was encouraging them not to think of the BCA as their only coaches association." The BCA was formed, but as a a second professional organization for black coaches, rather than as a competing alternative.

Teaff retired as Baylor's head coach in 1992 after twenty-one seasons, and in 1994 became AFCA's executive director. One of his responsibilities in that job was identifying a person worthy of receiving the AFCA's greatest honor: the Tuss McLaughry Award, which recognized "distinguished individuals who have made significant contributions to the American way of life." Presented only when AFCA leadership agreed that a deserving candidate had been identified, the award is named for the association's first full-time executive director. After serving in World War I, McLaughry directed the football programs at three of the East's most prestigious academic institutions – Amherst, Brown and Dartmouth – from 1922 to 1954, minus three seasons when he returned to active duty as a Marine lieutenant colonel during World War II. He was a key figure in building the Coaches Association into what it is today, serving as voluntary secretary-treasurer for twenty years before becoming AFCA's first full-time staffer, with the title of executive director. McLaughry was inducted into the College Football Hall of Fame in 1962, and in 1964 AFCA established the award in his honor. Among the twenty-seven recipients in the award's first thirty-three years were five U.S. Presidents (Lyndon Johnson first in 1966), five astronauts (Neil Armstrong, first man on the moon, among them), six military heroes (including Gen. Douglas MacArthur and Gen. Jimmy Doolittle), entertainers Bob Hope, Jimmy Stewart and John Wayne, and the Rev. Billy Graham. In 1996, Eddie became only the second football coach to receive the Award, joining Dallas Cowboys icon Tom Landry on that very short list.

"We rarely honor a coach for his lifetime achievements," Teaff said in announcing Eddie's selection in the November/December issue of AFCA's *The Extra Point* quarterly magazine. "We're taking advantage of this opportunity to honor Coach Robinson simply because he transcends the game with the way he has lived his life off the field . . . He has never wavered in his belief that a coach's primary role is to educate young people and to produce good citizens who will contribute to society in years to come. He has demonstrated throughout his lifetime that that is more important to him than any victory. He has always held that God and country are what have inspired him . . . and are the real reasons for his success. He has spread that message all over the world. He has been a goodwill ambassador for our game and for America . . . We should listen to his message: that the country he lives in and the democratic principles and values that have made this country great are the reasons he had an opportunity to be successful."

When Teaff called Eddie to tell him he would be receiving one of the highest honors of his life, Eddie told him, "I need to sit down, coach. I need to sit down because I can't believe I would be in the company of these men."

Eddie had attended virtually all of the past McLaughry presentations and had heard the distinguished honorees. He was sincerely overwhelmed. Teaff replied, "Eddie, you not only are in the company of these men, but you deserve to be in the company of these men." In an interview more than a decade later, Teaff explained why. "There's not any way to measure the extent of his influence," he began, "because in the teaching/coaching profession, when you affect one life, that can be like a pebble in smooth water. That life that you affected can affect other lives. So when you go back through the history of those that Eddie coached, and what many of them did with their lives, and how many lives they touched, you can't relegate a coach or a teacher to just what the individuals did while they were working with him. It just goes on. It spreads.

"His belief in America and his stalwart citizenship in America was translated to those young people who went out into America," Teaff continued. "And he had an effect on them. His mentality was, 'Do the very best you can do as an individual, and things will take care of themselves.' He knew as well as anybody about the world that he lived in, and that all minorities lived in. But his mentality has been verified to me in the election of Barack Obama. Eddie was not just a part of winning football games; Eddie was a part of making this country what it is today, because of the way he went about his business daily. Eddie wasn't somebody who was down marching in the streets and carrying banners and flags and all that. In his way, in his day, he taught as much about America and how you can succeed as anybody I've met.

"Part of it had to be that he had tremendous common sense. I'm from West Texas, and if you don't have common sense, you aren't going to last long in West Texas. So I recognize it, and I saw it so much in what he would do and what he would say. Common sense tells you that you've got, as a person, to do your job, and if you do your job in the environment you're in, you'll reach a level of success. Then, what you do with your success depends on you as an individual. To me, that appeared to be the secret. He didn't get into the broad strokes of why this or why that. He took the here and the now, and said, 'Do the best you can with it.' He also believed in America, that you have an opportunity to be what you want to be. It may not be easy, but you can do that."

Eddie's reaction to the accolades heaped upon him, whether it was something as major as the Tuss McLaughry Award or any of the lesser honors among more than two hundred he received, was always the same. "Anytime he received an award," said Wilbert Ellis, "Coach Robinson would always say, 'I never blocked. I never tackled. I never did throw a pass. It's in the name of Eddie Robinson, but it was my players, my coaches, my support staff who earned it. I'm going to receive it in their name.' Coach was an emotional person. He was so thrilled, so proud and so happy. He often cried."

Fittingly, Eddie received his Tuss McLaughry Award at the AFCA Convention held in New Orleans, a city that for a big part of his life did not welcome or accept either him or his athletes. "He has broken through barriers previously considered unreachable," Teaff said when he introduced Eddie as the McLaughry honoree on the night of January 10, 1996. In the acceptance speech that soon followed, Eddie chose to ignore race – as he typically did – and focus instead on the positive, hopeful view he imparted to his players for decades, even during the worst years of the Civil Rights Movement. "I've said so many times that the greatest thing that has ever happened to Eddie Robinson was to have been born in America," he told the audience, "where you can dream, and where, if you've got guts enough, you can make those dreams come true. I tell our football players every day that the vision that you glorify in your mind, the thoughts you instill in your heart, will form the super-structure of your life, and you become: 'As a man thinketh, so he is; as he continues to think, so he remains.' I have learned the American way from football. I've learned how to win without bragging. I've learned how to lose without offering excuses. I've learned how to give something back to this great society, the strongest and most powerful country in the world."

The Football Writers Association of America honored Eddie in 1966 – long before the Coaches Association ever thought about it. Formed in 1941, the same year Eddie began his coaching career at Louisiana Negro Normal and Industrial Institute, the FWAA used the occasion of its 25th anniversary to present a one-time award to the "Coach Who Made the Biggest Contribution to College Football in the Past 25 Years." There was no shortage of legitimate candidates that year: Clark Shaughnessy, who modernized the T-formation as a replacement for the single-wing, had coached at seven universities since 1915; Jess Neely, a past president of the coaches association, was finishing a 27-year career at Rice, which came after nine seasons at Clemson; Neely's successor at Clemson, Frank Howard, had won six conference championships and had recorded fifteen winning seasons since taking over in 1940; Volney Ashford had guided small-college Missouri Valley to the nation's longest winning streak, forty-one games during a 30-year career; "Scrappy" Moore had completed thirty-three seasons at Chattanooga; and Joe Aillet had been coaching Louisiana Tech, next door neighbor to Grambling, since the year before Eddie arrived there, and was one of the founders of the Gulf States Conference in 1948. Bear Bryant and Woody Hayes also were well into their illustrious careers, though neither had quite completed a full twenty-five years by then.

In the judgment of the Football Writers Association of America, however, in 1966 the "Coach Who Made the Biggest Contribution to College Football in the Past 25 Years" was Grambling's Eddie Robinson. It was a remarkable choice – considering that he was a black coach from a historically black college at a time when much of America still practiced various forms of racial discrimination, the Deep South violently resisted the end of Jim Crow segregation, and the white media largely ignored black college athletics. It was vindication of Eddie's faith in America. A search of FWAA files in 2009 did not produce any notes, press release or story clipping that explained the writers' basis for choosing Eddie over those obvious contenders (all future members of the College Football Hall of Fame), or any other coach who could have been considered. Retired FWAA members in Waco, Texas, Gainesville, Florida and Bloomington, Indiana, who were active in the organization in the 1960s and might have recalled the reasons, also drew a blank. Only 84-year-old R.L. Stockard could even attempt to explain the thinking. What he came up with sounded a lot like justification for the Tuss McLaughry decision thirty years later.

"People who really knew him knew what and how he taught his athletes," Stockard said. "He told them, 'This is the greatest country in the world, and if you invest in it, it will reward you.' He wasn't angered by the racial policy. He was the most patriotic person that you'd ever meet; he preached – he PREACHED – Americanism to his football players. This is one of the many reasons they honored him at such an early stage in his career."

Stockard began his pioneering newspaper career in 1953 when he visited the sports editor of the *Baton Rouge State-Times* and convinced him that the paper should publish coverage of Southern University athletics, particularly the football and basketball teams. "He said, 'I don't really see a need for anyone else on our staff,'" Stockard recalled. "I said, 'If you get the newspaper, any day of the week, look and see how much information is there for one of the local, four-year colleges – Southern University – as against what's there in representation of LSU. Now here's a four-year college with almost 10,000 students and hardly anything more than the score, and maybe who scored two touchdowns; no personal interest stories, no background stories.' He was surprised, I guess, that I read the paper. He said, 'Well, I don't really run this paper; I've got to speak to some people. Come back in a week and maybe I can represent the newspaper a little better than I'm doing now.' So I went back in three days. He said, 'You're right; we don't do anything on the sports page with Southern University.' He said, 'Okay, it's yours.' I had to do my own pre-game stories, my own statistics, my own game stories and my own post-game stories."

In 1958, Stockard became sports editor of a black weekly in Baton Rouge, and in 1960 he moved to New Orleans to pursue a graduate degree in historical geography, which led to his second career as a university professor. This time he didn't have to knock on any doors. The sports editor of the *New Orleans States-Item* called the day after he arrived in town and said, "I understand that you used to write for the afternoon paper in Baton Rouge. I could use you." Once again, Stockard was a Louisiana daily's first black sportswriter. For the next decade he covered not only Southern but also Grambling, other black college teams in Louisiana, and black high school sports in New Orleans. The sports editor told him, "Don't expect integration here. Remember, geographically, where we are."

By the time the Football Writers decided to honor Eddie for his first quarter-century of contributions to the college version of the sport, he had been attending American Football Coaches Association conventions and clinics for a decade, and had become well-known already. "He was a vociferous learner," Grant Teaff recalled. "He devoured everything he could get close to. Whenever he was around somebody and a conversation would start with a coach, he'd start quizzing them about things that he'd seen them do on television. He'd talk to them about it, and he'd write it all down. He read everything he could get his hands on. He went to every clinic he could go to. Every time you'd look out at our general sessions at the convention, Eddie was sitting in the front row. He's there, writing. He told me one time, 'Never stop learning. Never stop learning.' He was passionate about learning."

Stockard observed Eddie in those settings, too. "He would attend these coaches meetings, back before integration, and other coaches would come up to me and ask, 'Is that guy for real? Is he really that friendly?' I said, 'All the time.' Every time he went into a non-integrated situation, particularly in the 1950s and 1960s, he acted as if he had known these coaches for years. The guy was amazing. Even when he lost a close game, even if it was to his biggest rival, he would give the other team credit: 'We didn't play well today. We hope to do better next year. My kids played the best they could.' That was his approach. He talked to his players the same way after the game in the locker room. It's just amazing, a coach who had that kind of temperament dealing with his players, the public, the press and media. That was another reason they honored him.'"

Through the end of the 1965 season, Eddie's teams had won two-thirds of their games (156), lost a quarter of them (64) and tied ten. Grambling had won two SWAC football championships in its first seven seasons in the conference, and had been declared the black national champion once. He had pioneered the prominence of players from HBCUs in pro football, first with Tank Younger, whose breakthrough alone might have been enough for the FWAA to honor Eddie, then Willie Davis, who by 1965 was captain of the Green Bay Packers defense, and Buck Buchanan, the first overall number one draft choice from an HBCU. And he had accomplished it all while demanding conduct that often frustrated his players.

"If we were ever penalized for kicking or any kind of violent act," said Nemiah Wilson, "we were off the team. He didn't teach that. We played Florida A&M, and they did everything but shoot us. We went to the sideline and said, 'Coach, we have to fight back.' He wouldn't have it. If we hit anybody, we were off the team." Eddie required similar behavior toward officials. "On the field," said W.C. Gorden, "you'd never see Eddie curse an official or give one a hard time. 'You don't embarrass him,' he would say. 'He's the man in charge.' I asked him about it one time. 'You know the guy made a bad call,' I said. 'Why didn't you chew him out?' Eddie answered, 'I tell my players they can't chew anybody out and they have to respect officials. If I do it, I'm not teaching the philosophy I believe in.'"

That attitude did not go unnoticed or unappreciated among the men who wore the striped shirts. When Eddie died, the *Baton Rouge Advocate* created an online "book of condolences" as a place where the public could express whatever feelings each contributor wanted to share. By mid-afternoon the first day, the newspaper reported that messages from coast to coast filled twenty-nine pages. One man wrote: "I am proud to say I have officiated two of his football games. He had the most disciplined sideline I have ever seen on a collegiate football field."

"I've been around coaches so very long," R. L. Stockard said, "and most of them will do whatever it takes to win. Eddie Robinson wasn't like that, not like that at all. He wasn't a guy who did a lot of hollering and shouting. He wasn't a guy who cursed. He wasn't a guy who would go and grab the side of a guy's jersey, or as some coaches do, the chin strap on a player's helmet to get his attention. He wasn't that kind of a coach. But he did the same thing as the more typical coaches, and that is win. That's why I have such respect for him, because many people think you have to do what the winners do in order to win. But he didn't look at it that way. I would call him a perfect football coach."

23

EDDIE LOVED being a football coach, absolutely loved it. He often quoted Amos Alonzo Stagg, the prolific innovator who coached the University of Chicago and College of the Pacific for a combined fifty-seven seasons between 1892 and 1946, and won three hundred fourteen games. *"Coaching is the most rewarding profession in the world. No man is too great to coach the American youth."* He repeatedly recalled his childhood dream. *"I never wanted to be anything but a football coach since the fourth grade . . . I don't know any other place I would rather be."* He regularly referred to himself as "the luckiest man and happiest man in the world" because he had the opportunity to coach football. *"I love this coaching profession . . . It's just been a picnic for me . . . I just had a ball . . . I don't ever know any day that I didn't want to be out there."* And he spoke with reverence of meeting and learning from the great early coaches, not only Stagg but Pappy Waldorf, Carl Snavely, Fritz Crisler and Frank Leahy, too. A lifelong student of football and coaching, Eddie proudly told others he had at his fingertips the notes and summaries he had saved from more than fifty years of clinics and convention programs. *"I've heard the best . . . I can go back and get them all."* He didn't hunt, or fish, or play golf. *"I have no hobbies."*

Asked to explain his approach to coaching, Eddie answered: "I just believe that you can't really coach the player right if you don't love 'em. You have to understand that the people we coach today are going to be the leaders of this nation, and we have to fit them into society and help them become good, productive Americans. I want them to have a quality education. When an athlete comes here to Grambling to play football, I want him to leave here a better man." He also wanted them to be able to handle adversity. "It's not how many times you get knocked down," he said. "It's whether you're going to get up."

College football celebrated the one hundredth anniversary of the beginning of intercollegiate gridiron competition in 1969. Five days before the actual date of that first game between Rutgers and Princeton, played November 6, 1869, Eddie was the featured speaker at the Houston Touchdown Club's observance of the centennial. His remarks that day, expressed with an eloquence seldom heard in the history of sport, articulated the intrinsic value of competitive athletics, and football in particular. Forty years later, everything he said in 1969 retained its validity.

"The game of football is like life itself," Eddie said. "There are lessons to be learned, responsibilities to be accepted, obstacles to be overcome, disappointments, accidents and even defeats to be endured, sweet victories to be savored, and all played under the rules of the game. Football builds basic character in boys. It gives them strength enough to know when they are weak, and makes them brave enough to face themselves when they are afraid; to be proud and unbending in honest failure but humble and gentle in success; not to substitute words for action nor to seek the path of comfort but to face the stress and spur of the difficult and the challenge; to learn to stand up in the storm but to have compassion on those who fall; to master themselves before they seek to master others; to have a heart that is clean and a goal that is high; to learn to laugh but never forget to weep . . . to be serious but never take themselves too seriously. For youth, as it crosses the threshold of manhood, collectively speaking, athletics is a rallying point to build courage when courage seems to die; to restore faith where there seems to be little cause for faith; to create hope as hope becomes forlorn. Athletics may be the school's most enduring world of discipline, of sharp thinking, of a demonstrable connection between what one puts into anything and what he gets out of it.

"The boy is testing himself in a laboratory where everything works out pretty much as it does in life," Eddie continued. "He finds out that he gets out of the game just what he puts in it. He finds that proper preparation usually brings results. He finds out that the breaks of the game, many of them almost impossible to explain, occasionally give one side a tremendous advantage while imposing a handicap on the other side. But he learns that the breaks will continue to come and he cannot throw up his hands and quit when they go against him or his team. Secondly, the boy has ample opportunity to discover his weaknesses of character and to build them up. If he lacks aggressiveness, he will soon find out. He will learn, too, why aggressiveness is so necessary for success. Next is the business of performance under pressure, and being willing to face up to requirements . . . I am in favor of exposing young people to situations that require the highest performance on a regular basis. While football is a manufactured environment, there comes that moment when you stand face to face with doing – the moment, perhaps a fraction of a second, when you either do or don't. The student in the classroom . . . often loses all contact with the cause-and-effect world. In athletics this does not happen. On the playing field, a cause is always followed by an effect. In plain words, it's hit or get hit; fight or run; pay the price or fail . . ."

There is no better example of his belief in paying the price than a 1958 Collie Nicholson story in the *Chicago Defender* headlined: **"Grambling's Players Get Up At 4 A.M."** This is the story that began, in the classic fashion of Collie and Marshall Hunt:

> *"Coach Eddie Robinson rolls his Grambling College gridders out of the hay when most burglars are returning home from a hard night with the crowbar and wedge."*

In succeeding sentences, Collie explained:

> *"A strict disciplinarian who demands work as near to perfection as his athletes are able to give, Robinson starts his daily practice session at 4 a.m. 'We're up with the chickens every morning,' the coach confessed with a friendly grin. 'It's our only chance for survival.' Robinson and his staff are working overtime to transform the Tigers into a crisp-blocking and tackling squad thoroughly groomed in fundamentals."*

Besides drills from 4 a.m. to 7 a.m., he wrote,

> *"The daily treadmill schedule includes a 3 to 6 p.m. practice session and an 8 p.m. chalk talk."*

Collie concluded with player reaction.

> *"Several of the boys have accused coaches of having sundial trouble. 'We seem to work 12 hours a day,' they complain. The overtime schedule prompted a drawling 260-pound tackle to stretch his imagination. 'I wonder,' he asked, blinking quietly, 'what would happen if we were in the Arctic Circle where the days last six months.' His caustic conclusion was, 'We would probably stay up right through the football season.'"*

Nemiah Wilson came along a little later, but could have given Collie similar quotes (if indeed that unnamed big tackle was a real person). He could have told him the story of the hit song by the sightless African American superstar, Ray Charles. "When we started summer training," Nemiah recalled, "we had to be dressed and on the field at five o'clock in the morning. It was still dark. We waited for the sun to come up. Eddie had loudspeakers in each dorm. There was an old Ray Charles song called "Hit The

Road, Jack," and that would wake you up in the morning. It would start playing about five or ten minutes before time to get up. And then the minute that song started, Eddie would be walking down the hall blowing a whistle. I asked him one time, 'Coach, why would you play a song like that – Hit The Road Jack?' He said, 'Well, you know, we bring guys in here that we think can play, and we're wrong on some of them. But we don't have to cut any of them. They leave on their own. That's what that song is about; if you can't cut it, hit the road.' (How ironic that Nemiah "hit the road," only to be intercepted and returned.) We had guys who couldn't make it at Grambling, who became stars for other teams," Nemiah said.

Long after his successful 11-year career with Denver, Oakland and Chicago had ended, Nemiah recalled his introduction to pro football, and how different it was from playing for Eddie. "I'll never forget the first day I went to practice with the Broncos. I almost made all of the guys mad at me. We had practice, and it was only forty-five minutes. I made the statement, 'Hell, this is easy. We'd just be getting started at Grambling.' They said, 'What are you talking about!' That was the regimen I knew – four-hour practices.

"I always called him a slave driver because we worked so hard," Nemiah continued. "Eddie always felt he needed to have an edge. So what he did was, the whole practice field was sand that deep. (Nemiah held his hands about six inches apart.) We had to practice on that field every day – in sand, three to four hours a day. He figured the sand would make you stronger, would make you faster, and above all, his big thing was endurance. You were building up endurance. In the fourth quarter, when everybody else was tired, you were just getting fresh. It worked that way for a lot of us. Most of the wide receivers, defensive backs, running backs and linemen that came out of Grambling had the reputation of being fast. A lot of us didn't really think we were fast, but that was the net result of running in that sand every day."

The demands hardly lessened when the fall semester began. "He would make the schedule for us," Nemiah said. "He would say, 'You have to be dressed and ready to go for practice at three o'clock.' So you had to have seven o'clock classes and be through by two. Then you had to go down and get dressed and be on the field by three o'clock. If you were a minute late, or a second late, you had to run the bleachers fifteen or twenty times, and then practice. And after practice, every day after practice, it didn't matter what position you played, you had to run ten to fifteen 100-yard sprints. Most teams just run forty-yard sprints, but we had to run hundreds. Everybody – linemen and everyone; there was no out. That was just standard. After practice was over, about seven o'clock, we'd go to the cafeteria for dinner. We had an hour to eat, then we'd go back to our room for half an hour, and then we'd go back to the stadium because they had tutors there for us."

Players on scholarship received a small monthly allowance for incidental living expenses called "subsistence." The allowance – $10 – doesn't seem like much today. But it was real money in the 1950s and 1960s when gas was a quarter a gallon and a cold drink cost a dime, especially to guys who came from poverty-level backgrounds. Eddie controlled the disbursement of the monthly subsistence, and used it as a carrot (or maybe a stick) with his players. "If you didn't show up for tutoring," Nemiah said, "you didn't get your $10 subsistence. The second thing about it is, you had to go to church. He passed out the subsistence at church, so if you weren't at church, you didn't get it."

As much as he enjoyed everything that football represented, making a difference in the lives of his players gave Eddie his greatest satisfaction. His efforts began with training in social skills that were uncommon among boys from the rural South in the 1940s, 1950s and, in many cases, even the 1960s. "Long ago, when I first started at Grambling, whenever I went to New York or someplace, I'd take the restaurant menu back home with me so some of the kids could learn how to order from them," Eddie said. "I've even gone so far as to have people come in and show them what silverware to use at the table." He also wanted his student-athletes to make the most of a standard of living he knew would exceed what almost all of them had experienced before coming to Grambling. "We encourage our boys to take some business courses," he said in 1969, "so they will know what to do with their money. You know, investments are a new thing to blacks, and we want to help our boys get started right." Even before they learned about investing, Eddie made sure they learned the basics of handling a checkbook.

"Rob realized that if you prepare yourself as well as you possibly can, and you're given an opportunity, then you can take advantage of that opportunity," said Doug Porter. "But if you're not prepared when the opportunity presents itself, you're going to fail and you're going to hurt other opportunities for other people. So his concentration was to make sure that you are ready and able to step into mainstream life in America. He put a lot of emphasis on things that people today take for granted: being able to speak when interviewed . . . being able to give intelligent answers when interviewed . . . making sure that you know how to properly conduct yourself in a hotel when you're staying at a hotel as part of the football program. He put a lot of emphasis on those kinds of things and spent a lot of time with our kids. Consequently, when they were faced with those kinds of situations, being interviewed by maybe a national figure, they were able to handle themselves well, not make a lot of grammatical mistakes, not make a lot of statements that would come back to haunt them later on."

Of helping his football players learn to be poised and self-confident when interviewed, Eddie said: "Look at it this way. If a guy scores four touchdowns or runs a nine-second 100 yards, when it's over he's got to tell the American public how he did it. The microphones and the TV cameras will be there, so every chance I get, I encourage my kids to take public speaking and speech courses."

A recurring theme when he spoke about the coaching profession was that the job extended well beyond the field and outside the locker room. "You as coaches must be teachers, and I tell teachers they must be coaches," Eddie told his fellow coaches the year he was AFCA president. "I feel that you as coaches hold the substance of life itself in your hands because you teach the youth of this nation how to handle themselves in competitive athletics. You teach them they must dream, and work to make this dream a reality." In his acceptance speech after receiving the Tuss McLaughry Award, he told his colleagues: "You've got to serve as an inspiration to these young people. There are times you've got to be a father, a friend, a counselor, a teacher and a coach. My thinking really is, that nobody else can do it better than you can do it . . . to help shape the character and the careers, both on and off the field. We've got to be concerned about people, off the field."

Rod Paige heard that from Eddie when they were traveling together to an AFCA convention. It was a message that stayed with Paige after he quit coaching and began to champion educational reform, first in Houston public schools and later as Secretary of Education during President George W. Bush's first term. "One of my most vivid memories of Eddie," Paige said in 2009, "is when we were waiting in an airport – I think it was New Orleans. We were sitting on a bench, reading the newspapers, and there was an article that reported on the test results of one college in Louisiana where the black students did very poorly. Eddie made the observation, 'We'd all be much better off if coaches could become better teachers, and teachers could become better coaches.' He saw it that the teachers in the colleges were not as good, as coaches, as they might be, although they might be good teachers. He thought the two things should go together. 'You need to coach and teach,' he said. 'That's the way we solve this problem.'

"I remember looking at him," Paige said, "and asking myself, 'How do I interpret what this man just told me?' The more I thought about it, the stronger it became as a good idea. When you think about the aspects of coaching, it exceeds teaching. It involves a deeper relationship with the student or athlete, but it involves teaching because teaching is your main vehicle for moving both the student and the athlete forward. I carried that with me in my career. Every time I heard Eddie Robinson, that's what I thought about."

Eddie's emphasis on completing a college degree left a lasting impression on many of his players. "Eddie knew that education conquers all," said

Goldie Sellers, a three-year Grambling teammate of Nemiah Wilson. "He was educated himself, and he knew that nobody can take that away. He knew that if you've got an education, it opens doors when doors are sealed shut. He told us, 'Once the legs stop moving, you're going to have to have something else to depend on.' His philosophy was that everybody who came to Grambling should graduate."

Eddie's morning ritual in the players' dorm became one of the most frequently repeated parts of his legend. "He would go through the halls ringing his cowbell in the morning, Sellers recalled, "saying 'Get Up. You've got to go to class.'" Drowsy players would take turns answering the door, because they knew Eddie wouldn't move on to the next room until he saw a face to let him know the occupants were out of bed. "We had to show him our reports on what we were doing in class, and he would go talk to our teachers," Sellers continued. "This was a person who, in that particular era, was way ahead of his time."

More than the cowbell, Charlie Joiner remembered Eddie's early morning visits to some of his teammates' dormitory rooms. "If he found out you weren't going to a class," said Joiner, who never cut classes himself, "he'd come there at six o'clock in the morning and wake you up. He'd get you up, make you take a shower and walk you to that class. I can remember hearing that knocking on the door next to me. It would be Coach Rob, knocking on the door at six in the morning to get this guy up because he had already cut that class twice, and he wasn't going to let him cut it again. Coach Rob was really serious about it, and sooner or later the players got serious and he didn't have to walk them to class anymore.

"What had the most impact on me was his care for the person, his care for the players," Joiner said. "You were there to play football, but he tried to educate you on what it would be like in life if you didn't play professional football. He tried to educate you on why you should have a good religious background. He also tried to educate you as to why you should have a solid foundation like a degree from a four-year college. He said,

'You're going to need all those things because football is just a temporary career, and when you do leave football, you'll still be a young person and you've got to live the rest of your life.' That impressed me a lot, and when I became a coach, I tried to teach the same things: Have a good religious background, and if you haven't finished college, go back and finish."

24

UNDERSTANDING THE greatness of Eddie Robinson involves knowing him not only as an exceptional coach, resolute leader and avid American but also as a committed family man and uniquely caring person. Jean Roe Freeling, Dave Whinham and Doug Ireland are three of many who observed and experienced Eddie in those more private dimensions. Their stories help to define the full scope of his life and confirm the far-reaching impact of his example, which continues to ripple across generations too young to have known him.

The fifth of ten children born into the sharecropper family of Anthony and Carrie Roe of Minden, Louisiana, about forty miles west of Grambling in Webster Parish, Jean Roe had obtained a scholarship to Grambling through the efforts of State Representative Ernest Gleason, who owned the farm where the Roes lived and worked. "My oldest sister, Meredith, was their maid," Jean said. "I used to go up and help her when the Gleasons would have parties. I started helping her when I was in the seventh grade, and started babysitting Mr. Gleason's grandchildren then. Many times he would come in, and I wouldn't even know he was listening. I would be reading stories to those grandkids of his; sometimes I would recite poetry, and other times I would read Bible verses to them. I would just do a whole litany of things, like the Preamble to the Constitution, the Gettysburg Address and that kind of stuff."

Jean had finished her first college semester when she moved in with Eddie and Doris Robinson and their two children, Rose and Eddie Jr. "The Robinsons didn't know it until I had finished college," she said, "but they rescued me from being a homeless person. My scholarship paid for room and board, tuition and books – everything, really. At the end of that first semester, I received a letter from the university telling me that my scholarship was being reduced because of a state funding cutback, and for the next semester I would have only tuition and books, which meant I didn't have a meal ticket or any place to live." The letter instructed Jean to vacate her dorm room immediately, but she stalled, hiding out and avoiding contact with everyone associated with Grambling while she tried to figure out what to do next. "I was determined not to go back home," she said, "because I knew the only things that awaited me there was the cotton field and a white woman's kitchen, and that just didn't appeal to me. I'd been a reader all of my life and I'd been around white people, and I knew what life should be like. And the only way that I felt like I'd ever get there was to get educated."

Desperate, Jean finally visited her adviser, who first told her to go home and work for a couple of semesters, and return when she had saved enough money to finish college. When Jean told her that was not an option, the adviser – a woman – looked her over, asked if she had ever been told she was pretty, and suggested that she put herself through school by "entertaining" male faculty members. Jean was shocked, and her indignant reaction immediately made it clear that she was offended by such an idea. The adviser quickly moved on. "Do you know Coach Robinson?" she asked. "Of course I know Coach Robinson," Jean replied. "Everybody knows Coach Robinson."

The adviser then explained the opportunity that changed Jean Roe's life: "She said, 'Well, he and his wife usually keep a young lady in their home to help with the children and the housework, and she lives there and she just becomes part of the family, and she gets her education that way. Would you be interested in that?' I said, 'Oh, indeed I would.' So she got him on the

phone and told him about me. He told her they were still looking for someone, so she asked if he could see me. He told her to send me right over."
Jean had been living on corn flakes and powdered milk for a week because
she had no money, and was very hungry. Suddenly there was hope. "I went
on over to the back door of the gym," she said, "and just as I opened the
door, Coach busted through the door. I said, 'Coach Robinson! Where do
you think you're going? I'm Jean Roe and you have an appointment with
me.' He started laughing and he got so tickled he had to hold onto the door.
There were other students around, and they were laughing, too, because I
know they'd never heard anybody talk to him the way I was talking to him.
When he regained his composure, he said, 'Jean, I'm Eddie Robinson and
I'm so sorry, but President Jones has called me to his office and I'm on my
way to see him. But I'll tell you what. My wife teaches school down at Ruston, and she'll get off at 3 o'clock. If you'll give me your dorm and everything, I'll have her come by and pick you up.' I said, 'Okay. But you know,
you might forget to do that, too.' He said, 'Oh no, lady. You're one I will
never forget.'"

Waiting for Doris Robinson to pick her up, Jean actually hid under her
bed to avoid being evicted when two representatives of the university came
to her room to make her leave. "Mrs. Robinson picked me up later that
afternoon," she said, "and we went to the house." Eddie Jr., who was still in
elementary school, and Rose, who had started high school, greeted them
as they pulled into the driveway. The family's dogs bounded out, too, and
Jean immediately felt right at home. "My first night there was actually a
get-acquainted kind of thing. But when I got home with her, I helped prepare the meal, and straightened up the house. By this time, Coach was
home. After we had dinner, I asked her, 'Would you like me to fix you an egg
pie?' She said, 'I sure would.' I was very good at doing pastries; I learned to
cook when I was seven or eight years old. I cooked that egg pie, and they ate
it while I was there. Sweets were Coach's favorite. When they got through,
Coach said, 'Well, let's take Jean back to the dormitory and get her things,

because we can't let her live in that dormitory no more.'"

Life in the Robinson home in 1957, according to Jean, was about as middle class as the hit television show about a white suburban family of four of that time, *Father Knows Best.* "Meals were very special," she said. "We always had breakfast and dinner together when Coach was in town. He always said grace, then each family member would quote a Bible verse. Then Coach would start a conversation, and everyone was encouraged to contribute. He would ask how our days had gone, and 'How are your classes going, Jean?' – what a typical parent would want to know about their children. I think he did it because he wanted to hear what was going on in our lives. He rode shotgun on us just like he did those football boys. He was gone quite a bit of the time, but the time he spent with us was quality time, even to the point where many times Rose, Eddie and I traveled with him and the team. If Mrs. Robinson was in a meeting at school at night, he would take us with him."

Jean (Mrs. Freeling by then) wrote a tribute to Eddie for Father's Day a few years before he died. "Many of Coach's outstanding achievements in sports and education have been highlighted in words and on film," she wrote. "He is especially noted for the many young men he has lifted from poverty and turned into accomplished professional athletes and educators. Little, though, has been mentioned about Coach Robinson's contributions to, and positive influence on, the lives and education of many young women from similar backgrounds. I was proud to be one of those women. We were mentored, nourished and parented by Coach and Mrs. Robinson, and encouraged to complete our educations."

Although she chose to participate in the sit-ins in Ruston and Shreveport when they spread from Southern University in 1960, Jean appreciated Eddie's guidance regarding racial matters just as much as his football players did, and viewed them similarly. "He had an understanding that very few people had, especially about things like that," she said. "Even with the hideous things that were happening in civil rights, he said the main thing we needed to concentrate on was getting our education. He stressed that daily: Get your education. 'Times are going to change,' he'd tell us. 'We're in the midst of times changing. But get your education so whenever you get out of college, you will have something to fall back on.' He was a fantastic person."

Dave Whinham would certainly agree, based on his relationship with Eddie that began in 1985. The Opryland Hotel in Nashville was the site that year of the American Football Coaches Association annual convention, the gathering where coaches of all ages and experience levels, from schools of all sizes, learn the latest offensive and defensive formations from their peers, attend clinics on motivational and organizational techniques and myriad other topics, and make the contacts that might lead to their next coaching opportunity. More than a thousand football coaches filled the 600,000 square feet of meeting and exhibition space that January, including Whinham, then a young graduate assistant at the University of Cincinnati. Even though he had started coaching college football as an assistant at Grand Valley State, his alma mater, five years before, this was Whinham's first AFCA convention, mainly because it was the first time he could afford to pay his own way. It proved to be worth every penny, though not because of what he learned or the new coaching job he landed but because he met Coach Eddie Robinson.

"I had had an interview and was hustling back to the conference center to listen to one of the speakers," Whinham said in an interview long after leaving the coaching profession to start his own sports consulting business. "If you've ever been to the Opryland Hotel, you know how expansive those hallways are at the conference center. They've got to be miles long, and they're probably thirty yards wide. As I was walking down this very large, empty corridor, off in the distance I saw a gentleman walking toward me on the other side of this corridor. As I got closer, I could see that it was Coach Robinson. Being a young coach, and this being my first AFCA convention, I was very excited to see the great Eddie Robinson. In the fifteen seconds I had to plan, I thought I would just say, 'Hello, Coach' as I was passing by. We were both on our respective right sides of the hallway, but Coach Rob walked across to me. He offered his hand to me and said, 'Hello. I'm Eddie Robinson,' as if anybody didn't know who he was. And I said, 'Oh coach, it's a pleasure to meet you. I'm Dave Whinham.' And he stood there with me for ten or fifteen minutes, asking me where I was from, asking me about my college career and the early stages of my coaching career. Obviously, I was completely thrilled to have had the opportunity to meet Coach Rob, and thoroughly overwhelmed that he would walk over and visit with me. But as time went on, we visited at every AFCA convention that followed. He became a very caring friend who took a personal interest in me."

Whinham became a coach in the Arena Football League in 1988, and the AFL each year hosted a reception at the AFCA convention. "I'll never forget," Whinham recalled. "Coach Rob came into the reception – so the place was all abuzz because Eddie Robinson was in the room – and he was essentially going from person to person asking if they knew where Dave Whinham was." The relationship extended well beyond coaching and became more personal. "On the occasion of the birth of my older son, Will," Whinham continued, "Coach Rob wrote not me, but Will, a very beautiful letter. In it he wrote that both he – Coach Rob – and Will's father had spent many years working to build better men through the game of football. And he followed that statement by saying, 'And now the game waits for you.'" That was in May, 1997, when Eddie was approaching his fifty-seventh and final season as Grambling's head football coach. It was a stressful, disappointing time in his life, but it didn't keep him from reaching out.

"On an earlier occasion," Whinham said, "I told him about my niece, Ashley, who couldn't have been more than seven or eight; her parents had gone through a very difficult divorce. It was at a convention about 10 years after that first one. We were just sitting and visiting, and he asked me what was going on in my life. It just so happened that I had just gotten off a phone call with Ashley's mother. Coach Rob took the cover of a magazine called *Coach and Athletic Director,* with a picture of him celebrating his 400th victory, and he wrote, 'Dear Ashley: The greatest of all attributes is human courage.' Then he signed it as he signed all things that I'd ever seen from him, 'Eddie Robinson and the Tigers.' The original signed cover is still with Ashley. She has valued it even more as she has grown older."

The walk across the hallway to befriend a young white coach at his first national convention, the letter to a friend's newborn son, and the act of kindness to a little girl facing the kind of upheaval in her young life that Eddie experienced in his at a similar age are, in Whinham's view, measures of the man that Eddie Robinson was. "I came to learn over the years that as big as Coach Robinson became, as famous as he became, as in demand as he was, Eddie Robinson always, and I mean that word exactly the way I say it – always – endeavored to give a positive piece of himself to each and every individual he encountered. Now you stop and think about the content of that statement. I don't know how many human beings in the history of the world you could make that statement about.

"Everyone who even from a cursory level follows college athletics knows who Eddie Robinson the coach is, and is aware of his accomplishments, which are many and are great, no question. But his true greatness is that he was never too important, nor was he ever too busy, to pause for a child, for a young coach, or just a stranger. Anyone he ever encountered was not a stranger after that moment. He always took my calls and met with me when we were geographically convenient to one another. And I visited his home in Grambling a number of times. But based on what I experienced with him, he probably had ten million friends like me."

Doug Ireland grew up thirty miles from Grambling, watching the Eddie Robinson Show on television on Sundays. "I was familiar with the lore of Grambling football," he said, "but I didn't know Coach Robinson and had never had the opportunity to go to a Grambling football game." Ireland became executive director of the Louisiana Sports Hall of Fame in 1991, and in that role saw just what Dave Whinham was talking about. "The first time I was at a Hall of Fame event, he was there. It was a great thrill just simply to see him. I had the opportunity to find out right then that not only was he very approachable, but he also was one who valued each conversation he had. He had that very special quality of being able to treat each person he met with equal respect. The catch-phrase nowadays is that you 'big-league' somebody. You might turn away from a 'lesser' profile person to deal with somebody who has a higher profile. That was never in Coach Robinson's repertoire. He was always very considerate and focused on the person or persons he was speaking with, and really made them feel valued from the start.

"No matter who the inductees were, and what walk of life they came from," Ireland said, "they were always gratified and thrilled to meet Eddie Robinson. They were particularly impressed to meet him and find out how humble, how down-to-earth, and how compelling he was as a human being, not as a personality. He had time for everybody. He enjoyed telling stories, and he enjoyed *listening* to stories. So often, when you get that caliber of a personality, the scene revolves around them. But Coach Rob was very content to listen to other folks' stories. He loved a good laugh and a good time, as much as anybody."

Eddie and Doris attended Hall of Fame weekend every year, and were surprised, Ireland said, when he would call each year to confirm their attendance. "It was part of their lives. There was no way they'd miss it." The importance Eddie placed on the Louisiana Sports Hall of Fame and the sincerity of his interest were apparent every year. "He had a constant joy about being involved in the activities," Ireland said. "Because of his background and his humble beginnings, he understood what it meant to celebrate excellence and to be honored by your peers in your state. He gave great respect to the occasion, and to the people involved in every aspect of the occasion."

25

GRAMBLING POLICE Chief Claude Lamar Aker shared Doug Ireland's view of Eddie, based on his own observations and personal experiences. To Aker, and many others who interacted with him regularly, it was a simple matter of uncommon humility. "Rob was as down-to-earth a guy as you could ever find," Aker said. "Even as he came to the end of his career and his name was up in lights, you never would realize it just by talking to him. Rob was a guy you'd just meet on the street and just talk. You could chat with him about anything, ask his advice about anything. He would stop, and talk to you. He wasn't this guy who was so concerned with politics and everything. In the heyday of the news media, he really wasn't concerned with that. He would talk to you before he talked to the press. He was just down-to-earth." So much so, in fact, Eddie Robinson's home phone number was always listed in the local phone book.

Highly successful football coaches, especially ones who become fixtures on college campuses, inevitably acquire a larger-than-life persona. Their names and the names of their schools are spoken as one: Penn State's Joe Paterno . . . Notre Dame's Knute Rockne . . . Alabama's Bear Bryant . . . So it was with Eddie G. Robinson. "Rob's middle name should have been Grambling," said Aker. "He was a guy who could walk across campus, and everybody knew him. If Rob didn't know your name, he knew something about you – what you were doing in school, where you were from, or maybe even your part in those demonstrations on campus."

Aker himself was a toddler when his family moved to Grambling in 1945. His earliest memories of Eddie date to elementary school. "All kids in Grambling knew Coach Rob," he said. "That kept us all on our toes. We knew if we saw Coach Rob coming, whatever you were doing, if it wasn't right, you'd better stop." Aker's niece, Sheree Rabon, went through the same routine twenty-five years later when she was a teenager. "If there was something I did, or any of us did, that was too out of order, our parents knew about it before we made it home," she said. "Everybody knew everybody's telephone number because we didn't have to dial the exchange. You just dialed the last four numbers. So it was nothing for Coach to drop in any office, or his own office, and make a phone call. 'So and so did this.' And if Coach said it, there was no way out of it. As sure as Coach said it, it was a done deal; you were in trouble. Because he was not going to stop his busy day for anything that wasn't worth calling about.

"He was mindful of so many things," Rabon said. "When you didn't think he was looking, he was looking. I guess that's what made him such an excellent coach. He saw everything."

Her uncle learned to appreciate the "Coach Rob aura" after he became chief of police. "If one of his boys got in trouble, you didn't have to worry about taking the boy to jail," Aker recalled. "All you had to do was say, 'Look, son, I'm going to call Coach Rob.' He'd say, 'Oh, wait, officer. Don't do that. Don't do that.' If you caught a boy and smelled alcohol on his breath, and told him you were going to call Coach Rob, he'd almost get on his knees. 'Please, please, please don't.' Those boys were more fearful of you calling Rob than they were going to jail. It made the police chief's job a lot easier." Once, Aker said, a naïve young man thought it might work the opposite way, that Eddie might intimidate the chief. "I stopped a guy for speeding, and he said, 'I play for Coach Rob.' I said, 'Who?' He said, 'I play for Coach Rob. You know, the football coach.' I said, 'I don't know him, son.' And I continued to write my ticket. He thought he was going to get off because of Rob. All I had to do was just say that I'd try to reach the coach for him, and he was quiet."

Eddie's influence wasn't limited to his players, or even just athletes in general. Sailor Jackson, who became director of audio, film and video for the Louisiana Secretary of State's office, saw the effect Eddie had on the student body at-large in his first couple of weeks on campus in 1968, when he was a seventeen-year-old freshman. "My first experience of actually seeing Coach Rob was when he passed through the Student Union one day," Jackson recalled. "Everybody was cutting up. You know, you're sitting on the tables or you're sitting on the back of a chair. You've got your cap on funny; things like that. I noticed that, all of a sudden, it started getting real quiet. Then somebody says to me, 'Here comes Coach Rob. You better get right. You better get right.' It seemed like the more he walked through, the quieter it got. I'm telling you, that was *amazing* at that time. Everybody straightened up. They put their caps on right. They sat at the tables. Their voices lowered. It was just showing him respect. That made a big impression on me, the kind of respect he commanded. He didn't even have to say anything. He joked and talked with us, and then went about what he was doing. That was my first time meeting him."

Thelma Smith-Williams arrived at Grambling on October 1, 1956 from Charleston, West Virginia, as a new faculty member. Expecting to stay "exactly two years," she retired after thirty-one and never left. "I got off the train in Monroe – still thirty miles away and didn't know it," she recalled. "It was snowing in West Virginia when I left, so I had a fur coat on. And then I'm sitting there on my trunk in Louisiana, and it's eighty-six degrees! I got a taxi and we drove those red clay roads to Grambling. I'd never seen dirt that color in my life. I remember the driver's name was Price. I said, 'Do you know where you're going?' He said, 'You said you wanted to go to Grambling.' I said, 'Yes I did.' There were three women in the back seat of the cab in white dresses. Each one was holding a piece of my luggage."

Smith-Williams, who became a close family friend of the Robinsons, had been hired to teach health and physical education, which meant she would be teaching a subject that Eddie taught, and that he would, in effect, be her supervisor. "It wasn't that organized back then," she said. "The school just started growing and having divisions in the mid-fifties, but he was responsible for this area."

The taxi driver dropped her at Juitt Hall, the dormitory where new faculty members had rooms. That first night, she decided to try to find her new boss. "I found out where Coach Rob lived," she said, "and I went to his house. Doris was home, and she was very nice. I had my first red beans and rice that night. An hour and a half later, Rob walked in. Doris called out, 'Baay . . . bee! Here's your new teacher.' After we ate, he just wanted to talk. He wanted to know what I was interested in and what I felt my strengths were. He just wanted to hear your side of it. He was an excellent listener."

In addition to coaching football and basketball – which he would relinquish that fall – and assisting Prez with the baseball team, Eddie taught two phys-ed classes. "We didn't close our doors in those days," Smith-Williams said. "Everything was wide open, so I could hear him teaching his class. He was very humble, a very humble and caring person. In his classes, he always made sure his students knew what he was talking about." As her supervisor, Eddie would on occasion evaluate her as a teacher. "The first thing I really loved was that he wasn't a highly critical person," she said. "He respected what I knew. He would ask questions. He'd say, 'Why did you do that?' Whatever I did, he wouldn't criticize it, but he wanted to know why I did what I did."

As a freshman at Bennett College in Greensboro, North Carolina, Smith-Williams imagined becoming "the next Marian Anderson," the celebrated African-American contralto whose pioneering career extended from the 1940s through the 1960s. By the time she transferred to Morgan State in Baltimore, however, her artistic focus had switched to dance. After graduation, she went to Carnegie Hall and studied ballet for one summer before accepting the teaching job at Grambling. It was this training that enabled her to make an important contribution to the success of Eddie's football teams.

"I used to go and watch the team," she said. "I mean, we're in the country – no transportation. The fellas on the football team were always having trouble with their ankles, getting hurt. So I went to Rob one day. I always called him Co, as in co-worker. I said, 'Co, I want to talk to you.' He said to come on in. His door was always open. I started telling him what was happening, why the fellas were having trouble with their ankles. When they would make a pivot, they would put their foot down flat. I showed him the ballet movement of the pivot. I showed him how they needed to rise up on their toes, and I showed him the pivot we do in ballet. He said, 'Why, Co, that's what I need.' Rob made all those fellas take modern dancing." Dance wasn't just a part of practice, Smith-Williams said. It became a required one-semester course that she taught with Catherine Williams, also a member of the Grambling faculty and the wife of eventual Grambling mayor John Williams. "These were country boys," Smith-Williams said. "I don't have to tell you the language that came out of them. But it did cut down on the trouble they were having with their ankles."

Eddie's receptiveness to dance instruction for his players wasn't as surprising as it might seem. "Rob loved to tap dance," said Smith-Williams. John Williams agreed. "When the sororities and fraternities had social activities, faculty members were invited guests. My wife would go to a function and take her tapping shoes because she knew if Eddie was there, they'd tap dance. He loved to tap dance." Jean Freeling recalled a different dance experience. "Coach was good at calling square dances," she said. "When I first got to Grambling, they had what they called play night. Kids would live for play night on Thursday nights. That's when everybody would come to the gym and do everything from gymnastics and tumbling to square dancing. Coach would call the square dances."

John Williams was elected mayor of Grambling in 1994, just a few years before Eddie retired from coaching. Despite decades of change all around it, Grambling was still a self-contained, local business haven. Williams set out to change that during his two terms in office. "Grambling had no tax base. Food places and businesses were very limited. There were no franchise places," he said. "That was my big thing, improve the tax base." With Eddie's help, he succeeded in attracting national and regional fast food restaurants and economy retailers. "When they'd come to Grambling," he said of business representatives he was courting, "they'd all want to meet Coach Robinson. He was a great influence for the city."

Doug Ireland realized the extent of Eddie's celebrity status when Eddie was inducted into the College Football Hall of Fame in South Bend, Indiana in August, 1996. It caught him unprepared. "Wherever you were that weekend," he said, "when Coach Rob walked into the room, it was one of those head-turning moments. You could hear people: 'That's Coach Eddie Robinson. There's Coach Rob. Wonder if he'd mind if I went up and talked with him. Wonder if I could get his autograph.' He was absolutely revered, and that's something people in this area (Natchitoches, about ninety miles southwest of Grambling) never had a chance to appreciate. We knew him as Coach Robinson, as the fellow from Grambling, the Grambling coach. Our perspective wasn't as appreciative, until later, as it was around the country. He was revered."

Sheree Rabon learned that for herself after she left Grambling. "I really didn't see him as this famous hero, this larger than life person, until I moved away," she said. "When I would tell people, 'I'm from Grambling,' the first thing they would say is, 'Oh, Coach Eddie Robinson!' You heard about him in the news and saw more and more of him outside Grambling, and you realized that, 'Wow! This is nationwide.'"

Rabon's grandmother, Darline Davis, attended Grambling with Tank Younger and served as the campus switchboard operator for more than a quarter century, starting in the job before she graduated. A magazine feature story about her in 1972 documented her contribution and the appreciation and respect Eddie had for those who worked behind the scenes in roles that often were taken for granted and never earned acclaim. "Darline's one of our top recruiters," Eddie said. "She hangs in there and makes sure we get our man. The pro scouts know they can trust her to get a message through and get it through right. When these guys meet Darline after talking to her on the phone, they feel like they know her already. She's very personable. She knows how to meet people and talk to them. She devotes a lot of her time to our sports calls."

Darline saw Eddie's daily routine as few could. "Coach Robinson is always so busy on the telephone," she said. "He's got two lines, and if he's not on one, he's on the other. I don't see how he does it. From the time we open the switchboard in the morning until late afternoon, he's on the phone. We place so many football calls . . . setting up conference calls, answering fans, taking calls from pro scouts. I feel that getting his calls through makes me a part of his team, and I don't want to feel it could happen without me."

Eddie wouldn't have wanted her to feel any differently, and when she finally retired, he presented her with a Woman of the Year Award. "When he introduced my grandmother," Sheree Rabon recalled, "he said, 'There are three heroes in Grambling, and two of them are popular, and one isn't well-known.' And then he presented her with that award. He really showed her a wonderful time." When Davis died years later, Eddie made sure to attend the funeral service. "He gave me one of the most caring hugs," Rabon said, "and told me what a phenomenal woman she was. 'She was a very special lady and I am blessed to have been a part of her life,' Coach Robinson said to me. He never let his own glory stop him from seeing the good graces in others."

So what shaped Eddie Robinson? Was he born a leader? Who instilled in him such compassion, humility and determination, and how did he acquire that optimism and trademark patriotism in the face of exceptional racial prejudice growing up? Charlie Joiner had no idea. "All I know," he said, "is he passed it on to us." But Yvonne Byrd, who began observing him when she was still a child, had some theories. Her most traditional thoughts make a lot of sense, and her more alternative line of thinking is at least hard to argue with.

"Uncle Eddie was one of the more fortunate young men when he was growing up," began Adolph Byrd's daughter, recalling the years Eddie spent with Daddy Frank and his second wife, Ann. "He had more than the average young man did that was his age. He came from a home where both parents were working. Even though they didn't make a lot of money, they were allowed to do what they could do as African-Americans at that time. According to more than half of the people who were their neighbors and friends, they were living a good life. Because of that, Uncle Eddie was exposed to ideas, dreams, philosophies, expectations that many of the others were not. They always pushed him with the saying that you can be whatever you want to be. Working at Standard Oil, as his daddy did, was a step up; most unusual for a black man then."

As for Eddie's concern for others, this trait might have been something beyond anyone's doing, in Yvonne's opinion. "A lot of people are going to think I'm nuts to say this, but it has a lot to do with his astrological sign. He's an Aquarian. They always want to help somebody. It's something about liking the underdog and feeling like you can help everybody even though you know you can't. But if you can see any potential, you try. It was all about the young person."

John Williams didn't know about astrological signs, but he did see those Aquarian traits as far back as when Eddie was attending Leland College and starring on the football team in the late 1930s. Williams was a youngster, living across the street from Eddie's daddy and stepmother in Baton Rouge. "Everybody had to know Eddie," Williams said, "because he was a popular guy. We looked up to him as a leader in the community even as a college student, because Eddie was always trying to help people and do things to make things better, especially for young men. He was trying to get young men to go to school and do what you needed to do to have a better life. He was always trying to help somebody. He believed in doing things to help people. He would talk to youngsters – talk to everybody, really."

Williams attended McKinley High when Eddie's best friend and favorite pass receiver in high school and college, George E. Mencer, was McKinley's coach. "There were nine seniors on the 1951 McKinley team," Williams said. "Eight of them went to Grambling." Williams was one of them, and quickly found that Eddie, the college coach, was very much like Eddie, the young guy who lived across the street in Baton Rouge. "His big thing," said Williams, "was, 'Go to class. Go to class. Go to class.' That's all you'd hear. He instilled in you: 'You need to go to class, and you need to pass. You need to get your grades together.' That was his big thing." Williams played only one season. "I played guard and linebacker," he said, "and got in one or two games. I weighed about two hundred pounds, but most of the guys were bigger. I had the heart but not the physical attributes." The other seven stuck with it, and several were contributors as seniors on the unbeaten 1955 team led by Willie Davis. "When he first came, we weren't sure he'd make the team," Williams recalled, "and he wound up being better than everybody else."

The influence of Daddy Frank was apparent to Williams. "Eddie was a disciplined person because his father was a disciplined person," he said. A seemingly little detail also provides insight into Eddie's insistence that his players make a good impression with their appearance. "Everybody admired Eddie's dad for his car because he kept his car clean all the time," Williams said. "He was a very clean and neat guy. We lived on a muddy street, but he always kept his car shiny, shiny, shiny." Eddie was a reflection of his daddy in all but one way, Williams said. "Eddie's dad was a very quiet guy, not as talkative as Eddie. If Eddie was there, you knew it. Eddie was a very social person, and got along with everybody."

Charles Smith, a little guy who – despite his lack of size, or perhaps to emphasize it – was nicknamed Tank, played for Eddie from 1968-73, including a red-shirt year. What he remembered most was Eddie's motivational ability. "He was a man ahead of his time as a coach," Tank said, "because he really knew the Xs and Os and the ins and outs of football. But he probably should have been a psychiatrist because he had a knack for getting you to be the best that you could be. Coach Rob could relate to you and have you believing you were the best in the world, that nobody could beat you. He loved America. He'd say, 'This is America. In America, you can become anything you want to become.' He had you believing you could do anything.

"We'd practice long and hard," Tank continued. "He believed in doing it right. If you were going to do it, do it right. We might run a play twelve, thirteen times. But that was because he wanted you to do it right. And he'd sell you on that. He'd say, 'Man, you didn't do that right. We gotta do that over.' He had that way about him. You might get mad at him, but when the pressure was over with, shoot, if he asked you to, you'd run through a wall for him."

The leadership that Eddie's Baton Rouge neighbors recognized as early as when he was a student at Leland reminded Tank, thirty years later, of Martin Luther King. "Coach Rob had a way, just like Martin Luther King, of getting people to do things, of getting people to believe in things, of getting people to follow him," Tank said. "Coach Rob took all these different people, all these different personalities and different backgrounds, and got them to work together and do what he wanted them to do. He had a way of helping people, of showing people that you can be successful and that things are going to change. Coach Rob wanted us to be ready when things changed. He didn't want to look for excuses for failure. He wanted to find reasons to be successful."

Eddie's ability to relate to everyone is what always struck Wilbert Ellis. "Coach Robinson was a man who saw no color," he said "He just looked at people being people. He respected people, and in return he received a lot of respect. Eddie was a people person." Ellis described a collection of people who nurtured Eddie's interpersonal skills. "His parents encouraged him," he said, acknowledging that Eddie's exposure to them was one-on-one because of their divorce. "His mother was a strong woman, who had a good foundation.

Things that she was able to teach him about the way of life are some of the things that helped him." Eddie's college coach had a great impact, Ellis added. "His coach at Leland was a preacher. Reverend Turner took Eddie under his wing because he said Eddie had a lot of leadership ability and it just needed to be developed." And then there was Ralph Waldo Emerson Jones. Grambling's visionary leader filled the critical role of mentor and advisor for Eddie for more than thirty years. "President Jones, the man who hired him, was just like a father to all of us," Ellis said. "Prez took Coach as a young man right out of college. He took a chance on him, and believed in him. He believed he was going to be a great coach and a great leader.

"He believed he would put Grambling on the map, and he did."

PART FIVE

Pinnacle

26

JIM CROW never took up residence in the all-black enclave of Grambling, Louisiana. There were no "colored" drinking fountains or bathrooms, no "whites-only" lunch counters, and no separate schools for white and black children. "We were so self-contained," said Sheree Rabon, "I didn't understand racism and discrimination and things people were going through until I moved away as an adult." Segregation and discrimination were as close as all-white Louisiana Tech, literally next door, and the town of Ruston, less than ten miles away. But within this oasis in the most conservative region of the state, the indignities and affronts that fueled the protest marches, sit-in demonstrations and boycotts of the Civil Rights Movement simply didn't exist. "You had to leave Grambling to get involved in civil rights activities," said John Williams, a resident as far back as the early fifties. Charlie Joiner concurred. "We were kind of immune from demonstrations and riots and all that kind of stuff, because Grambling's in the middle of nowhere. The closest group of whites in those days was in Ruston. But even the people in Ruston kind of cherished Coach Robinson because he was THE PERSON in Louisiana, The Number One Person in Louisiana." Or, as Rabon put it: "The things Coach Robinson was doing made the whites want to come to us. They wanted to be a part of it."

That insular tranquility is what made it such a surprise when Eddie and his football team returned from the historic game in Jackson to find trouble brewing on the Grambling campus. "We went through some trying times," said Doug Porter. "We were faced with a situation where the National Guard was called onto our campus to ensure that we would have a homecoming football game, because a portion of our students had said they were going to stop the game from being played as a form of protest."

Ray Hicks was in his final semester as a student that fall. He would graduate the following January, and almost thirty years later – as Dr. Raymond Hicks – would serve as the fifth president in the institution's history. Claude Lamar Aker, meanwhile, worked in the grounds maintenance department. When the administration announced it planned to expand the campus police force, and asked if anyone was interested in police work, Aker saw it as his chance to "get off grounds" for a better job. He spent seventeen years on the campus police force before becoming chief of police for the City of Grambling. While chief, he assumed the largely ceremonial role of the uniformed officer at head coach's side, escorting Eddie on and off the field before and after each game the last ten years of his coaching career.

Because they witnessed the unfolding student demonstrations from different vantage points, Hicks and Aker came away with different views of what precipitated the uncharacteristic unrest. "The kids didn't like the way the school was operating, and they wanted to change it," Aker said. "You had what we called vesper hour," he said of an old-fashioned devotional prayer service. "One day a week you had to go to vesper hour. That was mandatory, and the kids didn't like it." Female students were not allowed to wear slacks or drive cars; off-campus dating was prohibited; and dormitories locked down at ten o'clock. "A boy couldn't walk a girl back to her dormitory," Aker said. "When he got on the grounds of the dormitory, he had to turn around and go back." Dorm rooms didn't have televisions, and the only telephones were pay phones in the hallways. "There were rules and conditions that had been in place from the time the school started," Aker said. "They thought it should be more relaxed."

While conceding that students wanted relief from restrictive policies that lagged way behind the more liberal social norms of the late 1960s, Hicks described a broader set of issues that had racial and political implications. "Louisiana Tech was three miles down the road," he said, "so it did include some racial factors in terms of, 'Why is the white school three miles down the road growing and getting everything they want from the state, and our president has to go down to Baton Rouge and beg for things?' Faculty members and people in administration were always making some kind of comment that Prez was down there begging the legislature to do something. The students felt it was time to stop begging. We paid tuition, so the state should try to keep up with what the white schools were getting. To that extent, it had a political aspect to it."

By 1967, Stokely Carmichael had succeeded John Lewis as the head of SNCC, and Stokely's "Black Power" militancy had replaced Ghandian nonviolence as the prevailing protest tactic. When "Rap" Brown, the McKinley grad, succeeded Carmichael as SNCC's leader in May 1967, the mood intensified. Authority would be questioned and the establishment challenged, to an extent and in ways never before imagined. Grambling was changing, too, and just as Eddie was beginning to expose his players to the world outside of Louisiana, students in general were being introduced to more points of view and were being encouraged to think more independently. "They brought in a lot of new professors," Hicks said. "We had white professors from Harvard and Wisconsin, and a couple of black professors from the West Coast. The kids in political science had a dynamic and diverse faculty, and that's where it started, in the political science department. They started seeing other universities, and reading about other colleges and life at other places. These kids were reading a lot. They were really well-read and understood international and national affairs.

"Twenty-three students organized the movement," Hicks said. "It started with them publishing their own newspaper. Everybody wanted to read it every time it came out. They were criticizing the university, criticizing the state. In getting all of us involved, these students said, 'We deserve better. Why don't we have this?' Then they focused on the administration, and said to President Jones, 'It's time to stop begging. We need to DEMAND to have these things.' Because the impression was that the school was being run in such a way because that's the way the predominant system wanted it to run. They said, 'You've got to change philosophy; open up.' Some of it got back to the legislators. Some national people came down and helped these kids take it to another level, demonstrating and demanding changes at both the campus and in the state in terms of black higher education."

At one point students initiated a boycott of classes and called for mass withdrawals from school. Representatives of the governor visited President Jones, ostensibly to negotiate a resolution but in reality to pressure him into concessions that would restore calm. Students occupied some campus buildings, including the library, and a fire broke out in one of the women's dormitories. Faculty members were sent in to secure every building, with instructions to keep the students from leaving. It was the fire that brought out the National Guard, which concerned Ray Hicks because two students had died when a group stormed a police barricade at Jackson State back in May that year, and a policeman had been killed during a student riot at Texas Southern less than a week after the deaths at Jackson State. He didn't know what might happen at Grambling. Eventually, the leaders of the student revolt identified themselves, and all twenty-three were promptly expelled. One sued for reinstatement and won, he said; the rest enrolled in privates schools in Louisiana or in public colleges out of state. "Everybody was in awe of the kids protesting against the university," reflected Claude Lamar Aker. "That was unheard of."

The turmoil was one of two distractions Eddie had to overcome as he worked to get his players to forget about the loss to Jackson State and prepare for a Texas Southern team that had won four straight to become a legitimate factor in the race for the SWAC championship. Along with that disruption in the normal routine, he also was opening his locker room and practices to a crew from New York that was on campus to film the scenes and record the interviews that would become *Grambling College: 100 Yards To Glory*, a groundbreaking documentary about the small black college in backwater Louisiana, its one-of-a-kind young coach, and the football program that was turning the heads and opening the eyes of scouts for virtually every pro football team.

Grambling College: 100 Yards To Glory was the idea of long-time Newark sports writer Jerry Izenberg, who wrote the script and supervised the on-location filming. The executive producer of the one-hour special – not the host or narrator – was Howard Cosell, whose name association brought the program far more status decades later than it did at the time. In 1967 Cosell was only beginning to revolutionize sportscasting with his provocative "tell it like it is" style of commentary. Despite the national exposure he was gaining with his coverage of boxer Muhammad Ali, he was not yet particularly well-known outside the New York radio and television market. It would be three more years before outspoken Cosell joined steady Frank Gifford and folksy Don Meredith to make ABC-TV's *Monday Night Football* a ratings hit and in the process establish himself as an American cultural phenomenon.

Cosell had produced a series of hour-long interview specials titled *Self-Portraits* for ABC's flagship affiliate in New York City, WABC-TV. He had recently chalked up his first network production credit with an acclaimed special on the NFL-AFL merger and Jets owner Sonny Werblin's role in it. When Izenberg pitched the Grambling idea to him, Cosell immediately loved it. But others in the ABC hierarchy weren't so sure a piece about a small black college from rural Louisiana would have either viewer appeal or commercial viability in the New York market. Without Cosell's commitment, the project never would have been funded. The immediate significance of the documentary was national exposure for Grambling. The show aired on WABC in January 1968, and was so well-received that the network bought it and broadcast it coast-to-coast as the lead-in to coverage of the

College All-Star Game in Chicago that July. "Once it aired," recalled Doug Porter, "it made Grambling a household name. And it became a name not just among the black community. It became a name that was recognized throughout America."

Izenberg's script acquainted the nation with the school that was producing pro football players in greater numbers than any university except Notre Dame, noting that pro scouts by the dozens were staking out Grambling practices and attending all the games. It revisited Grambling's impoverished turn-of-the-century roots and the obstacles Grambling football had overcome; acknowledged the usually poor and uneducated family backgrounds of its players, who were realizing an opportunity previous generations never had; restated the significance of Tank Younger's breakthrough; and highlighted the subsequent achievements of players from other HBCUs who had achieved NFL stardom. The program eventually was nominated for an Emmy Award, and several magazines – made aware by the TV show – published features about Grambling football.

"It helped enlighten people about predominantly black small colleges," said Joiner. "They are competitive and they do play great football. And some of these athletes are some of the best players in this nation. If you don't have stuff like that documentary, people would never know. Back in those days they didn't notice those teams that often." The script, of course, also heralded Grambling's own considerable success – two unbeaten teams and one hundred seventy-one victories in the past twenty-five seasons, two national championships, and more than sixty former players who made it into pro football in the twenty years since Younger, including Willie Davis, Buck Buchanan and Willie Brown.

Ironically, the emphasis at Grambling on sports in general, and on football in particular, was an issue with some of the students who were protesting – at the very time the story that elevated the football team's national reputation was being filmed. Two years later, *LOOK* magazine included a reference to the protest in a four-page spread about Grambling's football prowess: "Two years ago, the non-athletes staged a riotous demonstration. Their complaint: Athletics is fine because that's how we get attention, but what about the academic side?" An accompanying photo caption identified the student body president and two co-eds who wondered "if books should not be emphasized as much as brawn."

The student rebellion was approaching its crescendo when Collie Nicholson met Izenberg and his crew upon their arrival in Shreveport early the week of the homecoming game with Texas Southern. Collie expressed concern that the ugly disorder would interfere with filming, but Izenberg was determined to forge ahead. Avoiding the commotion on campus significantly reduced the production team's ability to film segments in the usual variety of settings, and at one point a ruse was employed to placate some demonstrators who threatened to interfere with the film crew's work. The students were led to believe their protest was being filmed and would be sent to the network for use on the evening news, when, in fact, the cameras aimed at them contained no film.

When the week of shooting was finished, there was no footage of student unrest or National Guard presence on game day. In addition to action highlights from a 20-14 Grambling victory, the edited video included scenes showing the Grambling choir, the Grambling marching band, President Jones in his office, the crowd at a local barber shop on game day, and Eddie in many different situations: retracing the car ride with Rams scout Eddie Kotel before Kotel agreed to sign Tank Younger for a price Eddie and Prez considered sufficient . . . at practice, where with typical repetition, he ran linemen through the same blocking scheme over and over until they perfected their execution . . . in a chalk talk session before practice, where he quoted a clinic speech by the legendary Frank Leahy of Notre Dame about setting the tone with a hard hit on the first play of the game . . . on the sidelines chastising a player who had been ejected – "You satisfied yourself. But think about the team. Look at the people you're letting down". . . and in the locker room at halftime, telling his players, "We teach you the technique, but when the pressure is on you've got to think," and imploring them to "Give it what you've got and try to do what we know how to do."

Racial discrimination was never raised or addressed in the hour-long program, but at one point Eddie was asked to reflect on the obscurity of black college football. "I wonder, " he said, "and I'm sure many Negro football coaches wonder, what it would be like to play before 80,000 people in the stands, and if you had all of these things that some of the other great coaches – Bear, Woody and the other guys – have to work with. If you don't think about these things, you're not real. You've got to wonder about it."

Eddie would never have facilities and resources to match Bryant or Hayes. But he would exceed their success on the field, and he would find out what it was like to play before those large crowds.

27

MICHAEL BURKE was general manager of the Ringling Brothers and Barnum & Bailey Circus, so he already knew something about putting on a show, when the Columbia Broadcasting System lured him away in 1956. Placed in charge of what became known as new business development, Burke soon told Chairman William S. Paley that CBS should invest in a new Broadway musical called *My Fair Lady*. A programming genius who built CBS into the dominant player in a new medium, Paley went for it and was rewarded with a smash hit. *My Fair Lady's* 2,017 performances broke the record for the longest run for a major musical theater production, and CBS profited. Burke later was responsible for the purchase of the New York Yankees by CBS, and served as president of the Yankees from September 1966 to 1973 when the George Steinbrenner era began.

Spring training was a month away for the 1968 edition of Burke's Yankees – destined to finish in fifth place, twenty games behind the Detroit Tigers and thirty-one game winner Denny McLain – and Mickey Mantle, by then a first baseman, was approaching the final season of his career, when Burke watched Howard Cosell's Grambling documentary on New York City's ABC affiliate that January. Promoter that he was, Burke envisioned another marquee production. He wanted the historic Yankee baseball dynasty and the history-making Grambling football program linked in the same headline. The way to do that was to have Grambling play in Yankee Stadium, which in its 45-year history had hosted a long list of historic college football games, boxing matches and other sporting events besides Yankee baseball games. Two of the most famous were the Notre Dame-Army football game in 1928, known for Knute Rockne's "Win One For The Gipper" halftime speech, and the Joe Louis-Max Schmeling rematch that Eddie had followed so intently on radio in 1938.

The death of Jim Crow in the mid 1960s marked the end of organized, large-scale southern protest campaigns, but the aftermath exposed the complexity of the civil rights struggle nationwide. Outside the South, the issues were not open lunch counters, freedom to register and vote, or unrestricted access to public transportation. Exclusionary housing practices, limited employment opportunities and unequal pay, and inferior education resulting from de facto school segregation represented more subtle forms of racial discrimination whose solutions proved far more elusive. In the black population of the North, East and West, family was not the defining cultural unit to nearly the same extent; respect for elders did not guide values and govern behavior as it did in Dixie; and the church was not the galvanizing center of activism, nor were ministers the acknowledged, unquestioned leaders of groups seeking social change. These seismic differences triggered urban rioting in many major cities and spawned more militant, radical leaders who exploited the latent anger of blacks who had fled Jim Crow only to find a way of life that was different but rarely better. Previously effective tactics failed to mobilize a new audience, and proved to be ill-suited for attacking vastly different problems.

Burke's interest in bringing the Grambling football team to Yankee Stadium afforded Eddie an opportunity to use the growing popularity of his program to join the effort to address this new set of racially driven conditions. Eddie had met with New York Urban League representatives who acquainted him with the organization's Street Academies, corner storefronts in Harlem and Bedford Stuyvesant where adults with minimal education could prepare with other adults for the General Equivalency Diploma test. Given the importance Eddie placed on education in general, and on seeing his players graduate from college, in particular, the Urban League's GED program would be a fitting recipient of funds from a benefit game. The nature and extent of urban poverty increased Eddie's sense of urgency. But despite Michael Burke's interest, the Urban League's obvious need and Eddie's desire to use football to improve lives, the pieces just weren't coming together.

Martin Luther King's assassination in April 1968 provided the impetus. Eddie attended Dr. King's funeral in Atlanta with Collie Nicholson, and found inspiration within the profound sadness of the moment. Eddie was determined to proceed with the first "Invitational Football Classic" benefiting the New York Urban League's Street Academy Program and its college scholarship fund. Before leaving Atlanta, he met with Florida A&M's Jake Gaither and Earl Banks of Morgan State to discuss the idea. Gaither passed, but Banks agreed: Grambling's first opponent on a national stage would be Morgan State – as close to a dream pairing as there could be. The two schools had shared the black national championship the previous season, and the team from Baltimore had not lost since the last game of the 1964 season, winning twenty-six games in a row. Banks wasn't quite Eddie Robinson, but he was known as a former All-American from the University of Iowa and was destined to join Eddie in the College Football Hall of Fame. Morgan State's Raymond Chester, who played offense and defense, would go on to a highly successful 12-year pro career with Oakland and Baltimore. Charlie Joiner led a list of Grambling players who would be taken in the NFL draft the following spring.

Collie, who visited a succession of advertising agencies until he had lined up a sponsor, then got to work publicizing the upcoming game, and hyped it with his usual flair.

*"Grambling and Morgan State, two Negro college football pow-
ers who guard their reputations like feudal lords, will play a charity
game Sept. 28 in Yankee Stadium to help students in the ghetto . . . It
is the first major attraction featuring Negro college teams in New
York City . . . efforts are being made to lure 60,000 fans into Yankee
Stadium to help underprivileged students who otherwise might be
abandoned in hopelessness and despair . . . Only Notre Dame has
surpassed the Louisiana school in the number of graduates toiling in
the American and National Football Leagues . . . While Grambling
was earning itself a niche in the pro ranks, Morgan State proved itself
irresistible and immovable on the college scene . . . one writer
observed, "facing this club is similar to playing Russian roulette with
a loaded pistol."*

Tickets went on sale the last week of August, and those associated
with the game held their breath. "So many people," recalled Doug Porter,
"didn't think two historically black schools, playing in New York City, could
sell out Yankee Stadium." The two schools barely had 8,000 students
between them, and one of the promoters admitted, "We weren't at all sure
what we had." They soon found out. The game was a sellout a week before
it was played, and the attendance of 64,204 was the largest crowd at Yankee
Stadium for a college football game since Army defeated Michigan 27-6 in
1950. The contingency plan for covering the loss if the gate was a financial
disaster wasn't needed. After all expenses were paid, the Urban League's
educational programs received about $200,000. Michael Burke was grati-
fied, and Eddie was proud.

With a population of approximately eight million, New York City in
1968 had roughly three times as many people as the whole state of
Louisiana. Manhattan, the smallest of NYC's five boroughs, was about four
times the size of the entire city of Grambling. Virtually all-black Harlem
had about 160,000 residents; all-black Grambling fewer than 5,000. In

short, it was a totally different world that Eddie and his wide-eyed athletes visited. "When we got to take that New York City trip," said Charlie Joiner, "I thought that was the neatest thing in the world. I had never been out of the South. That was true for most of us. Walking down Broadway . . . seeing the bright lights and the big city . . . going to Madison Square Garden and Yankee Stadium – that trip was one of the highlights of my career, one of the highlights of my life at that time." Manhattan's skyscrapers made the biggest impression on Doug Williams, who made his first trip to New York in 1975. "I thought the buildings were falling," he recalled. "I hadn't seen any buildings taller than two stories. Can you imagine walking down the street and seeing a 70- or 80-story building? You look straight up and you think it's falling on you."

Joiner's fondest memory was seeing the New York Knicks and former Grambling star Willis Reed play basketball at the Garden. Reed arranged tickets for those in the Grambling party who wanted to see an NBA game. O.K. Davis of *The Ruston Daily Leader,* who was the first white sportswriter to cover Grambling football as a regular assignment, recalled a reception for the Grambling entourage in 1968 where he was introduced to Howard Cosell and met Jackie Robinson. Doug Porter remembered Eddie introducing Jackie to all the Grambling coaches and players. Both Porter and Davis were struck by how low-key Jackie Robinson was. "You hardly knew he and his wife Rachel were there," Davis said. "They just blended in with the crowd."

Ernie Miles didn't attend the reception, but he still came away with an experience he would never forget. Collie Nicholson had hired Miles in 1960 to serve as the college's official photographer. He was responsible for everything from yearbook photos to pictures that went with press releases to sports action shots to go out with Collie's game coverage and feature stories. "I didn't know anything about shooting movie film," he said. "I was a still photographer." But Eddie wanted game films, so Miles started filming football games, too. "I missed one game in fifteen years," he said. "That was when my father died and I went to the funeral." The routine was always the same for Miles. "Wherever we went, when we got back, I had to go to Shreveport, sixty-two miles one way, to have the film processed. It took an hour or so, and I'd wait. That's what he wanted, right away, all the time. I'd bring them back and take them straight to his house. He'd look at them all day Sunday." Miles accompanied Eddie and the team to New York, expecting to film the game as usual. He did, but he also recorded a spectacle every bit as impressive as the sold-out game at the House That Ruth Built. "The Grambling band marched through Harlem," he said. "They had hundreds of thousands of people watching them. It was still an all-male band then, and they were really fast-moving. They put on a great show, and everyone loved it. It was quite a sight."

Baltimore, home of Morgan State, is a mere one hundred eighty-nine miles from New York City, a three-hour trip for Morgan fans, while Grambling is 1,356 miles away. Nevertheless, the Yankee Stadium crowd heavily favored the team from Louisiana. A close, low-scoring contest came down to the final minute when first-string quarterback James "Shack" Harris, who had not played because of a shin injury, entered the game and quickly marched Grambling to the Morgan State two-yard line with thirty-seven seconds left to play. Morgan State led 9-7. Eddie sent 235-pound Henry Jones up the middle. But Raymond Chester, who had scored a touchdown on a 52-yard pass reception and the safety that was Morgan's margin by blocking a Grambling punt, stopped Jones short of the goal line. A field goal that would have been shorter than an extra point seemed in order. But during a timeout with sixteen seconds remaining, Eddie is said to have told everyone in the sideline caucus, "Let's win it the right way." Jones again tried to crash into the end zone and again was ruled short. Time ran out, and Grambling lost by two points.

Eddie accepted all responsibility for the decision to go for a touchdown instead of a field goal, conceding that maybe it was the wrong call but insisting, "A man has got to go with what he believes." The second-guessing stopped at the locker room door. "I can't see anything wrong with any decision he made," Joiner said forty years later, "because he always seemed to be right. If there was a guy who always seemed to be right, it was Coach Rob." Expressing the view of Eddie's coaching staff, Porter said: "It wasn't that high percentage of a call, definitely not a sure thing. We didn't have the greatest kicker in the world, and we'd already had a punt blocked. We felt our running game was strong enough that we would score the touchdown. We were in accord. We supported the idea of going for the touchdown."

A year later, when Eddie spoke at the Houston Touchdown Club's observance of college football's 100th anniversary, he revisited his decision at Yankee Stadium and quoted the 26th President of the United States to explain it: "Teddy Roosevelt once said, 'It is not the critic who counts, not the man who points out how the strong man stumbles or where the doer of deeds could have done them better . . . the credit belongs to the man who is actually in the arena, whose face is marred by dust and sweat and blood . . . who, at the worst, if he fails, at least fails while daring greatly, so that his place shall never be with those timid souls who know neither victory nor defeat.' If faced with the same decision," Eddie told his audience, "I would go for the touchdown again, because a man has to do what he believes in."

That first Yankee Stadium game marked a breakthrough in many ways. Black college football gained national exposure through a full-length *Sports Illustrated* story by Pat Putnam, who was beginning what would be a twenty-seven-year career at the national sports magazine. "It was the turning point in coverage by the white press," said Doug Porter. And because Putnam went into Harlem and interviewed the very people the Grambling-Morgan State game was intended to benefit instead of writing only about the football contest, the critical importance of a good education – Eddie's message to all who would listen – received a public airing.

New York City also opened the door to America and beyond for Eddie and his football program, which in turn raised the profile of a tangible example of black achievement. Over the next decade Grambling would play in front of more than three million fans in major cities coast to coast, including New York eight times. "In all of those cities where we played there were so many people, particularly black people, who were from the South," Porter said. "This gave them a sense of pride and a sense of attachment when Grambling came to town. People in all those cities had the opportunity to see two historically black schools play, to see them play in a great stadium, and to represent themselves well."

The broad exposure and the team's striking success made Grambling football a national story in non-sports publications, as well. The December 16, 1969 issue of *LOOK* magazine was a perfect example. The cover story was a lengthy excerpt from the forthcoming book *My Brother Lyndon,* by Sam Houston Johnson. Also featured were Princess Grace of Monaco on her 40th birthday, Shirley Temple at the United Nations, Barbra Streisand and her twin Hollywood hits, *Hello, Dolly!* and *On a Clear Day You Can See Forever,* Robert Redford modeling the latest ski attire, and . . . Eddie Robinson and his phenomenal football program: **"GRAMBLING COLLEGE: WHERE STARS ARE MADE."** Not only was every other story in the 100-page edition devoted to white subjects, but all thirty-one of the sixty-four advertisements that featured people, whether in photographs or sketches, also featured only white people.

The rare four-page spread included photographs from Grambling's 30-12 victory over Morgan State in their 1969 Yankee Stadium rematch, a picture of members of the team dozing on the flight to New York City, and a shot of players leaning forward in a huddle at practice, showing mostly their ample backsides to accentuate the size of Grambling's players. The story recounted the program's gaudy winning record and (of course) reminded readers that only Notre Dame had produced more pro players. More important, it also acknowledged that Eddie was turning poor kids with bleak futures into successful, contributing citizens. "Eddie Robinson has produced 70 pro grid stars, but his real glory is that he makes men of them too," read the subtitle. "Like Coach Vince Lombardi," read a line in the story, "he believes it is more important to make football players into men than men into football players."

28

NEW YORK also represented the first national exposure for Eddie's entry into the world of integrated football. He had chosen Jim Gregory, a white all-star quarterback from Corcoran, California, to be Grambling's Jackie-Robinson-in-reverse. At the time, Shack Harris was Grambling's starting quarterback, a senior destined to make pro football history. And junior Frank Holmes, next in line, was a certain future starter. That meant Gregory's time to lead the team on the field, if it ever came, was at least a couple years down the road. Nevertheless, the novelty of a white player at the powerhouse of black college football made Gregory a celebrity even without stardom. "Writers always wanted to make big ink," he said, "and at that time, I was huge ink. It was all over the papers everywhere in the country." Others also saw a special story waiting to be preserved. During Gregory's sophomore year he agreed to collaborate with writer Bruce Bahrenburg on a book, *My Little Brother's Coming Tomorrow,* published in 1971. Ten years later his story was dramatized in a made-for-TV movie titled *Grambling's White Tiger* that was produced by former Olympic decathlon gold medalist Bruce Jenner, who cast himself in the starring role.

Gregory made the traveling squad in his freshman season – as the placekicker backing up the kicker Eddie chose not to use on the last play of the Morgan State game – so he was regularly an obvious pre-game story subject. "I got interviewed everywhere," he said. "I don't care where we went, I was interviewed." Almost always, the line of questioning was the same. "A lot of sports writers tried to bait him into making statements about the fact he wasn't starting," said Doug Porter, his position coach. "He never once fell for that. He always told them that the best quarterback was starting." And when the interviews shifted to hypotheticals about backing up the starter, Gregory was ready for that, too. "I'd say, maybe you should talk to Frank Holmes, because he'll be in the game a whole lot sooner than I'll ever see the field."

Gregory's home was a small agricultural community about fifty miles southeast of Fresno. Corcoran is best known as the site of the California State Penitentiary that houses Sirhan Sirhan, assassin of Robert F. Kennedy; killer-cult leader Charles Manson, and serial murderer Juan Corona. But it's ethnic diversity made the city an ideal training ground for the player chosen to break the color barrier at Grambling. The racial mix of the Corcoran High Panthers, Gregory recalled, was roughly 60 percent Hispanic, 10 percent Asian, 10 percent African American and the remainder white. The coaching staff included a Grambling alumnus, line coach Art Calloway.

"Coach Calloway and I talked about it a lot during the school year," Gregory said, "about Grambling and about what Eddie was looking to do. We had another white player on the team that Coach Calloway was talking about trying to get recruited to Grambling as a running back. He was really picking my brain to see what my feelings and attitudes were about the school and the program. He was feeling me out if I thought it was a good idea for a white kid to go to Grambling. He was always saying that Coach Rob was looking for a white player who could fit in the program and who could play and be a contributor, and who could handle the situation of being the first white athlete at Grambling."

Gregory never knew if Calloway's questions were being asked with his teammate in mind or if really they were a subterfuge designed to assess Gregory's own interest in and suitability for the groundbreaking role. Either way, he wound up with a decision to make. Eddie was willing to give him a full scholarship. "My dad was really good about it," he said. "He left the final decision up to me; my mom, also. They weren't going to say yes or no on something as important as my future education. And that's the thing about it. It was going to be a paid education. There were people in the community who thought my parents were crazy for letting me think about doing it, and some coaches who said it was going to be a tough deal, hard to manage for a young guy like myself. But I didn't look at it that way. I looked at it as an opportunity to go play football at a major football school and play for one of the top coaches. At that time Grambling was number two behind Notre Dame in terms of active pros. It was an easy decision for me. I never had any thought of not accepting the offer."

Eddie left it to Art Calloway to prepare Gregory in advance for the challenge of entering Grambling's all-black world if he decided to say yes. But Eddie did his best to counsel Gregory once he arrived on campus. "Guys from the South had never been around many white people, and especially had never lived with them, slept with them or ate with them," Gregory said. "These guys had to deal with one white guy coming in. My situation was totally the opposite. I'm the one small white guy in the picture. Eddie knew there would be struggles for both sides. The black kids, of course, had grown up with struggles. I was going to have a mixed situation with white society in the South and black society and culture in the South – both of them at times wondering why I was there." A scene from the *Grambling's White Tiger* movie captured it bluntly. Eddie, played by Harry Belafonte, tells Gregory, played by Jenner: "The Negro boy knows what it's like to be a minority. It's new for you." That's pretty much how it happened, Gregory said.

While admitting that he didn't "necessarily understand all the ramifications that went along with being the first white player at an all-black school," Gregory went into it with his eyes wide open in another regard. "I knew I was getting used in two ways," he said, "by society and by Grambling. I was helping to bring about an integration program that the federal government wanted to happen, and that Coach Rob wanted, so that funding for the school would stay, or hopefully get better. At the same time he wanted his athletes to deal with the situation. If you really wanted to be a pro football player, you should know how to deal with one white athlete on your team. He told them, if they were having problems with one white player coming into their program, how were they going to deal with playing on any of the pro teams that are owned by white individuals? He saw it as a natural thing that needed to happen for his other players to become better people. He was very adamant about trying to develop good people for this country. He wanted you to succeed. That was his goal for all his players. He didn't just want you to be there for four years and play ball, then let you go. He wanted you to graduate and get a job and be a part of society."

Many times in the decades after his Grambling career ended, Gregory said: "It was a great experience. I would do it again in a heartbeat." That doesn't mean, however, that it was always easy. "There were a few guys who didn't much care for me in the beginning," he said. "As we got to know each other, we became pretty good friends. I put it in the perspective that it was almost like basic training. We were doing two-a-days, and all you had time to do was eat, sleep and practice football until school started." There was plenty of trash talk from opposing players, too, once the games began. "I remember during warm-ups before one game, players on the other team were saying, 'White boy, you better not come out here. We're going to hurt you.' And I made some rash comment back, something like, "You better learn how to hit before you talk like that.' The guys on my team said, 'Hey, he's not afraid.' They were willing to back me up if there was a situation where anyone was trying to take a cheap shot."

Nemiah Wilson was in his fourth pro season, the first of seven with the Oakland Raiders, the year Gregory arrived in Louisiana. Looking back to that moment, he said: "When Eddie brought that white quarterback to Grambling, if it had been any other coach, that kid would have been dead. The attitude was, 'Why in hell does he want to come to our school when we can't go to theirs?' Only Eddie could have made him acceptable. His ability to communicate is what made it possible for him to pull things like that off."

Eddie, in fact, did tell his players that Jim Gregory was coming, and that he expected them to treat him like a brother and defend him as they would each other. He paved the way for Jim Gregory to be accepted as a full member of the team and embraced as a teammate. The title of Bruce Bahrenburg's book about Gregory's experiences at Grambling, in fact, is based on an incident at practice the day before Gregory arrived. It is indicative of the reception most of Eddie's players gave their white teammate. Eddie told his squad to count off, and when the pealing progression reached fullback Henry Jones, a team captain and the ball-carrier who was stopped short of the Yankee Stadium goal line a few weeks later, he was number ninety-nine. "Make that one hundred," Jones said. "My little brother's coming tomorrow."

Gregory arrived in Shreveport, the end of a string of stops and connections that went from Fresno through Los Angeles and Dallas. "It was quite an adjustment just to get on the airplane and fly back there," he said. "It was the first time I'd flown." Doug Porter, an imposing six-foot-five, met him. "He asked me what position I coached," Porter recalled, "and I said, 'I coach the quarterbacks.' So he asked me, 'Are all the quarterbacks as tall as you are?' I told him not all of them were." Gregory, who barely measured six feet, was still feeling a little airsick. After the exchange with Porter, he felt worse. "I'm a young, very little-traveled seventeen-year-old who wanted to play some football," he said. "I'm thinking, 'Oh geez! What have I gotten myself into?' We sat and had dinner, and we talked quite a bit. Talking to Coach Porter, I'm sure they were all wondering if I really was going to be able to hang in, make it, and graduate, because ultimately, that was the goal Eddie had for any player he had. When we got back to Grambling, they had just finished one of the night meetings. I met with Coach

Robinson, and then I went to the dorm. During summer practice I roomed with Charlie Joiner, Henry Jones and Alvin Richardson, a halfback. Tank was down the hall."

Charles "Tank" Smith was a freshman, too. He would go on to play eight years for the Philadelphia Eagles, catch more than two hundred passes and experience playing in the Super Bowl. He caught two passes in a 27-10 loss to Oakland in SB XV – despite a broken jaw. But long before that, he became Jim Gregory's best friend in college, a guy who could make him laugh. "Tank was a lifesaver for me," Gregory said, "a mainstay as far as someone who stuck with me. We would hang out. We would go to Monroe; we would go to Ruston. We became really good buddies." Tank red-shirted his first year and Gregory played very little, so they had plenty of time to work on their quarterback-receiver timing. It paid off in a game in 1970 when Tank caught Gregory's first collegiate touchdown pass – against Morgan State in the first football game played at Pittsburgh's Three Rivers Stadium. "When he and I were together, we were like brothers," Tank said. "You saw one, you saw the other."

Tank almost blew his chance to play for Eddie at the same time Gregory was pondering the pros and cons of attending Grambling. Eddie had gone to a recreation center in Monroe to offer him a scholarship. "But I hadn't played but one year of high school football," Tank explained, "and I was small. I'd already heard about Grambling: big people, always winning. I didn't think I was good enough or big enough to play at Grambling. So when he came, I slipped out the back door." As so often happened, one of Eddie's former players stepped in. Eugene Hughes, Tank's high school coach, told him to hustle over to Grambling before it was too late, and had an assistant coach give Tank's cousin money for gas to take him over there. "When I got there they had started summer training," Tank said, then added: "One thing about Coach Rob, he didn't turn anybody down. I told him who I was, and he remembered me. He had an assistant get me a dorm room."

Matt Reed, one of Tank's high school teammates and his friend since childhood, had caught Eddie's eye, too. "Actually, that's who he really wanted. It was sort of a package deal," Tank said, implying that Eddie thought Reed, who was a year younger, might be more inclined to choose Grambling if his favorite receiver was already there, waiting for him. "He and I had been together for years. We lived in the same neighborhood, so we were always together." Reed was another six-foot-five quarterback with a big arm, a Shack Harris prototype, which was not good news for Jim Gregory. "I saw the handwriting on the wall," he said. "My chances of getting the starting job were really getting slim. I'm looking at reality: Do I want to play more? Do I want to sit behind these guys? Can I beat them out? Are they going to get hurt?" Inevitably, Gregory decided to approach Eddie about a position change.

"I roomed with Charlie and Shack a lot," he said, "and I worked a whole lot with Charlie as a receiver. Besides learning more about route work, it made me a better receiver." When Gregory proposed catching passes instead of throwing them, however, Eddie wouldn't even consider it. "Every time I had the conversation with Coach Rob," he said, "it would come down to two issues. One, every black quarterback to that time had always been made into a defensive back or a wide receiver in the pros. He wasn't going to take the first white quarterback at Grambling and turn him into a wide receiver or defensive back. Second, my last two years I was sitting there behind Matt as his backup. Eddie wasn't going to take his second-string quarterback and let him run routes. If Matt went down, he'd have to go to the third guy. Fortunately, we won a lot of football games, so I got a lot of playing time."

Grambling won thirty-three games during Gregory's four seasons. He had not completed his degree requirements at the end of his senior year, but he returned the next year, graduated, then became a high school coach in Reedley, California. He and everyone who was part of those years at Grambling called them a success. "James Gregory adapted to that climate quicker than anybody I've ever seen, considering white and black," Charlie

Joiner said. "People took to him. He fell right in with us and became friends. He was always in on the domino games; he did everything with us. It was a great thing for Coach Robinson to bring him in, and a great thing for him to come. It gave us all some insight into how the world should be."

29

CHARLIE JOINER and Shack Harris were two of Eddie's biggest football success stories. They were starters by their sophomore seasons, and from 1966 through 1968 Grambling won or shared the SWAC championship all three years and shared one black national championship. Their record as starters was twenty-four victories, five losses and a tie. One defeat was the Jackson State game at Mississippi Veterans Memorial Stadium, and another was the loss to Morgan State in New York. Both went on to careers of distinction in the NFL. They were forever linked as namesakes of an era – the way Willie Brown and Buck Buchanan were – and Shack became the Tank Younger of his position in the historical sense.

No one, not even Eddie with his coaching prowess and tremendous optimism, would have imagined Charlie Joiner making it in pro football when Charlie tried out for his high school team in Lake Charles, Louisiana. "I'm not a very big guy," Charlie said, "five-eleven and one-eighty – maybe." And he was a neophyte, albeit a motivated neophyte. "I was in need of a scholarship to attend college, because my parents were very poor. So I started playing football my junior year in high school. I figured if I was good enough, maybe I could earn a scholarship."

As it turned out, Charlie was good enough, and Eddie's network did the rest. "All of my high school coaches went to Grambling except one,"

Charlie said. "So when I was able to put up some good numbers my senior year, I'm very sure they contacted Coach Rob and told him about me, and he awarded me a scholarship. That was a common practice in Louisiana because a lot of his former players were high school coaches in the state. I never met him before I signed the scholarship papers. I'd heard about him, but had never met him." Charlie never considered going anywhere else. "It was a tremendous honor to go to Grambling. I know it's a small school, a small, predominantly black school in some little hick town in Louisiana. But Coach Robinson was so famous across the country that people took notice of Grambling when they played, and you got your notoriety and you got your publicity just by being there. I didn't have to go to Michigan State to get my name in the papers. Just going to Grambling was good enough because of Eddie Robinson."

There was no hint of great things to come during Charlie's first season. "The thing that surprised me most about Grambling," he said, "was the size of the players. Everybody was so much bigger! For a kid going to a new place, man, that kind of scared me. But I needed the education and I wanted to make sure I didn't do anything to jeopardize my scholarship. So I just made the best of it. I was strictly a backup as a freshman – might have been fourth or fifth on the depth chart. I spent my first year on the "look" team and doing all the freshman jobs that you do for a football team." The "look" team is the unit that does its best to imitate the upcoming opposition so the regulars can get accustomed to facing the formations they'll see in the game ahead. Charlie always played defensive back for Tom Williams, the assistant coach in charge of pretending to be the next opponent. Little did he know it would be his ticket into the NFL.

The really great pass receivers have sure hands, above-average speed and, quite often but not always, good size. What separates them from others with those attributes is their ability to run precise routes, to be where they're supposed to be when the ball – which is thrown to a predetermined spot on the field before the receiver is even looking – arrives. With his self-discipline and attention to every step of every pass pattern, Charlie Joiner developed that kind of dependability, and ended his college career with one hundred twelve pass receptions, almost half of all the passes Grambling completed in his three seasons as a starter. Still, he couldn't see himself becoming a pro. "I thought I was too small," he said. "I really did. I was looking at the sizes of people in the professional ranks, and I just didn't match up. So my senior year, I worked very hard to get my degree. And I did it. I got it on time. I graduated on time."

While hoping that his accounting degree would enable him to start a business career, Charlie was chosen by the Houston Oilers in the fourth round of the 1969 NFL draft. He was the 93rd player selected. "When I got a chance to go to the pros," he said, "I was very surprised. I mean, very surprised. Fortunate for me, I went to a team that had an executive who knew me." That executive was Tom Williams, Charlie's old "look" team coach at Grambling. "He convinced the Oilers to draft me as a defensive back," Charlie said, "not as a receiver. I went back and forth my first couple of years. I would play wide receiver during an offensive period, and defensive back during a defensive period. My third year in Houston I became a full-time receiver."

Through all of the back and forth in Houston, Charlie stayed in close contact with Eddie. "I always called back to him," he said. "If I had a personal problem, I'd call Coach Rob. If I had a problem with my contract, I'd call him. He was my mentor." It figured, then, that Eddie would be the person Charlie would turn to when Houston traded him to Cincinnati in the middle of the 1972 season. "I was disappointed by the move," Charlie said. "Houston kept me close to my family in Louisiana. I called him and said, 'Aw, Coach, I really don't know.' He said, 'Hey, just go up there and show 'em what you can do. Just give it that good ol' Gramblin' try. I mean, give it all you got.' He was a true advocate of 'give it all you got.' Those words stayed with me throughout my career."

Cincinnati traded Charlie to the San Diego Chargers in 1976, and he remained there for eleven seasons. His old friend Shack Harris succeeded Dan Fouts, allowing them to be reunited for Charlie's last three years as a player. Charlie finished his improbable pro career with 12,146 yards gained receiving – more than all but fifteen receivers in the history of pro football. His seven hundred fifty pass receptions ranked 26th on the all-time list. And he played in two hundred thirty-nine games, more than all but forty-seven other men who ever donned an NFL uniform. When he was chosen for induction into the Pro Football Hall of Fame, he asked Eddie to be his presenter. Like parents who say they love all of their children the same, coaches never want to admit to having favorite players or teams. Eddie acknowledged that at the enshrinement ceremony in Canton, Ohio in August 1996, but said of Charlie, "he has to be a favorite."

As Eddie went on with his remarks, Charlie fought back tears, thrilled to be there but still finding it hard to believe he was receiving the ultimate honor in pro football. As Eddie spoke, Charlie was reminded of all that Eddie had emphasized during his years at Grambling. "Charlie is dear to me," Eddie told the audience. "Charlie has shown himself to be a man of courage, humility and integrity, as well as a scholar. My personal admiration for Charlie has grown through the years not only for what he has accomplished on the college and pro football field but also for the way he has conducted his private life. His devotion to his family, his civic and community involvement, and the excellence he brought to the coaching profession. When I talk about Charlie, it is not about just college and professional football, but it is about life itself. This man is someone who personifies class and dignity."

In contrast to diminutive Charlie Joiner, Eddie took one look at Shack Harris and saw a football player with the potential to make history. Already 6-feet-4 and 210 pounds when he was only eighteen years old, Harris figured to get bigger as he matured. He possessed a strong, accurate throwing arm, and had set numerous records during his high school career in Monroe, Louisiana. Eddie envisioned opening doors for black quarterbacks in pro football as he had done twenty years before for black players in general with Tank Younger. He handpicked Shack Harris to make a statement about the leadership ability of African Americans in that pivotal position. He was as sure about Shack as he had been about Tank.

"I had quite a few scholarships to major universities," Harris said in an interview published in the *Chicago Defender* in 1974, "but almost all of them wanted to convert me to another position. Eddie Robinson was the only man willing to give me the opportunity to play quarterback. He kept saying that someday there would be a black quarterback in pro football, and that I would be one of the first to break the color barrier." It didn't take an Act of God to convince Harris to believe Eddie Robinson, but the Word of God certainly had a lot to do with his decision to attend Grambling. "He would come by my house on a regular basis and bring his Bible," Harris recalled. "He and my mother would end up reading verses out of the Bible. Next thing I know, he had my mother recruiting me to go to Grambling."

The first black quarterback to start a pro football game was Marlin Briscoe, a 14th-round draft choice by the Denver Broncos from the University of Nebraska-Omaha. UNO is not to be mistaken for the University of Nebraska in Lincoln, home of the vaunted Cornhuskers. Smaller than Charlie Joiner at five-ten and one hundred seventy-seven pounds, Briscoe entered Denver's game against the Boston Patriots in the fourth quarter on September 29, 1968 – the day after Grambling and Morgan State played at Yankee Stadium. Denver's starting quarterback, Steve Tensi, had suffered a broken collarbone and his backup was ineffective. Briscoe's first play from scrimmage was a 22-yard pass completion, and on his second offensive series, he directed an 80-yard touchdown drive, scoring himself on a 12-yard run. That performance earned Briscoe the chance to make history the next week when he lined up under center on Denver's first possession against the Cincinnati Bengals. The date was October 6, 1968.

Briscoe set the Broncos team record for touchdown passes by a rookie with fourteen that season, a record no beginning quarterback, including

John Elway, equaled over the next forty years. But Briscoe was cut the next year when Tensi returned and the Broncos signed as his backup a white quarterback named Pete Liske, who had played the last four years in the Canadian Football League. Briscoe signed with the Buffalo Bills – and was converted to a pass receiver. He played eight more seasons and was a key member of two Super Bowl champions in Miami, including the undefeated 1972 team. But he never played quarterback again after the 1968 season in Denver. In that regard, he was like so many other black quarterbacks who had to change positions after college to gain or keep a job at the pro level: Eldridge Dickey of Tennessee State, who was the first black quarterback drafted in the first round (by Oakland) but was moved to wide receiver despite a strong showing in training camp and never played a pro down at quarterback; Ken Riley of Florida A&M, a four-year starter for Jake Gaither, who was moved to a safety by Paul Brown the day he reported to the Cincinnati Bengals; and Grambling's Mike Howell, who became a cornerback with Cleveland, to name only a few. It was this pattern that Eddie wanted to break.

"One day I asked Coach Robinson to switch me to another position so I might have a chance to play in the pros," Harris related in that 1974 *Defender* interview. "He wouldn't hear of it. He told me, 'You're a quarterback, and a darned good one. You'll remain a quarterback, and one day you'll make the pros.'" In his senior season, Harris completed 104 of 201 pass attempts for 1,827yards and eighteen touchdowns. In three collegiate seasons he threw for more than 4,000 yards and forty-three touchdowns.

"The guy had a great arm, an outstanding arm," said Joiner. "When we left Grambling, I didn't think anyone could out-throw him. Another thing, he had great touch. He wasn't just able to throw it far; he had great touch on it. And the guy worked harder than I did. We would practice for hours and hours on that passing game; just he and I throwing balls, and sometimes a couple other receivers." Joiner had no doubt that his college teammate could handle the mental side of the job. "James Harris is very smart, extremely smart. If they didn't give him a chance, and they tried to blame it on him not being mentally ready, that wouldn't be true. James Harris was a very smart quarterback. And James Harris was a competitor. That was just born and bred from going to Grambling and playing for Coach Robinson."

Buffalo picked Harris in the eighth round of the 1969 combined NFL-AFL draft, the last one before the competing pro football leagues completed the merger announced in 1966.

Rather than excitement at the prospect of an opportunity to play pro football, though, he felt only disappointment at being such a low draft choice. He considered not reporting to the Bills training camp until Eddie took him to Grambling Stadium for a heart-to-heart talk. "We sat on the bleachers, just me and him," Harris told William C. Rhoden of the *The New York Times*. "He told me that there was no question that I would make it as a quarterback; but if I didn't go, that I might be keeping other guys from getting a chance. If I didn't go, it would be hard for anyone else because he thought it would be a long time before another black quarterback came along with my ability."

The Bills had two veteran quarterbacks: Jack Kemp, a former AFL most valuable player who had led the Bills to consecutive league championships in 1964-65, and Tom Flores, an all-league player with Oakland who had come to Buffalo the season before to be Kemp's backup. Shaking off harassment that included anonymous death threats, Harris consulted with Eddie regularly and competed for the starting job. "I had never had much experience dealing with whites at the time," Harris said in a video tribute to Eddie produced the year he died, "and going to be the leader of a team, you understood the reason other blacks weren't making it – because they said they couldn't lead and weren't smart enough. So those were the challenges that I had. But I wasn't alone. Coach would call me every night." Ultimately Shack fulfilled Eddie's vision by beating out both Kemp and Flores, and thus became the first black quarterback to open a season as a pro team's starting quarterback – ironically with Marlin Briscoe as one of his receivers. But after suffering a torn stomach muscle in the midst of a lackluster first game, Harris played in only three more games the rest of the season. *The Defender* story related the ordeal that followed:

> *For Harris, the next three years were a period of frustration. He attempted fewer than 200 passes.*
>
> *"During those years my emotions underwent considerable changes," he recalled. "My first year at Buffalo was filled with high spirits. But as the years passed and my playing time did not increase, I saw my career going downhill. My confidence began to decline."*
>
> *In 1972 his career hit a low ebb when he was waived and no one claimed him. Harris went to Washington and worked for the U.S. Commerce Department's Office of Minority Enterprise. The pay wasn't comparable to that of pro football, but the rewards were of a different nature.*
>
> *"I helped recruit minority students in the top ten percent of their senior class and placed them in job opportunities relating to their projected areas of study in college," said Harris.*

Just when it looked as though Shack might be out of football for good, Eddie went to work behind the scenes. Tank Younger's playing days were long over, but Grambling's first pro had remained with the Rams as a scout. He stayed in touch with Eddie, and visited Grambling often to check out Eddie's top prospects. So Tank was quite comfortable with Eddie calling in the middle of the 1972 season and asking if Tank could get Shack a legitimate shot with the Rams. As a quarterback. The Rams followed Younger's recommendation and signed Shack. Eddie spoke with Shack almost daily, coaching him by phone on how to approach practice and to deal with the competition between him, Ron Jaworski and Pat Haden, and, above all, to steer clear of race in all of his comments. Eddie also placed a call to Rams owner Carroll Rosenbloom, asking him to take an interest in a talented young athlete who was still adjusting to life outside the South.

Harris led the Rams to back-to-back divisional championships in 1974 and 1975, and in 1974 became the first black quarterback to start an NFL conference championship game. Shack and the Rams just missed a trip to the Super Bowl that year, losing 14-10 to Minnesota amid an officiating controversy that changed the game in the third period. Losing 7-3, the Rams were inches away from the Vikings goal line after driving from their own one, and Shack was calling signals for what would have been a quarterback sneak to take the lead when Rams guard Tom Mack was called for moving before the snap. Television replays showed that Mack had not moved and that Minnesota lineman Alan Page had jumped offside. Pushed back five yards by the penalty, Shack was intercepted in the end zone two plays later. It was small consolation, but Shack capped a great season by leading the National Conference all-stars to a 17-10 victory over the American Conference in that season's Pro Bowl. He was named most valuable player. When he left the Rams for San Diego after the 1976 season, he had the highest career pass completion percentage in Rams team history, 55.4 percent.

Reunited with Charlie Joiner, Shack had a respectable first season with the Chargers but played sparingly his last two years in the league. His place as a trailblazer, though, was firmly established, and the continuing parade of black quarterbacks who excelled in the NFL afterwards – such stars as Randall Cunningham, Donovan McNab, Steve McNair and Grambling's own Doug Williams, among many – is his legacy, shared of course with Eddie, his irreplaceable mentor.

30

THE SIXTIES ended with a succession of history-making events. In January, 1969, Richard Nixon took the oath of office as the 37th President of the United States, succeeding a weary Lyndon Johnson, who declined to seek another term. In March, James Earl Ray pled guilty to the murder of Martin Luther King Jr. and was sentenced to ninety-nine years in prison. On July 20, Neil Armstrong told the nation, "That's one small step for man, one giant leap for mankind," as he became the first human being to set foot on the surface of the moon. Less than a month later, on August 15, an estimated 350,000 people attended the defining event of the counterculture movement – the three-day Woodstock Music Festival – at Max Yasgur's dairy farm in Bethel, New York. Before it ended, the 190-mile-per-hour winds of Camille, one of only three category five hurricanes to slam the United States in the 20th century, devastated Louisiana, Mississippi and Alabama, killing two hundred fifty-nine people and causing $1.42 billion in damage (about four times that much in end-of-the-century dollars). Also in 1969, the Boeing 747 jumbo jet took to the skies, the Public Broadcasting System (PBS) went on the air, the U.S. military gave birth to the Internet, and Wal-Mart was incorporated.

The decade had no such remarkable ending for Eddie and Grambling, at least not on the field. In Jim Gregory's second season, the Tigers won six and lost four – their worst showing since a four-win, six-loss record in 1959. The Grambling Road Show, though, picked up speed. The season opener, a 28-7 loss to Alcorn State, attracted more than 60,000 fans at the Los Angeles Coliseum, and a return trip to Yankee Stadium the next week, a 30-12 victory in the rematch with Morgan State, drew more than 62,000. It was the first time in history that a black college football team had played in major cities on both coasts in the same year, and the time in transit provided Gregory with the first lessons of an extracurricular education he wasn't expecting but which he treasured his whole life. "I wish I had a recording," he said. "I would love to bring back all the stories President Jones told on all the bus rides and plane flights. He always had the most amazing stories of growing up and being a part of Louisiana history, of Huey Long and all the things that went along with that. I just wish I could remember all those things that Prez had to say, and Coach Rob and Coach (Fred) Hobdy. They all had special things to tell you about how they lived and grew up in the South."

Gregory's first bus trip in his freshman season gave him a graphic demonstration of life in the South as his teammates and coaches knew it. Grambling was headed to Itta Bena, Mississippi, which is as far in every imaginable way as possible from New York City, the site of the previous week's game. "We still had to get clearance ahead of time wherever we were going to stop to go in to eat," he said. "I remember stopping at one place and we wound up not eating there because they didn't want us to come in." The way Eddie responded to it was enlightening for Gregory, particularly so as a white man directly experiencing racially-driven rejection and observing Eddie's example of restrained response. It gave him an appreciation for the example Eddie set.

"Coach Rob had to deal with that all the time, but he didn't emphasize it," Gregory said. "He didn't talk about it with the players or the team. Now he may have discussed it with his staff or some of the coaches, but we were never a part of any discussions about what was wrong in the country, or what's bad, or how this or that happened to him. He dealt with hardships growing up and coming through the South, but I literally cannot remember him ever bringing up issues like that. Eddie was never one to bring in the negative aspect of America, of how people had been mistreated. He never was one to push that side of his life, the struggles that he'd had. He just was always the most positive man. He never had a bad word to say about America. The main thing I can remember about Eddie is him stating that this is the greatest country in the world, and if you can't appreciate it, you must be crazy. He always had praise for the country and didn't tear it down on the bad issues of what we had to deal with. Eddie's philosophy of teaching and coaching was to make people better Americans."

O. K. Davis – everyone knew him as Buddy – was a student at Louisiana Tech, majoring in journalism, when Jim Gregory came to Grambling. That's when Buddy started covering Grambling football on a part-time basis for the *Ruston Daily Leader,* making the small afternoon daily, with circulation around 4,000, the first white newspaper in the state to pay a white reporter for coverage of a black sports team. Buddy, in fact, was still a Tech student when he accompanied the Grambling team to New York for the first Yankee Stadium game. "Back then," he recalled, "I caught some flack from people who just couldn't understand. They would say, 'Why are you wasting space on a predominantly black school?' I would say, 'Look, we don't even need to go there. You're wasting your time talking to me.' At that time, it was ridiculous if you *didn't* write a lot about them."

Buddy graduated in 1970 and immediately became *The Daily Leader's* one-man sports department, with the title of sports editor. Soon after that, he cast himself as a pioneer in Louisiana sports writing – the first white writer to cover a black sports team as a full-time beat. In 2009, his prolific career was doubly recognized – with induction into the Louisiana Sports Hall of Fame and presentation of the Louisiana Sports Writers Association's Distinguished Service Award,

"My publisher was a gentleman named Tom Kelly," Buddy said, recalling the day he proposed treating Grambling the same as any other sports subject. "I went to him after I joined the staff full-time. I said, 'Mr. Kelly, I grew up studying sports and appreciating the history of sports. And Coach Rob and what they have done at Grambling needs to be covered. This needs to be done. They deserve it. They should have it.' He said, 'Hey, I'm going on your opinion. You know what you're talking about.' He said, 'Go for it. I don't have any problem with it.'"

A native of Dodson in nearby Winn Parish, Tom Kelly had grown up with segregation all around him. "It was so much a part of the culture," he said, "that, really, that was just the way things were." Yet Kelly recalled experiences he was sure helped him become the kind of newspaper publisher who would believe in racially inclusive coverage as a matter of principle. When he was a little boy, four or five, "I remember there was a black man who worked at a country store that we went to, and the people who ran the store treated Ol' Dave with an attitude that made me uncomfortable, even when I was that young," he said. After he landed his first reporting job, "I began to cover school news and there were black teachers and principals working in the system who invited me to come out to their schools and cover events and so forth," he said. "That was when I first began to realize that they really had it tough. They had very little equipment, and they were scrounging for every little thing they had. But they were trying."

Kelly became a member of the Lions Club in Winnfield in the mid-1950s, and never forgot one particular incident from those days. "We had evening dinner meetings and met in the dining room at the Winnfield Hotel," he said. "Normally, the guest speaker came in, sat down and had dinner with the members. On this occasion, the program chairman said, 'He'll be here in a little bit.' When we finished the meal, he went to the side door and motioned for the man to come in. The man who came in was the principal of the black high school in Winnfield. He stood up in front of the crowd and, with a smile, said 'I can tell I've already missed the best part of this meeting.' He couldn't come in to eat with a group of white people, even under those circumstances."

Kelly came to *The Daily Leader* in 1962. He inherited a full-time news-room staff of three and a handful of country correspondents and ladies who reported on the goings-on at their churches, and a hundred-year-old letterpress that printed type just fine but wasn't much with photos. Daily circulation was around 2,500 copies. Until Buddy Davis was hired, a retired Army major wrote a column about sports, but there was little actual sports coverage other than whatever Buddy provided as a student contributor. Kelly wrote most of the local news stories himself. He hadn't been publisher very long – he called himself editor-publisher – when he was presented with his first defining decision. "I think there was a group in Grambling just testing the waters to see what would happen," he said. "They brought in a photograph of a black couple announcing their engagement. I published it.

"I was not unaware of the likely reaction in some areas," Kelly said. "There were a few eyebrows raised because that had never been done before. There were a couple phone calls and a few turned-up noses, mainly from some of the folks out in the country. But because I'm 'home folks,' people accepted it. If I had been from New York City, somebody might have decided to teach me a lesson."

Kelly's standing in the Ruston community was such that in 1968 – the year Buddy Davis accompanied Eddie and the Grambling football team to Yankee Stadium – the leadership of Lincoln Parish schools chose Kelly to be chairman of the biracial community committee to develop the federal court-ordered school desegregation plan for the parish, which included Ruston and Grambling. Once again his principles were tested. "The only reaction in the community to the desegregation order was the formation of a private school for the socially elite," he said. "They said we needed to make sure we maintained quality education. There was a group that came to me and wanted me to join their board and send my kids to the private school. I told them that part of what my kids learned in school would be how to live in the community that was developing, and I would continue to send them to public schools in Ruston. All three of my kids graduated from Ruston High."

As it always has been at every small newspaper, Buddy Davis did it all and had to hustle once he became sports editor at *The Daily Leader*. He wrote game stories, follow-up stories, columns, mid-week feature stories and game advance stories – and shot his own photos. In addition to Grambling, he covered Louisiana Tech's teams, local high schools, and anything else that belonged on the sports pages. "There were some instances when people there were having trouble adapting to it," he said. "Nothing vicious at all, but they'd ask, 'Why are you writing about them?' And they couldn't believe it when I would go on a road trip."

Traveling with Grambling was a curiosity wherever the team played on the road. "Coach Rob would introduce me at press conferences," Buddy said, "and I'd have media guys coming up to me and asking, 'How is it traveling with Grambling? You're the only white guy around.'" Almost always there was surprise when Buddy answered positively and enthusiastically. "Coach Rob was like a father to me," he said much later. "I made friends for life." Rick Hohlt, Buddy's publisher forty years later, affirmed the bond that developed between the two. "Buddy was more than a reporter to Coach Rob," he said. "Rob always said Buddy was like a son to him. It was a special relationship."

Buddy Davis arrived on the scene just as Eddie was reaching the pinnacle of his illustrious career. Between 1970 and 1980 Grambling won one hundred five games, lost only twenty-one, and tied one, an .827 winning percentage. Eddie's teams won or shared nine SWAC championships in those eleven seasons, and five black national championships. In addition to Yankee Stadium, Grambling played in virtually every famous stadium in America: the Rose Bowl, the Los Angeles Coliseum, the Orange Bowl, Soldier Field, Comiskey Park, the Astrodome, the Silverdome, Tiger Stadium, Giants Stadium, Shea Stadium, Three Rivers Stadium, Aloha Stadium, RFK (Robert F. Kennedy) Stadium, Philadelphia Veterans Stadium and Cleveland Municipal Stadium. "We're trying to give the country a glimpse of black football at its best," said Collie Nicholson, "by bringing it to the people in the major cities throughout the country." The longest winning streak in school history covered sixteen games, from late September 1974 to mid-October 1975. Games in Tokyo in 1976 and 1977 were the first played by an American college football team outside the United States.

No writer ever had more intimate access to Eddie Robinson than Buddy. Eddie loved old movies and would talk endlessly with Buddy about his favorite stars – Humphrey Bogart, Jimmy Stewart and John Wayne. "He often mentions the 'Duke' in pre-game and post-game talks," Davis once wrote. So impressed was Buddy Davis that he wrote and published *Grambling's Gridiron Glory – Eddie Robinson and the Tigers' Success Story* after the 1982 season. Buddy's appreciation for Eddie and what he had accomplished at Grambling was apparent in the book, but he stopped short of expressing his personal admiration in it.

"Coach Rob is the most compassionate, caring, understanding gentleman I've met in my lifetime," Buddy said when interviewed many years later. "He saw human beings as they were. He didn't make a big deal out of everything. The thing about him that just amazed me over thirty, almost forty, years of covering him is that he had to go through a lot of heartache and tough times in his lifetime, but you would never know it. He was always the most upbeat, compassionate guy you'd ever meet. We would sit around and he would just express his gratefulness for what he had at the time, and what they had been able to do at Grambling. His greatest line was, 'I'm the luckiest man in the world.' He thought he was the most fortunate guy in the world to achieve what he did. I don't think he spent a lot of time focusing on what happened in the past. He was focused on making those young men he had into good citizens, having them achieve in the classroom, and be a success. And all the players he turned out are a testament to that, and not just for what they did in the NFL."

In April 1970, during Buddy's last semester at Louisiana Tech, Eddie and Grambling achieved another media breakthrough that would parallel Buddy's first season of full-time coverage.

"Grambling College has signed an exclusive television contract with Black Associated Sports Enterprises, Beverly Hills, California, for 13 weekly football shows," the announcement story began. *"Jim Hunter, president of BASE and board chairman, said 'the complete Grambling schedule will be videotaped in color on location and edited for delayed telecast in major markets throughout the United States.' It marks the first time that black college football has been considered for major television distribution . . . . Willie Davis, ex-Grambling All-American and former all-pro defensive end with the Green Bay Packers, has been signed to host the weekly show. He will share the mike with Coach Eddie Robinson, who made the school a magic name in football circles."*

No story about Grambling football would be complete, it seemed then, without the following sentence.

"Grambling has sent more players into pro football than any other school except Notre Dame."

If playing before large crowds wasn't enough by itself to make Grambling a national name, the coast-to-coast television show every Sunday did the trick. The show created another "first-of-its-kind" opportunity, too. Eddie became the first black coach to appear in television commercials when he pitched Oldsmobile cars – with some truly classic scripts. *"Bein' in sports, you hear a lot of braggin' and big talk. But at Grambling, we let our record do the talkin.' And the Oldsmobile people do the same . . ."* Or, standing at a projector as though he were about to study some game film: *"Oldsmobile had a real strong showing last year. Let me show you . . . Cutlass S was one of the star performers on the team. And it looks even better this year . . ."*

Commercial endorsements involving black athletes and coaches were commonplace decades later, but it was Eddie who paved the way, as he had done in so many other ways. *Grambling's Playback* enjoyed a four-year run, 1971 through 1974, and led to live network telecasts of many football games involving HBCUs. Grambling appeared in ten nationally and regionally televised games between 1971 and 1982. All of this exposure also had a downside, however. It hastened the more aggressive recruitment of talented black players by coaches at predominantly white universities, including many that had refused to integrate or were limiting the number of black players they allowed on their teams. Change was coming.

31

AFTER COMPLETING his graduate studies at Indiana, Dr. Rod Paige resurfaced at Texas Southern in Houston in 1971, accepting the dual job of head football coach and athletic director on the unusual condition that he also be hired as a faculty member. He left coaching for good after the 1975 season, and eventually became dean of the School of Education at Texas Southern. He won election to the Board of Education of the Houston Independent School District in 1989, and was hired as superintendent of Houston public schools in 1994. On January 21, 2001 the United States Senate confirmed his appointment to President George W. Bush's cabinet, where he gained national prominence as the architect of the federal No Child Left Behind Act that attempted to enforce uniform higher standards for achievement on all school districts nationwide.

Two years into his coaching stint at Texas Southern, Paige's only sideline success against Eddie in seven tries had been Jackson State's victory over Grambling at Mississippi Veterans Memorial Stadium in 1967. As they prepared for their 1973 meeting, it didn't take a Las Vegas handicapper to figure out that Texas Southern was an overwhelming underdog in the upcoming game. Grambling was coming to Houston the winner in sixteen of its last seventeen games – ten straight to end 1972 and six of seven in the current season. The only loss had been to Tennessee State by a 19-13 score in what many considered the game of the year among black college football teams. John Merritt's team would finish unbeaten in ten games and win the black national championship. In contrast, Paige's team was 2-4-1 by late October. Also, Texas Southern had lost to Grambling seven years in a row, twice since Paige took over. But there's a reason teams go ahead and actually play the games even when it seems hopeless for one side. This, it turned out, was a perfect example.

"You looked at Eddie's teams," Paige explained years later. "What you always saw was a group of big, strong, talented athletes, especially on the defensive line. These guys were BIG." In fact, Grambling's defensive line averaged two hundred fifty-seven pounds per man, bigger than some pro teams at that time. "They outgunned us in terms of size," Paige said. "Our coaches and I were discussing this fact, and we agreed that if we have our guys offensively confront those guys defensively, 'You know what? We are dead men walking, because those guys are gonna murder us.' So we had to figure out a way to get around them.

"Charlie Lattimore, our defensive coach, and I were watching television the Saturday before we played Grambling, and the game on was USC. (Southern Cal was playing Oregon.) USC had Anthony Davis at tailback, and they had a play they called student body right and student body left. Simply, they'd turn around and pitch the ball to the tailback, and he ran a sweep play to either side. We said, 'That's it!' What we saw was, we won't play ball between the tackles. We'll take that space and just give it up. Because we know they're bigger and stronger than we are. Let's move the game out to the sidelines, between the hash marks and the sidelines. The way we're going to do that is we're going to use this sweep play that USC has, and we're just going to take our whole team and run out to the sideline and see if they can get out there in time to play the game."

John McKay was the head coach at Southern California, and one of the most respected minds in college football at the time. "We got on the phone and called Coach McKay," Paige said, "and told him we wanted to come out there and take a closer look at that. He allowed us to come out there and sit in his film room and break that whole toss play down. I don't think we saw him the whole time. He just turned us over to his film guy. We watched film for two days, and we got it down to a science. We came back and we taught our guys how to run that play."

The final score was Texas Southern 35, Grambling 21, but the game was never that close, according to Paige. "The game was really not a football game. It was a track meet," he said. "Before they could turn around, we were up on them. We were up on them real big, real quick. They finally scored some to make it that close." That stunning upset begat another upset of sorts. "I don't remember Eddie coming to the middle of the field and shaking my hand," Paige said. "I think he went directly to the locker room. Eddie was so shocked – and by the way, we were a little bit, too. I think he was really disappointed that they lost that game. They got outgunned, but it wasn't outgunning with physical skills. He was out-strategized."

It was obvious, thirty-five years later, how satisfying it was for Paige to outsmart the legendary Robinson on that one occasion. "He was a tough, tough adversary," Paige said. "When you were going to play Eddie, you had an awful lot to think about. In the first place, you knew his team was going to be very well-coached, and you knew they were going to be very talented players. You didn't have to spend a whole lot of time studying Eddie's films, because everybody who played him knew exactly what he was going to do. But nobody was going to be able to deal with it very much. It was execution. You knew that Eddie's idea was going to be uncomplicated, very focused, very clear, and very fundamentally sound. For example, if Eddie was going to run a trap play up the middle against you, you had to figure that one out pretty quick. Otherwise, Eddie was going to keep coming at you the same way. He would eat your lunch the rest of the ball game running the same play."

In a recorded interview, Shack Harris told a story that illustrated Paige's point perfectly. "One particular day we were playing Alcorn," he recalled, "and Coach had been running the same plays for so long that they knew the play. They called it by name: one twenty-six counter. So I say, 'Coach, they know the play. They're calling the play.' And he says, 'Oh yeah? What did they call?' I said, 'One twenty-six counter.' He'd always grab you when he was sending you in the game, while he was talking to you. He sent me in the game, and I said, 'What's the play?' He said, 'One twenty-six counter.' So I go in, and – reluctantly – I call one twenty-six counter. Essex Johnson goes sixty-two yards for a touchdown. I come off the field, and Coach says, 'blockin' and tacklin'.'"

After ambushing Grambling, Texas Southern lost two of its remaining three games and finished with a losing record. Grambling won its next two and needed to end the regular season with a victory over Southern University to secure a berth in the NCAA Division II national playoffs with a final record of nine wins and two losses. Interest in the rivalry had outgrown the capacity of Grambling's small campus field several years before, so Eddie went to President Jones with an idea: move the game to the big-time stadium in Shreveport, which could accommodate a crowd of more than 40,000. The money to be made in Shreveport appealed to Prez, but Southern balked, and even threatened to boycott the game. At 3:30 in the morning the day of the game, Southern finally signed a contract providing for a 50-50 split of the gate. Grambling won 19-14 before a record crowd of more than 41,000. Eddie was in the national playoffs, and, though not even Eddie realized it at that moment, the stage was set for the Bayou Classic.

Grambling wasn't the only north Louisiana school to qualify for the national playoffs in 1973. Louisiana Tech from nearby Ruston lost its season opener by two points at Eastern Michigan, then reeled off nine straight victories – allowing no more than a touchdown in any game and holding three opponents scoreless. If the two north Louisiana neighbors could both win two playoffs games, historically black Grambling and historically white Louisiana Tech would play for the national championship – their first meeting in history. That possibility said as much as anything could about how racial attitudes in intercollegiate athletics were changing. A victory over Delaware put Grambling in the national semifinals against Western Kentucky, and Tech beat Western Illinois to earn the other semifinal berth against Boise State.

The playoff game between Grambling and Western Kentucky was called the Grantland Rice Bowl. It was played in Baton Rouge, and televised by ABC – the first time a game involving Western Kentucky had ever been shown on network television. Western had allowed only sixty-two points in an undefeated regular season in which the average score for ten games rounded off to 38-6. Grambling went ahead 7-0 on a 15-yard pass, the only touchdown of the first quarter. But Western Kentucky scored three times in the second period, the go-ahead touchdown coming on a pass after a fake field goal attempt fooled the Grambling defense enough to pick up a first down that maintained possession. Another Western Kentucky touchdown resulted after Grambling was forced to punt from its own end zone. After the punt return, Western was only twenty-five yards from the Grambling goal. An 85-yard pass interception return by Robert Pennywell enabled Grambling to cut Western Kentucky's lead to 21-14 in the third quarter, and a touchdown pass in the fourth put Grambling in position to tie the score. The extra point kick, however, was blocked. That forced Grambling to take chances on offense and defense, and Western Kentucky took advantage, scoring on a 25-yard pass late in the game. Grambling lost 28-20.

What Jim Gregory admired most about Eddie during his years at Grambling was on display immediately after the opportunity to meet Louisiana Tech in the national championship game had been denied. (Tech edged Boise State 38-34 to reach the title game.) "I always respected Eddie's attitude about the results of a game," said Gregory, who coached in California for thirty years. "There was never blame on a player or individuals at all. He was always one to say, 'It's my fault.' Eddie would say, 'Evidently, I didn't have you prepared to win this game. I take responsibility for it.' That's a philosophy I used my whole coaching career."

Western Kentucky coach Jim Feix (pronounced Fikes) described the post-game scene in a Kentucky public television special a few years later. "I guess the Grambling-Western game will always be one of the most outstanding football games in Western history," he began. "After the ball game – and it was a big game for us and we were thrilled to death – they had the press conferences and interviews, and with Eddie Robinson's great reputation, all the ABC cameras and newsmen flocked to him. The question was, 'What was wrong? What happened? What was wrong with Grambling? Why did Western win?'

"Eddie just got his back up," Feix continued. "He said, 'Wait a minute you guys. I want to tell you something. There's not a thing wrong with Grambling. They played a great game today. Western was just better.' Then he launched into socially lecturing the media: 'I can't understand in our society why it is that every time something goes wrong, somebody's got to be blamed. There's no blame here. It's credit. And credit is due to Western Kentucky.'

"I thought of what a great man he had been all these years," Feix said, "and it had to be a heartbreaking loss for him, and such a thrill for us. I was just overwhelmed with this attitude. It was a great coaching lesson that I learned from Eddie Robinson and will always carry with me. He was a tremendous man, a great builder of young men, and an outstanding coach – a real monument in my profession."

Western was no match for Louisiana Tech the next week, losing 34-0. It was the most points Western had allowed in seventy-six games, covering almost eight years, and the first time Western had failed to score in eighty-nine games, dating to the third game of the 1965 season. Looking back, Feix focused on the Grambling game, though not the victory it represented. "It was a great honor to play against Eddie Robinson's team," he said.

Whether it was a surprising or disappointing loss, or a prospect who went elsewhere, Eddie never wasted time on "what could have been" or "the one that got away." But the outcome of the 1974 Rose Bowl, which was played less than a month after Grambling's unexpected loss to Western Kentucky, may have caused him to privately engage in a little wistful thinking. Ohio State beat Southern California 42-21, and the game's most valuable player was sophomore quarterback Cornelius Greene, the first black quarterback in Ohio State's history. Greene passed for almost one-third of Ohio State's total offense – one hundred twenty-nine yards – and ran for forty-five more. A performance like that might have been enough to beat Western Kentucky, and a quarterback like that might have brought Eddie a national championship victory over Louisiana Tech. "I was set on going to Grambling," Greene said after the Rose Bowl, "when Ohio State entered the picture."

32

GREAT RIVALRIES in college football are contested on the field, but their origins lie in status differences, some real and many merely claimed, between the alumni groups, student bodies and, often, even the faculties and staffs of the competing universities. Rather than heartfelt animosity, it is pride and a sense of superiority – or the desire to feel superior – that fuel the intense emotions surrounding annual renewals of these tradition-rich battles on the gridiron. No two institutions of higher learning could better exemplify such differences in style, reputation and heritage than Grambling and Southern when the Bayou Classic was born in 1974.

"Looking at the two long-time presidents gives you a feel for the two universities," said R.L. Stockard, who was in a position to observe both men during most of their long tenures. "Ralph Waldo Emerson Jones was more of a people person than an academician. Southern's President, Felton G. Clark, had a PhD in philosophy. And marginal students don't get degrees in philosophy. Clark's daddy was president of Southern before him. Prez's dad was a dean at Southern. One president was the baseball coach for over forty years. He loved coaching more than he did administering as president. I don't think you'd ever see Felton G. Clark at a baseball game. Dr. Jones couldn't wait until five o'clock to begin coaching the baseball team, and the Southern guy would go into his reading at five o'clock.

"When Felton G. Clark came in to address the Louisiana State Legislature," Stockard continued, "only the legislators who came up to him shook hands with him. He made no attempt to shake any of the politicians' hands. When he addressed the legislature, half the guys didn't know what he was saying because of the tone and the nature of his language. He was very eloquent. At that time many of the persons in the legislature in Louisiana were very ordinary people, milkmen, postmen and so forth. They were not academicians. So they disliked Dr. Clark because many of them couldn't understand what he was saying. He wasn't saying anything derogatory. He was simply using language that academicians use, and unless you're an academician, you're not going to understand what he's saying. So he was not a person the legislature was very friendly to and with.

"But Ralph Jones – everybody knew him as Ralph. When he went to the legislature, he was shaking hands and saying, 'How do you do Mr. This and Honorable That.' Every summer he gave a barbecue for as many Louisiana legislators as would attend. Many of those from south Louisiana were not about to go up there to Grambling, but everyone from central Louisiana northward would attend. So they looked at the two presidents differently, because they were different. The two men kind of mimicked the two schools they administered. Both are state schools. One is a large school in a metropolitan area, and the other is a small school in a rural area. Southern U. was an urban school, and the students were urban people, and they didn't find Dr. Clark strange at all. They found a guy like Ralph Jones, whose student body was from small towns, much different."

Coupled with these sharp contrasts, the difference in the ages of the two schools and their football programs – and, most of all, their status as the most prominent black universities in the state – made them natural rivals. Southern, established by the Louisiana State Legislature in 1880, played its first football game in 1918, when a squad coached by "Mr. Osborne and Mr. Woodard" lost 10-0 to Bishop College. By the time Louisiana Normal played its first game in 1928 – under the direction of coach Ralph Waldo Emerson Jones – Southern was into its ninth season, resuming competition that year after a two-year hiatus. The two schools played five times between 1932 and 1946, and Southern won every time, by the composite score of 151-0. The Tank Younger team ended that dubious streak with its 21-6 upset in 1947, then Southern held Grambling scoreless again, winning 18-0 the next season.

"That 1947 game was really The Big Game for Eddie Robinson," Collie Nicholson once said. "They came to Grambling highly touted, the SWAC champs, and we beat them. It was something they thought could never happen. Southern used to treat Grambling like the little brother. There were times when Southern was not interested in playing us. They'd play Wiley or Prairie View, and stop over and play us a practice game a day or two before their big game, and work on their plays. They'd beat us, of course."

Southern's shutout victory in 1948 was the last time the two schools played each other until Grambling was admitted to the SWAC in 1959. That 1948 game had ended with a melee on the field, and though it was brief, Ace Mumford of Southern considered it an indication the budding rivalry was getting out of hand. His solution was to refuse to schedule Grambling in the future. Forced to reconsider when the matchup became part of each year's conference schedule, he won three straight close games then retired. After that, Eddie's teams won eight of the next eleven head-to-head meetings, the last one the contentious spectacle in Shreveport that demonstrated the immense gate potential of this yearly pairing.

Ever the big thinker, Eddie envisioned a showcase event at a neutral site after the success in Shreveport. The series belonged in New Orleans, he believed, and it needed an identity – a unique name. Joined by Collie Nicholson and Southern University's athletic director, Ulysses Jones, Eddie called on the committee that managed Tulane University Stadium, also known as the Sugar Bowl because it was the site of the annual New Year's Day bowl game with that name. The Shreveport example was enough to convince committee members to welcome Louisiana's marquee black college football programs to a stadium that, not many years before, had been off limits to blacks. It was a proud day for Eddie, a day when another of his dreams became a reality. With establishment of the Bayou Classic, his words again rang true. *America is the greatest country in the world . . . if you work hard enough, dreams can come true.*

The first Bayou Classic was big news as far away as Chicago, where *Defender* sports columnist Doc Young continued to write about it for almost two weeks after the game was played.

> *New Orleans. Saturday, November 23. History in the making.*
>
> *Nature has patched small, fluffy white clouds into the blue of the sky, and it is a photographer's delight. Sunbeams dance between the floating clouds, brightly illuminating gray, old Tulane University Stadium . . . The humidity is a bit high, but no one in the huge crowd of 76,753 fans is irritated by it. This is the day of the first annual Bayou Classic . . .*
>
> *The crowd, largest in the history of black college play, would do proud the promoters of football anywhere, from Notre Dame to Trojanland, L.A. The behavior of the fans, 99 44/100 percent black, is impeccable.*
>
> *The rivalry on the field is as intense as that between the Buckeyes and the Wolverines . . . Both Grambling and Southern field Big Ten-sized marching bands which are musically superb.*
>
> *It's been a long time coming, but gone are the days when Grambling and Southern played before small, student body-sized crowds in rickety campus "stadia." Gone are the days when the major communications media ignored their games as if they weren't being played. Gone are the days when black college coaches and their players felt inferior, gaping in open-mouthed awe as they watched Notre Dame battle USC, Michigan battle Ohio State, or Army battle Navy on network television . . .*

* * *

. . . as that Dixieland jazz band played, the fans nearby swung and swayed. The handsome young men were a show all by themselves. One set was dressed in green: Green, wide-brimmed hats. Green suits. Green shirts. Green underwear. Large green feathers in hand. Green face towels, believe it or not, for the wiping of perspiration. Those guys were something else.

They swung and swayed to the music. They danced in their seats. They cheered and they laughed and made friendly bets . . . They had a good old time. But they never got out of line . . .

* * *

Grambling beat Southern . . . with a hard-hitting, stingy defense and a potent offense, which was directed by a freshman quarterback, Doug Williams. The lad is something else. If he improves as much under Coach Eddie Robinson's tutelage during the next three years as one has every reason to expect, he will probably force Grambling fans to "forget" James Harris . . .

"I was scared to death," Doug Williams admitted on several occasions about playing in the first Bayou Classic. "You run out there on the field and you look up in the stands, and there isn't an empty seat in the house! Tulane Stadium holds about eighty thousand, and you've got almost eighty thousand AFRICAN AMERICANS – in one place! Truly amazing. Unbelievable. As a kid from Zachary, Louisiana, all I'm doing is looking around, trying to figure out where all these black people came from. It was soothing to know that something like that could be pulled off."

Not many years before, Williams had regularly experienced a not-so-

soothing sight as he grew up. "Every Friday night there were cross-burn-ings," he said. "We weren't allowed to walk the streets after dark. When LSU played Ole Miss in Baton Rouge, the street I lived on – they called it Plank Road, La. 67 – went from Baton Rouge all the way up into Mississippi. They came from Mississippi with those Rebel flags on their cars, and they'd throw things at us if we were walking the streets, so we weren't allowed to be out."

As Eddie surveyed the scene at Tulane Stadium, his eyes filled with tears. His thoughts were of all the years when blacks were not allowed to play in that stadium, the times when he himself had been turned away. To him, walls were coming down before his very eyes. Yet he kept these feelings to himself, as he always did.

"He never talked about his feelings with the team," Williams said. "Coach didn't get us involved if it wasn't about going to class, if it wasn't about being a good citizen, if it wasn't about playing football when it was time. You would have thought that Eddie Robinson didn't grow up on the other side of the tracks. What he went through never ever came up. Through the five years I was there as a player at Grambling, and the years I knew him after those years, Coach Rob never talked about what he had to go through. We never heard that there were days when I'm sure they had no lights. He never talked about what his mom and dad had to go through. He never talked about what he had to go through – never ever, and that is amazing. But we knew. I saw crosses burned when I was eleven years old. If I saw them at eleven, I can imagine what Coach saw and what he had to go through. But not one time did Eddie Robinson ever mention it.

"I used to say to him, 'Coach, you're the most Americanized man I know,' because he always preached America," Williams continued. "He waved that American flag more than anybody, and you knew a guy his age had to have gone through some tough times early on in life. Yet he waved that flag. One of the things he used to tell us was, 'If it can be done, Amer-ica is the only place to get it done.'"

In that sense, the Bayou Classic became a monument to Eddie Robinson's belief in America. Played the Saturday after Thanksgiving and televised nationally, the game attracted attendance just short of 2.3 million from 1974 through 2008, and became the cornerstone for a weeklong celebration of African American culture and pride. Each year Southern University's "Human Jukebox" marching band squared off with Grambling's world-famous "Marching Tigers" in a pitched Battle of the Bands on the eve of the series renewal. Fraternities and sororities from both universities – known as The Divine Nine – competed in a high-energy Greek Step Show, and elaborate formals, a job fair and dozens of small parties were part of the festivities. The weekend ended with the Gospel Brunch on Sunday morning. The happening has been called "the ultimate black family reunion" and "showmanship at its best," and was indisputably acknowledged to be "Black America's biggest football game."

In the inaugural Bayou Classic, the long-term impact of one of Eddie's wisest coaching decisions became evident. Forced to change quarterbacks after winning four of his first five games in the 1974 season, Eddie had put unproven Doug Williams in charge of his offense heading into game six against Mississippi Valley State. After surviving his first start, 20-14, Williams took the field against Jackson State and Walter Payton, whom many consider the greatest running back in football history. Grambling won 26-13 with the rookie quarterback throwing two touchdown passes. Three weeks later against Southern, the tall freshman with the big arm led Grambling to a pair of touchdowns in the first quarter, and directed a 99-yard drive for the final touchdown in the fourth quarter as Grambling won 21-0 – the only shutout in the first thirty-five years of the event. The next week he passed for two hundred seven yards and was named most valuable offensive player in a 28-7 victory over South Carolina State in the Pelican Bowl. It was Grambling's seventh straight victory with Williams running the offense, and completed an 11-1 season that earned a share of the black national championship.

As if to ensure that he would not be overshadowed or forgotten, as

Doc Young suggested might happen, Shack Harris made the Pro Bowl later that year and won the most valuable player award. But the *Chicago Defender* columnist was absolutely right about one thing. Doug Williams indeed was "something else." His next three college seasons, and an eleven-year pro career highlighted by a memorable Super Bowl performance, would prove that beyond all doubt.

33

DOUG WILLIAMS was a well-known and highly regarded prospect at Chaneyville High in Zachary, then a country town about fifteen miles north of Baton Rouge, when Eddie began working on Doug's mother, Laura Williams. The pitch that landed Willie Davis and James Harris eventually worked again. "Late one night I heard the phone ring," Doug said, beginning one of his favorite stories, "and my mom answered it. I heard her talking for a while, and I didn't have any idea who she was talking to. Eventually she came in and woke me up, and told me I was going to Grambling. She told me Rob was on the phone and I was going to go to Grambling. I said, 'Okay.' The next morning I asked my mom, 'Why'd you say I'm going to Grambling?' Because, you know, a few other schools were recruiting me, too. She said, 'Well, Coach Rob said you're going to go to church; you're going to go to class; and you're going to graduate.' That was it. Case closed."

Doug actually was, in his words, "overwhelmed" that the great Eddie Robinson was interested in HIM. By then Eddie had recorded more than two hundred victories at Grambling, his teams had won three black national championships and seven SWAC championships, and more than a hundred of his former players had made it into pro football. Henry Dyer, one of Nemiah Wilson's Grambling teammates who played for the Los Angeles Rams and Washington Redskins from 1966-70, had been a

Chaneyville star when Doug was still in elementary school. Being good enough to follow Dyer to Grambling was heady stuff in itself.

The first lesson Doug learned when he reported to Grambling in the summer of 1973 was the same one Willie Brown, Nemiah Wilson, Charlie Joiner and even Bobby Mitchell had quickly learned. "From the early Sixties to the middle Seventies," he said, "when the black athlete couldn't go to any of the major schools in the South, Grambling could have lined up with any school in the country." In Doug's case, the starting quarterback was a junior and the backup was a freshman. He found himself red-shirted – allowed to practice with the team but withheld from game participation for a year to preserve his four years of eligibility. On top of that, he was two hundred fifteen miles from Zachary, and homesick. He considered transferring to Southern University, he wrote in his book *QuarterBLACK: Shattering the NFL Myth*. But he said Eddie told him, "You may think you want to, but you're not going to." At that time it looked to Doug like he might have to wait four years to play one season.

That, of course, changed in the fifth game of the 1974 season after the senior starter, Joe Comeaux, suffered a broken wrist against Tennessee State. When Terry Brown, the second string quarterback, was ineffective, Eddie called on Williams. After Doug led a long touchdown drive and Grambling won 21-7, he started every game for the next three and a half seasons, with storybook success. Grambling won thirty-five of his forty starts, including 10 out of 11 twice, and won or shared three black national championships and three SWAC championships in four years. Of all the eras named for their dominant player or players – Tank Younger, Willie Davis, Buchanan and Brown, Harris and Joiner – the one named for Doug Williams was by far the most eventful and far-flung of Eddie's illustrious Grambling career.

Grambling football made news in Doug's sophomore season even before the games began. **"Black gridders in 'dome,"** read the headline in the Big Weekend Edition of the *Chicago Defender* on Saturday, June 21, 1975.

It was another indication of how much things were changing in Louisiana and the rest of the South. The story began:

> *A new chapter in small college football history will be written this fall when Grambling and Alcorn State play the first college football game in the Superdome.*
>
> *Governors Edwin Edwards of Louisiana and Bill Waller of Mississippi made the announcement Monday during ceremonies attended by officials of both schools and the Superdome Board of Commissioners.*
>
> *They emphasized that it was an honor for two black schools to occupy the prestigious ceremonial place of honor.*
>
> *"Here we are," Governor Edwards said, "two white governors signing for two black schools to get the Superdome out of the red."*
>
> *. . . . The joust, part of the official Superdome opening . . . is expected to attract a capacity crowd under the big top.*

Billed as the largest fixed domed structure in the world, the Louisiana Superdome has been the site of numerous headline events since it opened in 1975, including six Super Bowls and four NCAA Final Four men's basketball championships (through 2008) plus the annual Bayou Classic. But it was built, first and foremost, to be the home of the New Orleans Saints. National Football League commissioner Pete Rozelle awarded an expansion franchise to New Orleans on November 1, 1966, and seven days later voters approved a $46 million bond issue to construct the massive building that would house the team. It was supposed to be completed in time for the 1972 NFL season, but work didn't begin until 1971. Upon completion in 1975, the delays made the final cost $165 million.

"Eddie was very opportunistic in promoting Grambling and the Southwestern Athletic Conference," said Alcorn's Marino Casem. "We were content to play in our own pond and beat each other's brains out. But Eddie was looking to promote. He had a real good relationship with the people who were promoting the 'Dome in the beginning, and they were looking for some headline acts to get people interested in the new stadium. They knew we were drawing real well. Grambling was playing all those road games. The conference was drawing real well. And the bands were real popular. In my opinion they knew that, for the 'Dome to get out of the red, they were going to have to attract the black population. They knew they had two good-drawing schools to come in there and play."

Casem's Alcorn team had denied Eddie a perfect season in 1974 by winning 19-14 at Grambling the second week of the season – three weeks before Eddie put Doug Williams in charge of his offense on the field. The rematch at the Superdome was played on September 6, 1975. Williams threw four touchdown passes, and Grambling won 27-3 before a crowd of 61,000.

Steve Richardson, who became the executive director of the Football Writers Association of America in 1996, worked in the sports department of the *Shreveport Journal* during the 1975 season. He covered Grambling's Superdome opener against Alcorn and one of three games Eddie played that season at Grambling's modest campus field, Memorial Stadium. The contrast between the two worlds of Grambling football was shocking to him. "I had been told, 'Don't expect much,'" he said. "Still, when I got there I was just stunned. The first game I covered was in the Superdome, so I'm going, 'What's this?' They had this little, bitty press box, and bleachers on both sides. There were lights just kind of strung up, and the school was over to the side. It looked like some high school field. They played in New Orleans twice, Washington, Honolulu, Portland, Nashville and New York City that year. When they could go to places like that and get big crowds, they weren't going to play at Grambling very much."

Richardson was awed by the depth and versatility of Eddie's 1975 team. "The talent was phenomenal," he said. "I attended Missouri, and I had covered Oklahoma and Nebraska, so I had seen good players. These guys were just amazing. James Hunter was a guy who could line up anywhere on the field. They had him all over the place, offense and defense. Sammy White and Dwight Scales were their receivers. And Doug Williams could throw the length of the field. I remember this one time, I couldn't believe it: He made this great play, a 30- or 40-yard pass, and it was called back for some penalty. They turned around and ran the same play, and this time it was a 50-yard completion. The athleticism was just tremendous. They had guys on their second and third string that obviously could have played at any of the Southeastern Conference schools. If they had been at a major school, they would have been on TV more, and I'm sure more guys would have been seen and more would have been drafted by NFL teams."

As it was, eight members of the 1975 team were taken in the 1976 draft and seven others signed as free agents. Three more, including Williams, were drafted in 1978. Among them, White played ten seasons with the Minnesota Vikings; Hunter seven with Detroit; Scales eight with the Los Angeles Rams, New York Giants, San Diego and Seattle; Mike St. Clair seven with Cleveland and Cincinnati; Ron Singleton five with San Diego and San Francisco; Robert Pennywell four with Atlanta; Carlos Pennywell four with New England; Robert Woods two with Houston and Detroit, and Williams nine with Tampa Bay and Washington plus two in the United States Football League.

After opening the Louisiana Superdome with such an impressive performance, Grambling won its next five games to set a school record with sixteen straight victories – the last thirteen with Williams at quarterback. Eddie called number fourteen in that winning streak, a 19-12 victory over Oregon State of the Pacific Eight Conference, "the biggest and most important victory in our history" because it was the first time Grambling had ever played a team from a major conference. Made possible by an open date on Oregon State's schedule that Eddie eagerly filled, the game provided a platform to challenge the bowl establishment and, within the SWAC, sparked controversy and hard feelings.

"We would like to state publicly that Grambling is available for the

Astro-Bluebonnet, Liberty, Peach, Sun, Fiesta, Gator or Sugar Bowl," Eddie declared in early November, a month after beating Oregon State. He was speaking at a press conference in New York, called to promote Grambling's upcoming game with Norfolk State at Shea Stadium. "This would mark a significant step for college football during the Bicentennial celebration in this country. It represents a 200-year leap that could be made in one season. We might be very competitive. And, more importantly, we can pack 'em in. We've played to 251,906 fans this season." With uncharacteristic bravado, he added: "We have a broad national following that has made us the Muhammad Ali of football."

Norfolk coach Dick Price, whose team would be shut out 26-0 by Grambling ten days later, was more blunt. "A lot of top schools are running away from Grambling, Jackson State, Tennessee State," he said. "They have everything to lose and nothing to gain. There's no reason why Grambling couldn't play Division 1 schools. Grambling could play with anybody in the country." Despite the compelling arguments, bowl committees weren't persuaded by either gate potential or on-field competitiveness. While Grambling finished with a 10-1 record, the Peach Bowl invited No. 20 West Virginia and unranked North Carolina State – with a 7-4-1 record, and the Sun Bowl matched No. 15 Pittsburgh (8-4) against unranked Kansas, with a 7-5 record.

Playing Oregon State when the opportunity presented itself led to Grambling forfeiting two games to Prairie View and almost undermined the SWAC. As the unseemly situation unfolded, R.L. Stockard was working as the conference's sports information director. "Eddie had been seeing the Oregon State coach, Dee Andross, for several years at the coaches conventions," he explained, "and every time Eddie would say, 'Let's line up a football game.' Coach Andros would always say, 'You know I can't play you.' But Eddie kept jabbing him, and finally Andros said, 'Okay. I've got this date open. I can play you on this date. I can't play you on any other date.' All of the schedules had been finalized by then, so he didn't think Eddie would be able to take the game. But Eddie called the athletic director at Prairie View and said, 'I've got a chance to play Oregon State. Can we get together and change the date of our game?' The athletic director said, 'Yeh, man, go ahead and do it. I wish you luck.' Next day, Eddie told Andros, 'The game is on.' Was he surprised!"

It had been a decade since Prairie View's back-to-back black national championships in 1963-64, and Grambling hadn't lost their annual game since then. In the last six games the two schools played, Grambling put up fifty-eight, fifty-seven, thirty, thirty-six, thirty-seven and sixty-one points – while allowing a total of fifty. The hopelessness of the matchup, however, mattered not to Prairie View alumni, who objected vociferously to the schedule change. In the face of this pressure, according to Stockard, the athletic director reneged, telling Prairie View's president, "We haven't signed any papers changing the date."

"I asked the conference commissioner, 'What are you going to do?'" Stockard said. "He said to me, 'What CAN I do? It's a matter between two schools.' I told him, 'That's what a commissioner is for.' So he declared Grambling ineligible for the SWAC championship. In those days, Grambling was playing 'classic' games and providing most of the operating support for the SWAC office. Grambling said it wouldn't make any more payments to the conference until the commissioner was changed. The SWAC didn't have a commissioner for ten years."

One forfeit turned into two when Grambling, still resentful that Prairie View reneged on its agreement to change the 1975 schedule, refused to play their 1976 game. Doug Williams, for one, was fine with two losses in games never played. "We could have played Prairie View," he said. "We had an open date that they could have played us. But they didn't want to move the game. If that's the only way they can win, you give them the win. Coach said, 'You don't get an opportunity like this very often.' You don't pass up that opportunity." The rivalry resumed at Grambling in 1977, with a predictable outcome. "My senior season," Williams said, "we took it out on them, 70-7. And we did that with the past two years in mind. No question."

The school-record winning streak came to an end on October 25, 1975, in the third game following that watershed victory over Oregon State. Jackson State, which had lost two straight, pulled a 24-14 upset – the first loss of Doug Williams' college career. Grambling started another winning streak with convincing victories over Texas Southern, North Carolina A&T and Norfolk State (in the New York City game), then the 1975 season ended ominously right where it had begun, in the Louisiana Superdome. More than 73,000 fans turned out on November 22 to see Grambling beat Southern 33-17 in the second Bayou Classic. Bigger news than who won, though, was that Doug Williams had suffered a serious knee injury. A week later he underwent reconstructive surgery, leaving his future in doubt.

34

TOKYO, JAPAN is 6,637 miles from Grambling, Louisiana. Flight time alone is at least sixteen hours. The most popular sports are sumo wrestling and baseball. All, however, were no more than minor obstacles in the audacious mind of Collie J. Nicholson. After learning that heavyweight boxing champion Muhammad Ali and Japan's heavyweight wrestling champion, Antonio Inoki, were going to square off in a ring showdown in Tokyo, Collie's immediate reaction was that Grambling should play a football game in Tokyo, too. It would be the first regular season American college football game ever played on foreign soil, but . . . why not?

Eddie wondered if "the man with the golden pen" had finally gone over the promotional cliff, and Ralph Waldo Emerson Jones feared it, too – at first. But Prez couldn't get the off-the-wall idea out of his mind. It would further raise the Grambling profile, he told himself, so he summoned Collie and Eddie to talk it through. In the end his conclusion was, 'It's an opportunity.'

Collie's first call was to Mackay Yanagisawa in Honolulu. They had become friends when Grambling started playing the University of Hawaii in 1972, and were two-of-a-kind as promoters. In fact, when Lenny Klompus, one of Yanagisawa's former business partners, described him in a story in *The Honolulu Advertiser,* it was as if he were speaking instead about Collie.

"Mackay Yanagisawa defined innovation long before it was used in such a general and cavalier way," Klompus said. "He dreamed bold ideas and always delivered big. In Mackay's world, anything was possible." Yanagisawa even had a nickname. Bill Kwon of the *Honolulu Star-Bulletin* dubbed him the "Shogun of Sports" because "he was a man of all seasons, a powerful figure in local sports," Kwon wrote. "Like a shogun, Mackay once commanded the attention of everyone – community leaders, politicians and prominent college football coaches."

Yanagisawa founded the Hula Bowl college football all-star game in 1947 – the year of Grambling's first-ever victory over Southern – and was known to take out a second mortgage on his home to keep the event solvent during tough times. He staged a wide variety of unusual events, including a race between black American Olympic sprinter Jesse Owens and a thoroughbred horse, and the Hopalong Cassidy Wild West Show. And he brought the Harlem Globetrotters and New York Yankees to Oahu. In 1980, he was instrumental in convincing the NFL to move its Pro Bowl post-season all-star game to Honolulu, and in 1982, he established the Aloha Bowl post-season college football game. Most important to Collie, Yanagisawa had contacts in Japan who could make a Grambling football game in Tokyo a reality.

Yanagisawa lined up tutors to teach Collie enough Japanese to get by when meeting with potential game sponsors, who might have been offended if certain names and phrases were mispronounced or misused. Through the Japanese Embassy, he arranged for Collie to meet an influential businessman who was a member of the American Football Association of Japan – and who not only had *heard* of Grambling but also had *watched* the Grambling highlights show on television. In the end, he assisted Collie in negotiating a million-dollar contract with Pioneer Electronics and Mitsubishi Motors. Accustomed to working on their own, "the man with the golden pen" and the "Shogun of Sports" formed quite a team.

Sheree Rabon saw the Tokyo adventure come together from a very different vantage point. Twelve years old at the time, she lived with her grandmother, who was Grambling's switchboard operator. A sixteen-hour time difference meant Collie would be calling in the wee hours, Louisiana time, so Darline Davis had to be there. "My grandmother had to get out of bed – I don't know the time, but it was probably three or four in the morning," Rabon said, "to wait for the calls to come in from Tokyo. Coach Robinson was in his office, and President Jones was standing there with my grandmother. I think the three of them were the only ones awake on campus, waiting for those calls from Tokyo. I was there for all of the calls, over on my little pallet. Every night it was like, 'Okay, time to go.' Those nights stood out because we had to get out of bed and go. The call would come through, and they would say whatever they had to say, you know, grown-up business stuff. And everyone was excited."

It was not lost on the Japanese government that this historic American college football game would be played during America's Bicentennial year. The formal invitation issued to Grambling by Japan's Minister of Finance, in part, called attention to the ideal, if coincidental, timing:

> *"Happy Birthday, United States of America!*
>
> *"The people of Japan and the American Football Association of Japan extend a formal invitation to the Grambling State University football team and marching band to visit Tokyo on September 24, 1976 for a game and a series of field concerts as part of a special bicentennial celebration emphasizing United States-Japan friendship.*
>
> *"A similar invitation has been extended to Morgan State University, Baltimore, Md., to have its excellent team accompany Grambling to Tokyo for the friendship classic.*
>
> *"The appearance of the outstanding Grambling football team and band for the first regular season game outside of the Western Hemisphere will make the event one of the major international sports attractions of the Bicentennial year.*

"Special plans are being made to entertain United States military personnel and their dependents quartered on Air Force, Army and Navy bases in Japan. Performances on military bases by the spectacular Grambling band and public appearances throughout Tokyo offer a once in a lifetime musical opportunity never seen in this country."

The meaning to Eddie of what was about to happen cannot be overstated. The football teams from two historically black universities were going to represent the U.S.A. on an international stage during the 200th anniversary year of the founding of the country he believed in so steadfastly. His players and the school's musicians would not only be accepted, but welcomed as celebrities in a country with a miniscule African American population. And he would be reminded of that night in his youth when Joe Louis fought Max Schmeling. In Tokyo, Japan, Eddie Robinson would be called an "American" for the first time in his memory.

"It was a total new experience," said Doug Williams. "JAPAN! To see that many people and that many cameras, it was almost like a freak show. You go to the stadium to play football, and it's packed to the max. And you figured most of them didn't know what they were looking at. But they did know one thing: It was exciting! And I'm sure most of them looked at it like a gladiator sport, because we were running into each other and tackling and running fast."

As Collie and Mackay Yanagisawa hustled to sell a game that many believed could not be sold, Williams was rehabbing. Knee surgery was different in 1975, and so was the drudgery of recovery. Doug wore a sixty-pound cast for six weeks and couldn't move his leg. Then came almost nine months of exercises to strengthen the joint and restore flexibility. Spring practice passed without him, but he was ready to test his new knee when the 1976 season arrived.

Marino Casem and Alcorn won 24-0 in their season opener versus Grambling – the only game in Doug's entire college career in which he did not throw at least one touchdown pass. Despite the shutout, though, Doug was encouraged. His knee withstood sacks and other hits, and felt fine. A long bomb for a touchdown with thirty-three seconds left in the game denied Grambling a victory the next week as Temple won 31-30 in Philadelphia. Grambling went to Tokyo winless in two starts, but clobbered Morgan State 42-16 before a full house at Korakuen Stadium. It was the first of eight victories in the last nine games of the season, including a third straight Bayou Classic conquest of Southern. Grambling finished with an 8-3 record (8-4 if you count the second Prairie View forfeit), and by every measure, Tokyo had been a success. Heading into 1977, everyone could only wonder: What will Collie think of next?

The Heisman Trophy is awarded every December to the "most outstanding college football player" in America as determined by vote of past winners and media electors nationwide. The recipient of the most prestigious individual award in college football – the "best" player in the nation, according to Heisman criteria – was either a quarterback or running back in all but five of the award's first seventy-three years. Over those years the Heisman winner always played for a "major college" team, and until 1961 was always white. Ernie Davis of Syracuse University edged Ohio State's Bob Ferguson by fifty-three points that year in the closest vote in the first twenty-six years of the award (and second closest in the first fifty-three years). After that, six of the next fifteen winners were black. With racial prejudice apparently no longer an insurmountable obstacle, Collie Nicholson figured it was time to try to beat the major college bias heading into the 1977 season – especially since he had a stellar player at one of the favored positions.

It was summer, and Doug Williams was getting ready to play in a fast-pitch softball game with his brothers when his mother told him Collie Nicholson was on the telephone and wanted to talk to him. "He said, 'I just want you to know that we're going to put you up for the Heisman,'" Doug recalled. "I actually laughed at him. Grambling . . . Heisman? That don't correlate."

Doug's reaction was understandable. No player from an HBCU team had ever been seriously considered for the Heisman Trophy up to then. Three years before, arguably the greatest running back of all time, Walter Payton of Jackson State, didn't even make the top ten in Heisman voting (when black running backs Archie Griffin of Ohio State, Anthony Davis of Southern California and Joe Washington of Oklahoma finished one-two-three). Bob Hayes, named "the world's fastest human" for his success as a sprinter, played wide receiver at Florida A&M and earned induction into the Pro Football Hall of Fame after a record-setting career with the Dallas Cowboys. But he wasn't even considered for Heisman honors in 1964. Nevertheless, with a return to Tokyo a seemingly certain success, Collie made the Heisman Trophy his next mission. "From Day One of training camp," Williams said, "he just pushed it. He got all kinds of press on campus. They took pictures. They did interviews. He just pushed and pushed and pushed."

Williams did his part, too. In the season opener, Grambling put up the most points any of Eddie's teams ever scored on a Marino Casem Alcorn team, winning 42-17. Doug's personal highlight was a 94-yard touchdown pass. The following week he impressed the New York City media by passing for three hundred seventy yards and four touchdowns in a 35-19 victory over Morgan State at Yankee Stadium. He appeared on network talk shows and was featured in *The Sporting News* and *Football News*. The payback game against Prairie View came next. In that 70-7 drubbing, he threw for five touchdowns and three hundred twenty-nine yards. Grambling lost only once all year – 26-8 to Tennessee State in a battle of unbeatens that took place in a driving rain in Nashville. By the time he returned to Tokyo for the final game of his college career, he had won his fourth straight Bayou Classic, and several NCAA passing records were within reach. The 1977 Heisman Trophy Dinner, where the winner of the award would be announced, was that same weekend in New York City.

"They had it set up that I was going to go to the dinner in New York," Doug said, "and then fly to Tokyo. The promoter in Japan was going to take care of everything." The Heisman Dinner custom was to invite the top three finishers in the voting. Doug knew he had not won as soon as he learned he was not invited to the dinner. "When I wasn't invited," he said, "I just went to Tokyo with our team." The opponent in Japan was Temple, the team that had stunned Grambling with a last-minute touchdown the previous season in Philadelphia. The 1977 game would also go down to the end, but with a different outcome.

Temple was leading 32-28 with time running out when Williams scrambled to the Temple 10-yard line on fourth down. He picked up a first down, but there was time, most likely, for only one more play. The Heisman Trophy was out of reach, but a quarterback for San Diego State University, Dennis Shaw, had set the NCAA single-season record for touchdown passes with thirty-nine in 1969. Doug Williams was sitting on thirty-eight with one play left in his career. Eddie called a timeout, and Williams came to the sideline. In the exchange that followed, the record was more important to Eddie than it was to his star quarterback.

"What pass are you going to throw?"

"We ain't going to pass, coach," Doug said. "We're going to run it."

"What do you mean? You don't need but one to tie the record."

"Coach, everybody in the stadium knows we're going to throw the football."

"Well, what running back do you want?"

"Let the running back that's in there, stay in there."

The second-team running back was in the game, "You don't want Odell?" Eddie asked,

"Coach, if you send Odell in there, they'll think we're running it."

The vision of that game-ending, career-ending play remained vivid in Doug Williams' mind more than thirty years later. And so did one scene in the locker room afterwards.

"We ran a thirty-seven sweep," he said. "They rushed two guys and dropped nine guys into the end zone. Floyd Womack walked in for the winning touchdown. After the game, Coach Rob stood up with tears in his eyes and said, 'I don't care what anybody says. The Heisman Trophy winner is in this room tonight.' To me, that was the greatest compliment ever to be paid."

Earl Campbell of Texas won the 1977 Heisman award – the first black player on a historically segregated southern team to receive the honor – and another running back, Terry Miller of Oklahoma State, was a distant second. Notre Dame tight end Ken McAfee was third, and Doug Williams fourth. "For a guy from a historically black college to finish fourth – in 1977," Williams said, "you take it as a first." While he passed on the chance to tie the NCAA single-season record for touchdown passes, Williams did finish with career records for touchdown passes with ninety-three and passing yardage with 8,411. He also set a school record with four hundred eighty-four pass completions. He became the first player from an HBCU team to be named to the first-team Associated Press All-America team, and in the 1978 NFL draft he became the first black quarterback ever selected in the first round when Tampa Bay chose him with the 17th pick.

It was shortly after the end of the 1977 season – before Doug Williams went so high in the draft – that Eddie interviewed with the owner Carroll Rosenbloom of the Los Angeles Rams about the NFL team's vacant head coaching position. Eddie would have been the first black head coach in the NFL had he gone to the Rams, and there was a part of him that wondered what it would have been like to have moved up, whether to the NFL or to a major college program. But his loyalty to, and love for, Grambling was too great. In his heart he didn't really want to leave. At the same time, as much as Rosenbloom was intrigued by the possibility of what Eddie could have accomplished with the Rams, he worried about the ill will he might create by luring black college football's king away from his kingdom. So they talked, but more or less agreed that it wouldn't be right for either.

Something positive did come from the episode, though. Rosenbloom invited Tampa Bay owner Hugh Culverhouse to join him and Eddie at dinner one evening. During the meal Eddie recounted the exploits of his star quarterback, and told them both what a great person and leader he was. After Tampa Bay made history by drafting Doug Williams a few months later, Eddie thought back to his dinner with the two club owners and concluded that what he thought was just casual conversation very likely convinced Culverhouse to do what no other NFL owner had ever done.

Eddie also was rumored to be a candidate for the head coaching vacancy at the University of Iowa after the 1978 season. But that most likely was because Iowa is where he earned his master's degree. Iowa athletic director Bump Elliott was friends with Hayden Fry, who had enjoyed a successful six-year career at North Texas State after coaching Jerry LeVias during eleven seasons at Southern Methodist. Fry had never been to Iowa, but got the job and stayed for twenty years. "Writers say I've been passed over," Eddie once said. He rejected the notion, saying it was his choice to remain at Grambling.

35

BEAR BRYANT died on January 26, 1983, less than a month after he retired from coaching. His final game was a 21-15 victory in the Liberty Bowl, the 323rd of a 38-year career, which was the most any college football coach had ever recorded. Eddie felt a personal loss when his legendary counterpart with the houndstooth hat succumbed so suddenly to a heart attack – the day after he passed a physical exam, no less. Eddie and The Bear became close friends in the mid-1970s, with Bryant speaking at the Grambling football banquet one year, and Eddie appearing as a guest speaker at Alabama's coaching clinic another. In the last year of Bryant's life each presented the other with a special honor. Eddie delivered a stunning tribute when Bryant was recognized for his illustrious career at the Liberty Bowl luncheon the week of his final game in Memphis, Tennessee. Earlier, The Bear insisted on being the presenting speaker after the Walter Camp Foundation announced that Eddie would receive its 1982 Distinguished American Award.

Walter Camp, who played and coached at Yale in the late 1800s, was nicknamed "the father of American football" by a *Harper's Weekly* columnist in 1892. He is recognized as the driving force behind the evolution of football from the brutal, rugby-like brawl it was in its early years into the orderly, though still physically punishing, game it became. His innovations are as numerous as Amos Alonzo Stagg's. In addition, he helped establish the National Collegiate Athletic Association, and originated the selection of the "All-America" honor team comprised of the best players by position in American college football. The Walter Camp Foundation, established in his memory in 1967, presents a variety of annual awards, including coach and player of the year and the distinguished American.

"The recipient," stated the Foundation's description of its Distinguished American Award, "is an individual who has utilized his or her talents to attain great success in business, private life or public service, and who may have accomplished that which no other has done. The recipient does not have to have participated in football, but must understand its lesson of self-denial, cooperation and teamwork, and (be) a person of honesty, integrity and dedication. He or she must be a leader, an innovator, even a pioneer, who has reached a degree of excellence which distinguished him or her from contemporaries, and who lives within the principles of Walter Camp." In announcing that Eddie would receive the sixth annual award, Foundation president Samuel A. Burrell Jr. said: "Coach Robinson left his imprint on thousands of young men who have played for him since he became involved in athletics at Grambling over forty years ago."

The designation "Distinguished American" had a particularly gratifying ring for Eddie. For decades he had been telling his players, students, friends and colleagues, *America is the greatest country in the world . . . I learned very early on that despite a lot of obstacles, America gives you opportunity . . . The best way to enjoy life in America is to first be an American, and I don't think you have to be white to do so . . . I don't believe anybody can out-American me . . .* Eddie was the first black recipient of the prestigious award, and one of only two African Americans honored in the first thirty years of its existence. The other was Gene Upshaw, head of the NFL players union, almost twenty years later.

The awards luncheon at Yale was held February 12, 1982, which made it like a birthday party for Eddie. He was 63 the next day. He had completed his 39th season at Grambling, and was sitting on two hundred ninety-seven victories. He seemed a cinch to join Pop Warner, Amos Alonzo Stagg and Bear Bryant as the only college football coaches ever to win at least three hundred games. In fact, it happened that September.

Grambling opened the 1982 season in New York, beating Morgan State 42-13 for number two ninety-eight, and checked off two ninety-nine against Alcorn the next weekend in Shreveport, when Eddie bested Marino Casem 31-14. The first chance for Eddie's 300th victory came September 25, 1982 in Tallahassee against Florida A&M – next to Grambling, the most storied black college football team in the nation. For a half, it was even, 14-14, and early in the fourth quarter A&M broke the tie. Then another of Adolph Byrd's discoveries, wingback Trumaine Johnson, took over the game. He caught a 13-yard pass from quarterback Hollis Brent for the tying touchdown, then barely a minute later in game clock time, returned a punt sixty-four yards to put Grambling ahead. Soon after, he was in the end zone again, on the end of a 20-yard pass from Brent. The final score was Grambling 43, Florida A&M 21.

Asked about No. 300 afterwards, Eddie answered in typical fashion, saying he owed "so much to so many." Commenting on the game itself, he said, "We came back. Showed the character you need in life." No one in the media brought up salary at a moment like that, but it is worth raising the pay issue in retrospect. The fourth coach to win three hundred games in the history of college football would earn less than $50,000 in his 40th year at the same school. There were white coaches with a fraction of three hundred victories who were making three to five times as much.

While Eddie was winning his 300th, Alabama was beating Vanderbilt 24-21 for Bear Bryant's 318th. Eddie would finish 8-3 in 1982, giving him three hundred five victories in forty seasons. Alabama closed the regular season with three straight losses, to then-unbeaten LSU, in an upset to Southern Mississippi the next week and by one point to in-state rival Auburn, to leave Bryant with a 7-4 record and three hundred twenty-two wins heading into the Liberty Bowl.

Eddie was quite proud to be asked to present the award to The Bear at the Liberty Bowl banquet. By then Bryant had announced his retirement, effective following the bowl game. Eddie was told he had three minutes for his remarks, and fretted and fussed because he knew there was no way he could say everything he wanted to say about Bear Bryant in three minutes. Doris finally calmed him by pointing out the truism of all speaking engagements: Once you've got the microphone, they can't shut you up. So Eddie heaped praise on his friend, telling everyone he was the greatest of all time, and why. It was already more than The Bear expected or thought Eddie should say. But Eddie was just getting warmed up. As only a great coach and motivator can do, Eddie whipped the audience into an emotional salute. He even managed to work in a story about Lincoln at Gettysburg before he finished. No one had ever seen Bear Bryant cry, but he broke into tears almost as soon as he tried to speak after accepting the award from Eddie. A few weeks later he was gone.

Grambling opened the $7.5 million, 19,600-seat Robinson Stadium – with its imposing sunken field built into what had been a wooded area that surrounded a pond – on September 3, 1983. There to see it was Mama Lydia, who would come to live with Eddie and Doris later that fall. At that time the state-funded facility was named not for Eddie, but for the Robinson family, because Louisiana law prohibited honoring a living person. "We all know who the distinguished member of the family is," said Governor Dave Treen as he dedicated "this magnificent facility to this institution, and to a person who is an institution – Coach Eddie Robinson."

It was the season opener, and Marino Casem again was Eddie's sideline opponent, and again Eddie prevailed as Grambling shut out Alcorn 28-0. The victory left Eddie eight short of tying Amos Alonzo Stagg's career mark of three hundred fourteen, and seventeen shy of Bear Bryant's all-time record of three hundred twenty-three. He would exceed both totals with home field victories alone during the remainder of his career. In fifteen seasons at "The Rob," as the stadium quickly came to be known, Eddie won thirty-seven, lost fourteen and tied one.

Special recognition for Eddie in his home state didn't stop with naming a stadium in his honor. In June, 1985 – after he had passed Amos Alonzo Stagg but before he caught Bear Bryant – Eddie was elected to the Louisiana Sports Hall of Fame. It was his fourth of what would be eight inductions into various halls of fame, and put him in the company of the first hundred competitors and coaches enshrined since the Louisiana Hall's first class in 1959. Included were baseball greats Mel Ott and Lou Brock, coaching legends Clark Shaughnessy and Ace Mumford, basketball stars Bob Pettit and Pete Maravich, former Heisman Trophy winners Billy Cannon and John David Crow, and Grambling's own Tank Younger, Willie Davis, Bob Hopkins and Willis Reed. Boxer Ralph Dupas, his race no longer an issue, would be added in 1994. Also during 1985, a 1.1-mile stretch of South 13th Street in Baton Rouge became Eddie Robinson Sr. Drive, giving Coach Rob streets in three cities (also Grambling and Jackson).

"What he meant to Louisiana goes so much past sports," said the Louisiana Hall's Doug Ireland. "He debunked myths and stereotypes. He influenced generations of people, white and black. I shudder to think how much we would have missed had Eddie Robinson not gone into coaching. It was always a treat to hear Eddie. He was determined to remind us of what we had to celebrate, not only as it related to the person being honored, but also because he was extremely patriotic. That was the central theme of his remarks at nearly every ceremony I ever saw him be involved with."

Eddie won more games against Prairie View A&M – thirty-five – than any other opponent, even though between 1946 and 1965 he was 8-10-1. Two of those victories were his 50th, in 1949, and his 150th, in 1965. Thereafter, he won twenty-seven of twenty-eight games that Grambling played against Prairie View, forfeiting two others for the chance to play Oregon State in 1975. It was hardly a surprise, then, that Prairie View acquired the dubious distinction of loser in the milestone victories in 1984 and 1985 that enabled Eddie to surpass first Stagg, then Bryant.

Prairie View A&M University was established in 1876, a product of Reconstruction. It was the first state-supported college for Negroes, and is the second-oldest institution of higher education in The Lone Star State. Prairie View played its first intercollegiate football game in 1907, beating Wylie College 7-0. The school began fielding a football team on an annual basis in 1923, and played twenty-two seasons before experiencing its first losing record. Under College Football Hall of Fame coach Billy Nicks, Prairie View won five black national championships and seven Southwestern Athletic Conference championships between 1952 and 1965, and had a 112-27-5 record. For four decades, Prairie View, very simply, was a powerhouse. But in the forty years between 1968 and 2007, PVAMU finished the season with a winning record only twice, and from November 4, 1989 through September 19, 1998, lost eighty games in a row.

PVAMU was no match in Eddie's Stagg-shattering 315th victory, going down 42-0 on September 29, 1984. A year and a week later at the Cotton Bowl, the score was closer, 27-7, but nonetheless Eddie had victory three hundred twenty-four, the all-time record. Ironically, he had tied The Bear the week before by beating Oregon State 23-6 in Shreveport. Known for crying – before games, in the locker room during halftime, and after games (win or lose) – Eddie broke into tears after surpassing the coach he so admired. He had more than the usual cause for emotion in this instance, though. Daddy Frank was terminally ill in Baton Rouge, and the media turnout in anticipation of the Bear-breaking victory prevented Eddie from visiting him all that week. It's doubtful that Frank was even aware of his son's tremendous accomplishment.

Sports Illustrated put Eddie on its cover following the victory that pushed him past Bryant. It was the first time in the magazine's history that a black college football program was featured on its cover. He appeared as a guest on *Good Morning! America,* and was the subject of a feature narrated by the preeminent college football broadcaster of his time, Keith Jackson of ABC. Dissenters argued that Bryant should remain the record-holder for collegiate coaching victories because all of his victories were against major college – then called Division I – teams. Eddie's response was straightforward and true: He played who would play him, often wherever and whenever they'd play. Though he didn't say it himself, others were quick to add that, with the talent that segregation virtually handed him, he could have beaten the all-white big boys with regularity if they had been willing to step on the field with his teams.

Eddie was sixty-six when he passed Bryant. He won five more games that year, to finish 1985 with three hundred twenty-nine victories. Grambling went 9-3 that year and won the SWAC. He needed to win seventy-one more games to reach the seemingly unattainable total of four hundred. It appeared that Louisiana law, which mandated retirement at age seventy for a state employee such as Eddie, would stop him short. In the 1987 regular session of the Louisiana State Legislature, however, Act 264 removed that obstacle. As long as his health allowed (and success on the field sustained him), he could continue coaching at Grambling.

In Eddie's 50th season as Grambling's coach – his 52nd year because of the World War II hiatus – his golden anniversary team went 10-2, his ninth season with ten or more victories, and won the last of his nine black national championships. Grambling would have won the SWAC championship too, but Alcorn snatched it away with a comeback victory, 35-33. Quarterback Steve McNair – a future NFL most valuable player known for his toughness – exhibited what would become his trademark as a pro, ignoring a leg injury to lead a long, late-game drive, and diving into the end zone in the waning seconds for the winning touchdown.

If that dramatic loss was the season's great disappointment, beating Southern in similar fashion for his 13th Bayou Classic victory in nineteen tries was an especially satisfying tradeoff for Eddie. Marino Casem had come out of retirement to coach Southern in 1991, and the 1992 Bayou Classic was his final game. Southern scored first and led by 14 in the third quarter. "Eddie beat me on the last play of the game," Casem said. "It was a quarterback sneak. On the previous play, they called pass interference. I was so upset I got a penalty. That put the ball on the one-yard line." Even in defeat, Casem considered it a fitting conclusion for two coaches as close as they were. "Eddie was my total friend," he said. "There's nothing like beating your friend." Eddie felt the same way.

After fifty seasons, Eddie had won three hundred eighty-one games, and showed no signs of slowing down or losing his edge – except to some of those closest to him.

Adolph Byrd said he was told by a former player who was on the side-line in Eddie's last few seasons that, "Coach was calling somebody to go into the game who had graduated." Byrd's daughter Yvonne added: "When we would watch a game, my brother would say, 'See that? Eddie forgot the play. He sent out the so-and-so play, but in this situation he usually sends in the such-and-such play.' He could tell that sometimes Uncle Eddie would forget the play and send in another play."

Marino Casem said Eddie was aware of the whispers in the waning years of his career. "He knew they thought he was suffering from Alzheimer's," Casem said. "He would say, 'They think I'm losing my mind.' But that wasn't new. Coaches forget. It's like parents calling one child by the name of another. They thought it was a lot worse, but I don't remember it being that bad."

Whether or not Eddie had started to slip, a movement to impose what Louisiana law no longer could was gathering steam.

PART SIX

Passage

36

Ray Hicks, who was finishing his Grambling undergraduate education during the campus unrest of 1967, eventually earned a doctorate at Southern Illinois University and entered higher education in both instruction and administration. He returned to his alma mater ten years after the demonstrations, at the invitation of one of Eddie's former players, Dr. Joseph B. Johnson. Dr. Johnson had become only the third Grambling president in almost a hundred years, following the retirement of Ralph Waldo Emerson Jones. He asked Hicks to leave his administrative position at the Southern University branch in Shreveport to develop a human resources department at Grambling. It was in this capacity that Dr. Raymond Hicks and Eddie Robinson began a relationship that would alter both men's lives 20 years later.

"He was a hands-on administrator," Dr. Hicks said of Eddie. "When I was building Human Resources, he would come in and follow up on paperwork for his coaches and his office staff. He didn't just submit paperwork; he came in personally. If I was the person he needed to talk to, he would ask me what he needed to do. 'Is everything all right?' A couple days might go by, then he'd come there again. If what he needed was taken care of, he'd come back and thank you. That's just the kind of person he was."

Hicks moved to the faculty of the College of Education once his human resources project was completed, and the interaction with Eddie continued. "When I got into academics," he said, "the main thing was making sure these kids were eligible, doing their work, meeting academic standards. Again, he was hands-on. He was always making sure that these kids were going to class, doing their work. He wanted the teachers who had athletes to submit a report to him. Because he was hands-on, you had a chance to see him. Just moving about the campus, you'd see him. He didn't hide."

Family matters required Dr. Hicks to leave Grambling and go back to Southern in Shreveport for a period of time, but his interaction with Eddie left lasting impressions that influenced his actions after he returned to teach in 1993 and quickly found himself in charge of the university. "I started viewing Coach as an icon when I was in college," he said. "I remember going to the first football game at home, and actually seeing him coaching. Everybody said, 'Here's our icon coach.' I always saw him as an iconic figure.

"The thing that amazed me about him," Dr. Hicks continued, "was that he was so humble. In person, and when he wasn't coaching, he was just a humble person. We read about him all the time in the paper and magazines. He was getting all these awards and things. As things got better, Oldsmobile gave him cars – recognized him. We always read about him doing something. But when he was on campus and you'd see him, he may have been in the paper about doing something in New York, but when you saw him on campus the next day, he was just a humble guy, a real humble, down-to-earth guy, always smiling. He had a good sense of humor, liked to tell jokes. He was the most humble person that I've ever come across. I had this impression of him that he was just a decent person who had achieved some national status but was very humble about it.

"We all knew he still lived in the same house he bought in the '40s. He just bricked it and modernized it a little bit. He drove an old car. They tried to give him cars, and finally he took one from Oldsmobile, so he held on to that for a long while. He was just a guy who took something, made something outstanding out of it, and handled it in such a humble way. It was always about the university. He would always make a point that everything he did was because he wanted to make sure the university got its recognition – because he would be nothing without Grambling. He always made that clear."

At seventy-three years of age, Eddie was still brimming with energy and passion for the game that was his life. He relished the challenge of relating to a different generation of players than he had known for much of his career. He acknowledged the increasing challenge of coaching the modern player in an interview with *Coach and Athletic Director* magazine around this time. "It's more difficult because of what's around in the world," he said, "the opportunities, both good and bad, that are open to everyone. Athletes can play basketball, soccer, baseball at any university. This can make a player tougher to motivate, tougher to coach. And never before have we had so many players involved in drugs and things like that. You have to look at it and be realistic. The youth today are not really bad. They're just looking for something to do, and if it's out there, they're gonna find it. We want to give something to the boys who come from broken homes, one-parent homes, from homes where the mom and dad are not married. There are so many of these homes in this country. We have to put more emphasis on educating our offspring. They are the center of our society. We should keep them in mind in everything we attempt to do."

A 7-4 record in 1993 left Eddie with three hundred eighty-eight victories in five hundred forty-three games, a .715 winning percentage. Only five teams in fifty-one seasons had had losing records. Understandably, he felt secure in his job when former student Ray Hicks was appointed interim president in July 1994.

"When I became president," Dr. Hicks said, "Coach was one of the first persons to come and meet with me, wish me well and offer anything he could do to be helpful. We talked and made sure we understood the role of athletics in college administration. I think he was concerned whether or not I might be anti-athletics because Dr. Johnson was an athlete at Grambling and Coach Rob had coached him, so they had a good relationship.

He wanted me to be open to him coming and meeting with me before the season and after the season. Before the season he wanted to tell me what his goals were. After the season he wanted to do an assessment. He would meet with me weekly, usually on Mondays after the games, and assess what happened. After the season he would always talk about his budget, what he was trying to do, and why he needed all of that. I had a chance to work closely with him, and it was a unique experience because he was so humble."

Dr. Hicks had been interim president only a brief time when he realized that Eddie Robinson was vulnerable as well as venerable. "There was an issue swirling almost as soon as I got there," he said, "about whether or not it was time for Coach Robinson to step down. That argument was being pushed by the national alumni association and a couple of former athletes who, I think, wanted Doug Williams to be the coach and wanted him to get the job as soon as they could make it happen. The national alumni people approached me about Coach Robinson, and I said, 'Well, I'm just getting here. We'll see how it goes. I'm going to evaluate the athletic department just like I would evaluate academic departments. Those people started visiting me. Even some of the athletes started calling me. They wanted Coach Robinson terminated before the start of the '94 season. I just told them I was not going to engage in any of that kind of conversation. I told them, 'I'm sorry. I've got other things I'm working on. Athletics are straight for this year. I'll look at it after the season. We can visit then.'

"But then they started really playing a heavy political game," Dr. Hicks continued. "The president of the University of Louisiana System, Dr. James Caillier, the person I reported to, called and told me there was a lot of pressure there. Maybe I should replace Coach Robinson before the start of football season. I told him that if I was directed to do such a thing, I would resign immediately. In fact, I made a statement to him, 'I can resign today.' I hadn't been in the presidency two months." It was not an idle bluff; Hicks was serious. "As a Grambling graduate, " he said, "I would never, never terminate Coach Robinson. I think they were afraid I would quit before I even got my presidency started, and announce to the public why. So they encouraged me to stay on. But all that year, it was always these people getting together politically to remove Coach Robinson."

Eddie's 1994 team did nothing to support the argument that he should be replaced. The opening game, a rematch with Steve McNair and Alcorn, attracted the largest attendance in the history of The Rob: 25,347. Eddie's quarterback, Kendrick Nord, passed for four hundred eighty-five yards and seven touchdowns as Eddie achieved his only victory in four tries against the superstar McNair. The two teams combined for 1,318 yards of total offense, and Grambling won by the incredible score of 62-56. Grambling averaged 49.4 points per game while reeling off nine straight victories to start that season, and came within four points of the all-time school scoring record of four hundred eighty-three, which had been set just two years before. Playing a typically grueling schedule that included road games in Baltimore, East Rutherford, New Jersey, Dallas, Shreveport, Houston, Miami, New Orleans and Atlanta, Grambling tied for the SWAC championship, the seventeenth time Eddie won or shared the title. The final record was 9-3 – his forty-fifth winning season – leaving him just three victories short of the unimaginable total of 400 for his illustrious career.

"They were kind of disappointed that he succeeded," Dr. Hicks said of those who were pushing for a coaching change. "But the pressure never stopped." After six months as temporary president, Dr. Hicks was asked to apply for the vacant regular position. The "interim" tag was removed after the 1994-95 school year ended. "The same thing started again the next summer, 1995," he said. "I needed to get rid of Coach Robinson before the start of the season. I said, 'Well, I'm ready to resign.' So we got through that. But the pressure just kept coming."

Three losses by a total of six points – one decided on the last play of the game, another in the final minute – left Eddie with a 5-6 record, only his sixth losing season in 53 but his second in the last five. Coaching victory number 400, however, came that year, on October 7 on national television.

Mississippi Valley State, winless in its first four games, fell behind 21-0 in the first half and lost 42-7. After the game the world-famous Grambling marching band filled the field in a special "400" formation. There were fireworks, and telephone calls from President Bill Clinton and Louisiana Governor Edwin Edwards. In the days that followed, Eddie and Doris were guests of honor in a parade at Walt Disney World, and Eddie was inducted into the Blue-Gray Football Classic Hall of Fame in Montgomery, Alabama – where the Civil Rights Movement in the South began with Rosa Parks and the bus boycott, and ended with the arrival of Dr. King and the Selma marchers.

Some of Eddie's oldest and closest friends called after victory No. 400, too, but not merely to congratulate him.

"I tried to get him to retire then," said Adolph Byrd, "me and Collie J. I called him and said, 'Coach, are you going to retire now?' He said, 'No, Byrd. I'm going to coach a few more years.' He didn't really give a reason. He would tell you over and over and over: 'One wife, one school, one job.' He just couldn't give it up." Eddie's future plans became a topic at the annual AFCA convention, too. "I'd ask him almost every year," said Grant Teaff. "I'd say, 'Eddie, you gonna retire?' And I'd just get that look with a little smile." Marino Casem publicly opposed any attempt to force Eddie to step down. "I spoke out against that. I came out hard. I thought they were very, very wrong in forcing him out." But, he added, "Collie and I talked. He didn't think Eddie should step down under pressure. He wanted Eddie to step away on his own." Behind the scenes, that's exactly what Casem was trying to convince his good friend to do.

"I said, 'Eddie, you know yourself. But if you're not making a contribution, you need to leave while you're on top. My wife always said, leave the stage when they're still applauding. Walk away after you made a speech while they're still standing. You think about that. Don't leave when it's bad and times are tough, and they're looking down on you. Leave while you're still on top.' Eddie said, 'That's what I want to do. That's what I want to do.' But he couldn't do it. Eddie didn't want to step down. He thought he still had something to offer the game. He constantly said he would know when it was his time."

Did Eddie stay too long? Was it necessary to force the issue regarding his departure? Or should Grambling, its anxious alumni and the state board for higher education have been more patient? As the story-setting line in the hit musical *Jersey Boys* goes, "Ask four guys and you'll get four different answers."

Willie Davis could see both sides but came down on the side of loyalty to his former coach and mentor. "I would be the first to tell you, in all honesty, that he probably stayed a few years beyond when he should have," Davis said. "I was down at one of the Bayou Classics, and I was in the locker room. I'm hearing the coach, and the kids in the back – you couldn't hear him for their own conversations. I stood up and said, 'Dammit! Shut up. Don't you hear Coach talking?' It was like dropping a bomb or something. It's unfortunate, because if you had to tell them to be quiet and listen to Coach Robinson, that in itself said something."

Not even that scene, however, moved Davis to be part of the faction calling for Eddie to be replaced. "I refused to be a part of it," he said. "There was a movement at one point to try to get him to step down. I stayed a mile away from that. I said, 'Absolutely, I'm never going to be a part of asking him to step down,' because of all he meant to Grambling. I was hoping we could find some way, maybe rather than asking him to step down, to find another way for him to play a role that he would feel good about – not having any idea what that might be. It would have been better for his legacy."

No one asked Charlie Joiner at the time, but he would have argued for compassion and respect if they had. "I was not involved," he said, "but my opinion is, if a guy of Eddie Robinson's stature wants to coach, you let him coach. You let him coach as long as he wants to. He is no dummy, and we know it. He would know when the end comes. You just don't take those things away from a person like him. Let him retire the way he wants to retire. The man is a peerless legend, okay? He's a legend not just in Louisiana, but all across America. He's one of the biggest legends in the black world – in black America – there ever has been. Why kill his heart? Don't kill his heart when he's a little vulnerable. Let him play it out."

Doug Williams tried to stay out of it as things unfolded, but later spoke to the other side of the debate. "Shack Harris is like a big brother to me," he said. "We used to talk about it, and Shack always told me, 'You know what? You can't get involved.' Because it wasn't about the job, it was about respect for Coach Robinson. Because at that time the program was no longer what we thought it should have been, and we wanted Coach to go out on top. That's what it was, more than anything else: Don't stay too long.

"There comes a time when it still has to be about the university," Williams said. "Even though Coach gave his life to the university, somewhere along the line the university is still going to stand. I'm not a firm believer in the view that a guy who stays that long and gives that much and has contributed as much as he did deserves to go out whenever he wants to go out, even if he isn't doing well at the end. I would hope that when I fade to that point . . ."

Even the coaches closest to Eddie had differing views. Marino Casem left on his own terms but related to the grip that coaching can have on a man, especially one who spent his life at one place. "Everybody can have some lean years," said Casem. "His length of service entitled him to stay." Grant Teaff looked beyond victories and defeats. "Whether he was as successful in the latter years or not is totally immaterial," he said, "because those youngsters who were with him, even in those fading years, got to hear him and sit at his feet, and listen to that which he taught on a daily basis. Maybe the record wasn't as good, maybe it wasn't as glamorous as it had been, but there was still a huge value in it." W.C. Gorden said simply: "Eddie definitely stayed too long. After all that time it was hard for him to give it up."

37

EDWIN EDWARDS was elected Governor of Louisiana four times and served sixteen years as the state's chief executive between 1972 and 1996. The last time he won the statewide race, his opponent was David Duke, a former Grand Wizard of the Knights of the Ku Klux Klan, whose stated belief as an avowed white supremacist was that "all people have a basic human right to preserve their own heritage." That was in 1992, Eddie's jubilee season as Grambling's coach. Four years later Edwards announced that he would retire rather than seek another term as governor. For much of Eddie Robinson's coaching career, most blacks couldn't even vote in Louisiana. In the 1995 election, a black man, Cleo Fields, was the Democratic candidate to succeed Edwin Edwards. Fields lost to State Senator Mike Foster, but the contest itself was further confirmation of Eddie's lifelong belief in the opportunity America afforded all of its citizens who got an education and worked hard. Though the black candidate lost, he received more than a half-million votes.

Following the election of Governor Mike Foster, in the spring of 1996, Dr. Hicks began to realize the inevitability of his football coach's demise. "The final time, when it really, really got hot was when the governor's office got involved," he said. "That's when I started having conversations with Coach Robinson. I said, 'Based on what I see, these people are politically connected. They've been involved in politics, and somebody owes them a favor. And the favor might be, coach, to get you replaced.' He was shocked that I had the conversation with him. I just told him I was getting pressure, and I thought it was time to start talking about it. When it came that time where the pressure was, 'Hicks, either you get rid of Coach or we get rid of you,' I knew that he and I had to start really talking about it because I was going to step down, and if I wasn't there, whoever they put in was definitely going to fire him because that was going to be part of the deal. I told him, 'I would never terminate you. I would step down as president before I would ever do that.' Now whether he believed me or not, I don't know. But I made that clear to him."

President Hicks continued to meet with the man he first encountered while a student thirty years earlier. "I'd say to him, 'If the pressure gets hot enough, you've got to have a plan.' We kind of left it at that. I really think, looking back on it, Coach Robinson probably never had an idea that pressure would ever result in him being in that kind of position. I mean, he was an icon. Here's a man who's been wined and dined, at the governor's mansion, with the legislature, having their pictures taken with him. He was trying to resolve, 'How did I get to this position? I'm Coach Robinson.' He started with nothing, and built it up. He even lined the field. Everybody knew where Grambling was because of what he had done. Most of the students who were attracted from out of state were there because of the football team and the band. He built the Bayou Classic. He had done so much. I think he was surprised."

Almost three years into his own retirement, Marino Casem became Eddie's confidant within the coaching profession. The apparent role of some former players in the movement was particularly upsetting. "Eddie would call me at night," Casem said, "and want to talk. He'd say, 'Cat, they want to tell me what to do. I raised them. I taught them. I ought to be telling them what to do.' It hurt him. He thought of his former players as his sons. Eddie loved those kids. For them to be counseling him to come out of it –

Eddie thought that was wrong. He told me that. It really hurt him that 'his sons' had lost confidence in him."

As the 1996 season approached, Dr. Hicks tried to fashion a strategy that would preserve Eddie's dignity and self-respect while satisfying the forces pushing for a coaching change. "Coach, you've got to be able to go out when you want to go out, on your terms," he told Eddie, speaking then as if Eddie were someone else. "I'm prepared to say I would like Coach Robinson, once he's stepped down from coaching, to help raise money for the university and move us forward, because he can open doors that I would never be able to open. We'll pay him an outstanding salary."

"To show him I was serious," Dr. Hicks related, "I drafted a letter for him to take a look at – to look at, not to sign. I think when that letter was drafted, it really affected Coach. I think he shared it with his family, and their attitude was, 'the audacity of me to even think about doing something like that – remove him from coaching!' So we had a couple conversations after that, and I said, 'Well, Coach, it's probably going to happen, but I promise you, I will not terminate you. What you've got to do is call your own shot. If I were you, I'd say, 'Two years from now I'm going to retire.' The pressure here is that you say something, because these people are not going to stop. I could tell. They were getting a source of power that, if a telephone call was made, it could happen."

In a story published during 1996 in the campus newspaper, *The Gramblinite,* Eddie remained steadfast in his resistance to a compelled exit. "I don't think I can go on forever," he said, "but I think I have the right to decide when I want to go out. Sooner or later I will make a move. But I feel I've earned the right to make my own decision." With no plan in place, Eddie needed at least a winning season in 1996, if not something comparable to 1994 to withstand the rising tide. Instead, Grambling finished 3-8. Langston College, which finished 1-7, got its lone victory at Eddie's expense. Mississippi Valley State, which had beaten Grambling only three times in 39 years, won 19-10, and Texas Southern, which had only one victory over Eddie in the past thirty seasons (Rod Paige's surprise), won 20-7. In the Bayou Classic, Southern won for the fourth straight time.

As if he were being lifted up then thrown down by competing forces beyond his control, the American Football Coaches Association presented him the prestigious Tuss McLaughry Award in January 1996. But in April, an investigative story in the *Monroe News-Star* alleged that grades for up to seventy of Eddie's players had been altered during the 1994-95 seasons. Soon after the National Collegiate Athletic Association announced it was investigating eight charges of rules violations by Grambling's football program. The NCAA said the charges included "lack of institutional control" over the football program, impermissible contact with recruits and offering money to athletes. In November, four of Eddie's players were charged with the rape of a fifteen-year-old girl in a dorm room following the homecoming game with Alabama State, a 7-0 victory that was his third and final success of the troubled season. Eddie dismissed the players from the team and the charges eventually were dropped, but the developments distressed him greatly. "I don't mean the same thing to kids now that I did earlier in my career," he lamented. "Today, when you talk to kids, it's like you're hitting a wall. I know they're good people, but there's something we've lost along the way. I'm sure some people are wondering, 'What the hell is Eddie doing over there?' I teach them as much as I can to be the best human beings possible."

President Hicks, for one, found the timing of the NCAA charges very suspicious. "They were minor things," he said, noting that Eddie's son, an assistant coach, was accused of observing players working out on their own, and recalling instances when Eddie had given players money for transportation home in times of family emergencies. "Some of those people who wanted him out of there filed the complaints. They figured that was one way to get him out of there – destroy him with NCAA violations." Six months later the NCAA exonerated Eddie. By then, however, Dr. Hicks had been blindsided by a report on the national sports cable network ESPN, and embattled Eddie had surrendered.

"I was going to an accreditation meeting in Nashville," Dr. Hicks said. "When I landed in Nashville, I was passing through the lobby of the hotel, and ESPN flashed on with a news break that said, 'Grambling to fire long-time Coach Robinson.' I just turned and looked at it, and people were reacting. I walked up and got a closer look, and I turned around and went straight back home. I didn't even attend the meeting. I called them and told them something had happened on campus and I had to get back.

"I don't know who leaked that information," Dr. Hicks said, "because Coach Robinson didn't get a letter saying he was fired. The letter was, 'When you decide to retire, if you retire this year, this is what our plan is.' When I got back, ESPN – Jeremy Schaap – was on campus, and I was hit with that. I called Coach Robinson, and I said, "Coach, I have not fired you. Nor will I fire you. Somebody's leaked this out to the media. So you've got to decide what you want to do."

Dr. Raymond Hicks immediately was portrayed as the villain, the cold-blooded university president responsible for dumping a national hero in his waning years. **"For Shame, Grambling,"** read the headline on a column in the *New York Daily News* that was representative of the sentiments expressed around the country. The column quoted former NFL star Everson Walls, a freshman on Eddie's second Tokyo team in 1977 and a key contributor on outstanding teams the next three seasons. "What this goes to show you," Walls was quoted, "is my old school has arrived. Grambling has gone from a black university to a major university. Eddie Robinson is the sole reason the school exists as it does today . . . And now they're trying to put him on his butt. The ironic thing is, if it wasn't for Eddie Robinson, the guy who wants to fire him wouldn't even have the job to do it."

A report in the hometown Ruston paper, headlined **"Robinson saga is hot topic across nation,"** quoted radio talk show hosts from New York City and Cleveland. "His name is linked nationally to not only black college sports, but sports in general," said Warren Jacobsen from New York. "Why shouldn't a man of his stature and success be given one more year to do what he's done for over 50 years? He's earned that right and it would be a disgrace if they don't let him do it." Recapping events after the controversy concluded, another newspaper wrote: "The notion that Robinson was being forced out set off a groundswell of support for him. Hicks' office was flooded with faxes and letters, including one from entertainer Bill Cosby, until the day he announced Robinson would coach another year. Robinson was given one more season only after Gov. Mike Foster and the state's board of regents, which sets policy for all of the Louisiana's university system, came to his defense."

If those on the outside had only known what was happening in the office of the president of Grambling State University. "I got calls from the University of Louisiana System (the alternative name for the Board of Trustees for State Colleges and Universities) and from the governor's office: They all wanted to know: What was I going to do?" Dr. Hicks said. "I told them I was not going to terminate Coach Robinson. I would meet with him and we would work out when he might step down. There was a lot of pressure: 'You've got this opportunity. You've got to do it now.' And I said, 'No. I'm not going to do that.'

"It went on for three or four days," Dr. Hicks said. "Coach and I met every day. Coach Robinson would ask me every time we met: Why, after he had given so much? I told him it was about power. I think he believed me, but he just couldn't understand. I think he always wondered if there was something I could have done. What I tried to show him was, this is politics. When I'm willing to give up a job I didn't think I would ever get – when I'm getting the chance to run a university I was a student at, and I'm willing to give that up for you – then you know it's got to be something I can't even deal with. I think he wondered if I would really resign. He probably lived with some questions, even about me, until he passed.

"Finally, I said, 'Coach, if I were you, I would ask for another year. That way you can go out on your terms. You can have a last year and you can be celebrated.' I think he thought about it. I told him if he would make that decision, that's what I would support. And if I couldn't get support for it, I would step down. I kept getting a lot of pressure about when I was going to work this out. I told ESPN I would announce it on graduation day, after (mid-term) commencement. So I called Coach Robinson and told him I was going to write two letters. One would be a letter of resignation if he didn't accept their conditions. In the other letter, if he accepted their conditions, I was going on record saying that I'm going to recommend to the board that Coach be given a final year so he can be celebrated properly."

When the day of decision arrived – Friday the 13th, no less – President Hicks still didn't know for sure what Eddie and Doris had decided to do. "I had a resignation letter in my left pocket, and an endorsement letter in my right pocket," he said. "I was met by somebody from the governor's office and asked what I was going to do. I said, 'You'll have to come to the press conference.' They said, 'You can't tell us now?' I said, 'No. I'll tell you when I get over there and visit with Coach and Mrs. Robinson.' When I got there, they were there. I had a good cordial conversation. I said, 'Coach, are you ready?' He said, 'Well. Let's go with the final year.'

"So when I got up, I announced my decision," Dr. Hicks said. "I told them, 'Coach Robinson has informed me that he plans to retire after the next football season. He asked me to allow him to do that. I'm calling this press conference to announce that I'm honoring his request. This is going to be a great opportunity.' I also said, 'Let me put to rest the question of would I have ever fired Coach Robinson. The answer is no. I would have resigned before doing that because, as an alumnus and a faculty and staff member, I never would want it on my record that I terminated Coach Robinson. So I was prepared to resign, and in fact, I am prepared to resign if the Board does not approve this request I am making today.' Somebody from the University of Louisiana System was there, so they interviewed him afterward. They asked, 'Are you going to support Dr. Hicks' recommendation?' And the man said yes."

A story published by *Diverse: Issues In Higher Education* attempted to report what happened, but didn't quote Dr. Hicks. It noted that almost a week had passed between the report that Eddie would be fired and the announcement that he would return for the 1997 season, and then retire. James Bradford, Grambling's director of its national alumni association, lamented the public relations black eye, which he implied was the result of the university mishandling the situation.

"With all the media attention, things were blown out of context," Bradford said. "The way things came out made it look like we were trying to run him out. That's not so. Nobody dislikes him. He's done a great job. But there comes a time when it's time to move on. We don't want to see him destroy what he has built up." Bradford also said, "Grambling started losing more than it ever had, and people got concerned when he never said anything about retiring. They felt he just might try to go on and on."

38

THE END came sooner for Dr. Hicks than it did for Eddie. **"Hicks gets sacked by Grambling State,"** read the headline on a story in *Black Issues in Higher Education* in October of 1997. It was, in Hicks' opinion, more than coincidence that this development followed by mere months his successful effort to secure one more season for his embattled, aging football coach. "After that, my days were numbered," he said. "I was at-will. I didn't have a contract. They got rid of some of the supportive board members, who really supported Coach Robinson, supported Grambling and supported me. The handwriting was on the wall. When it got rough, I resigned and went back to the faculty."

The story reporting the end of his presidency attributed the change to "ongoing financial and administrative problems." But in fact, most of those issues had preceded Hicks and were reasons for his appointment. Near the end of the account, the misperception that Hicks initiated the effort to force Eddie to retire, and that only public pressure and intervention by the governor had provided Eddie the opportunity for a graceful exit, was perpetuated. At the time it was all anyone would believe, leaving Ray Hicks to set the record straight years later with the few who would listen. "I did not ask Coach Robinson to step down," he said. "I stand by that."

As the time neared when President Hicks would go down for the count, Eddie, who had celebrated his 79th birthday that February, already had begun experiencing the very kind of celebratory sendoff Dr. Hicks envisioned in their discussions. The National Football Foundation applied the provision of its eligibility criteria that states, "Active coaches become eligible at seventy-five years of age. He must have been a head coach for a minimum ten years and coached at least one hundred games with a .600 winning percentage." Eddie was inducted into the College Football Hall of Fame the summer before his farewell season. He joined Jake Gaither, Earl Banks and John Merritt as the only black coaches in the Hall of Fame at that point.

"Eddie Robinson Football Classic to feature major college foes," read a headline later that summer above a story, dateline COLUMBUS, announcing that "Ohio State University and the University of Wyoming will open the 1997 season here Thursday, August 28, in the first annual 'Eddie Robinson Football Classic,' named for the famed Grambling coach." The report provided President Hicks with a rare opportunity to be quoted praising the man who most people thought he was running out of town. "Coach Robinson . . . built a dynasty at Grambling by making the most of an impressive array of talent," Dr. Hicks said. "Getting to the top of the mountain is one thing, staying there is another. Robinson kept Grambling in the thick of championship races year after year. He deserves his term in the spotlight."

The SWAC paid homage by publishing an eight-page tribute brochure with the heading *Salute To A Legend . . . Eddie Robinson . . . The Farewell Season.* It included his comments on nine subjects, such as being an American, having people call him a legend, memorable moments from his career, and what he'd like for people to say about him years later. It listed his milestone victories and all seven Hall of Fame inductions (to that point), summarized his career and accomplishments, and presented personal commendations from SWAC Commissioner James Frank, NCAA Executive Director Cedric Dempsey, Doug Williams and Yankees owner George Steinbrenner, who brought his Yankees to Grambling three times between 1982 and 1997 to play exhibition games against the university's baseball team as a show of his regard for Eddie.

"As a former assistant football coach at Northwestern and Purdue Universities," wrote Steinbrenner, "it's very difficult for me to understand any man being the head coach for 57 years at one institution. Eddie Robinson is one of the most unique and admirable men I have ever met, in or out of athletics . . . He's a man with an immortal presence. The lessons he teaches are lessons which can solve the problems of our great nation. . . .'" Commissioner Frank praised the "highly exemplary manner that he's conducted himself and represented Grambling . . . while achieving all of his greatness." Dempsey wrote, "His tenure . . . teaches all of us the values of loyalty and commitment to self, others and our communities." And Doug Williams shared a bit of wisdom his coach had imparted. "Coach would always tell me before each game, 'Doug, you have good eyes, which will serve you well on and off the field. Always remember to look in several different directions to determine which way you want to go.'"

At the end of September Eddie received a letter that most people would frame or at least mount in a scrapbook. The letterhead read:

THE WHITE HOUSE
WASHINGTON

It was a personal note of congratulations from the 42nd President of the United States, Bill Clinton. Included was a paragraph that read:

"More important than your record on the field has been your influence on the lives of the young men you've guided. The sportsmanship, self-discipline and commitment to athletic and personal excellence that you inspired in your players will be a lasting legacy long after you've coached your last game."

About the same time the leader of the free world was writing to Eddie, Steve Richardson, the new executive director of the Football Writers Association of America, was orchestrating an enduring tribute.

"FWAA renames coaching award for Robinson," read the headline on an Associated Press story announcing that the Football Writers Association of America was renaming its coach of the year award for Eddie. The FWAA had been the "voting group" that selected the winner of the Coach Bear Bryant Award, sponsored by the Houston Touchdown Club and the American Heart Association, since 1986. The Bryant Award would continue, but without the involvement or endorsement of the FWAA. (In 2009 there were four coach of the year award programs in college football, including the Bear Bryant Award still based in Houston, American Football Coaches Association awards for coaches of teams in each of five size classifications, and two Eddie Robinson Awards. One was sponsored by The Sports Network for coaches of Football Championship Series-level teams (formerly called Division 1-AA), and the FWAA's Eddie Robinson Coach of the Year Award for coaches of Football Bowl Series teams – formerly Division 1.)

Writing in the September/October 1997 issue of *The Fifth Down,* the FWAA's newsletter, FWAA President Blair Kerkhoff of the *Kansas City Star* explained the move away from the Bryant award program: "There were scheduling conflicts and some philosophical differences with the group in Houston which could not be overcome. And since the FWAA did not 'own' the Bear Bryant name, it had no recourse but to bow out . . . As a coach of a program once considered small college and later classified as Division 1-AA, Robinson never won the FWAA award. Now, Eddie Robinson IS the award."

Issues with the Houston-based sponsors of the Bear Bryant Award notwithstanding, Richardson had other reasons for making the change. "There were concerns on my part that we needed to evolve into a more diverse organization," he said. "Not coming from the South myself, I thought there was too much of being a Southern organization. Some of our members were not happy. Here's this new guy coming in, and he's not only getting rid of Bear Bryant – he's bringing in Eddie Robinson! What a 180-degree turn! You can imagine what they were saying, but it went through."

Richardson's rationale for choosing Eddie to be the namesake for the FWAA's coaching excellence award was, simply, "How can you go wrong with this guy? It's a no-brainer." He was referring to the man, not his number of victories, championships or star players. "He was a great example for black America," Richardson said, "but he was never wearing it on his sleeve by any stretch of the imagination. He was all about doing a hard day's work and leading by example. It was, like, the all-American story: being married to Doris for – fill in the blank – number of years, leading an exemplary kind of life and making the players responsible for their actions and their education. There was quite a bit of discipline involved. People probably don't realize that as much as they should. Whenever he was talking, it was about American youth and doing the right thing."

Eddie and Doris were invited to a reception in Dallas the weekend Grambling played Prairie View. Richardson wanted to show off the bust of Eddie that would be the award, and he had presents for both of them. Eddie's first reaction, though, was that he needed to be with his team and coaches, and concentrate on the game. In that regard, not much had changed in his last season from the days when he was oblivious to historic happenings, such as events surrounding the Grambling-Jackson State game at Mississippi Veterans Memorial Stadium in 1967. Richardson was apoplectic. "I said, 'C'MON! IT'S PRAIRIE VIEW,'" he recalled. Once-proud Prairie View had lost 71 straight games dating back to the last two games of the 1989 season. "They finally decided to come," Richardson said. "He was there for a couple of hours. They enjoyed themselves." The next day, Grambling won easily, 33-6.

"Walking out a winner would mean a lot to me – more than walking out on your worst season," Eddie had said in December 1996, as his future was being decided. With the Prairie View victory, four games into his final season, Grambling had won two and lost two. A 20-13 victory over Mississippi Valley State at Grambling the next week raised hopes that he might be able to go out with that winning record he so wanted. But something Collie Nicholson said, back when Eddie's farewell season was announced, proved prophetic. "We don't want anyone, including Eddie Robinson," Collie said, "to think that somehow, someone is going to wave a magic wand and he'll automatically have a winning season." Grambling lost the next four, three of them each by a touchdown or less. With Eddie's final home game at Grambling and his final Bayou Classic all that remained on his last schedule, a 3-6 record eliminated any chance of a 48th winning season.

November 15, 1997, was cold and rainy in northern Louisiana, the dreary kind of day a fiction writer would choose as the backdrop for an unhappy ending. Despite the ugly weather, Yvonne Byrd and her children drove up from Baton Rouge to see "Uncle Eddie" for the final time in the stadium named for him. "We got there early in the morning," she said, "about 9 or 10 o'clock. We had breakfast with them. At 10 o'clock the doorbell started ringing. There would be thirty or so guys bringing their families. They had footballs. They had baseballs. They had basketballs. When they couldn't find a football, they just brought whatever ball they could find to get Uncle Eddie to write his name on it."

The parade of well-wishers to 234 Adams Street, where Eddie and Doris had lived since 1951, continued through the morning. "He sat right in the kitchen," Yvonne Byrd said. "He'd sign and sign and sign. And then that crowd would leave, and right away here comes another crowd. Every size, height and color was there. Whatever you thought you wanted in a man came through the door. I didn't even want to go to the game, but we had to. When we came back, same thing. He would sit in the kitchen at the table. The living room was to the right, and the kitchen to the left. People didn't even have to come all the way into the kitchen."

Visitors to the house didn't really outnumber the fans who showed up for Eddie's home farewell against North Carolina A&T, but it almost seemed that way. Some reports put the crowd at the game at a single thousand; most said four times that. Either way, 19,600-seat Robinson Stadium was mostly empty when Grambling kicked off. Eddie had conducted a full-pads practice the night before to ensure that his team was primed, but A&T jumped out to a 23-7 first half lead. At halftime he implored his players to "remember who you are. You're Grambling." They responded by scoring 28 points but still trailed by two in the final minute. When the visitors recovered Grambling's onside kick, it was only a matter of running out the clock. Final score: North Carolina A&T 37, Grambling 35.

Fittingly, Eddie bowed out at the Bayou Classic: Game No. 24 in the series he started. It easily received the most extensive coverage of any game in its history – more than two hundred fifty media credentials were issued, overflowing the Superdome's capacity of one hundred seventy-five press box seats. Unfortunately, it also was one of the least competitive. More than 64,000 fans at the Superdome and a national television audience watched the curtain drop with a 30-7 loss to Southern that may not have been even that close. Grambling gained only one hundred twenty-three yards total offense and made only eight first downs. Eddie left the field tearfully in the embrace of Doris, to an ovation from both sides of the stadium. "The feeling on that last day, in his last game," his son told a reporter, "is something you really can't describe, even if you lived it."

The unique prose of Collie Nicholson, who had moved on from Grambling almost twenty years before, resurfaced in print one last, nostalgic time as Eddie entered the final month of his final season. In a column written for *The Gramblinite*, Collie summed up decades of experiences and feelings as only he could:

> "He has been a coach half the time that Black college football
> has been in existence . . . Robinson's tenure at Grambling is 16 years
> longer than any other coach at one school . . . Regretfully, the 1997
> campaign is twilight time for the fabled mentor, a man many regard

as a national treasure . . . His hair is thinner now and he has mellowed somewhat . . . but Eddie Robinson, at 78 years-of-age, still reports to the football field each day with missionary zeal, a bounce in his gait, and a smile on his face, like a teenager who just got his driver's license . . .

"The story of his life . . . is like stepping into a time capsule before plastic helmets, face masks, television, concrete stadiums, football gloves and low-quarter shoes . . . Grambling's barber-shop, blue-collar, hard-hat, boondocks inner-city following is only surpassed by Notre Dame's subway fans . . . Grambling has played in 28 of the 50 states, plus Washington DC, a record no school can match . . . Without social stratification, people from all walks of life embrace him as a national hero . . . Robinson estimates that he has coached over 4,500 varsity athletes in football, basketball and baseball with an 85 percent graduation rate . . .

"Football has been his job and his love . . . His immersion has been total. He will be missed, but his legacy will remain for the ages.

"Here's to you, Mr. Robinson . . . Thanks for the memories."

39

SUPER BOWL XXII will always rank as one of the most shocking pro football championship games ever played, though not because the Washington Redskins beat the Denver Broncos, or even because the final score was a lopsided 42-10. No, it's the stunning reversal of fortunes that distinguishes this one from most others. Denver scored a touchdown on its first play, a 56-yard touchdown pass by John Elway, and kicked a field goal the second time it had the ball to take a 10-0 lead. The sputtering Redskins, meanwhile, dropped two third-down passes and had a 25-yard run nullified by a holding penalty on their first three possessions. When their starting quarterback went out with a sprained knee on the next offensive series, their prospects could not have looked more bleak.

That quarterback was Grambling's Doug Williams, the first black man ever to start a Super Bowl game at that position. After Tampa Bay made history by drafting him in the first round in 1978, he played five seasons for the Buccaneers. An expansion franchise that began play in 1976, Tampa Bay lost its first twenty-six games and was the butt of many jokes on late-night television shows before Williams arrived. He led the Buccaneers to the NFL playoffs three times in four seasons following his rookie year, and in 1979 took them to the brink of Super Bowl XIV, losing 9-0 to the Los Angeles Rams in the NFC championship game. A free agent following the

1982 season, he left the Bucs rather than accept a take-it-or-leave-it offer from Hugh Culverhouse, who refused to pay Williams a salary comparable to white quarterbacks with similar records of success. He lost his wife, Janice, to a brain tumor in 1983, and sat out the season, signing in 1984 to play in the newly formed United States Football League. When the USFL folded two years later, he returned to the NFL with the Redskins.

Suppressing the pain in his knee, Williams answered "Yeah" when Washington coach Joe Gibbs asked him, "Hey, you OK?" at the start of the second quarter against Denver. What unfolded in the next fifteen minutes of play may never be duplicated, especially in a game of such magnitude. Less than a minute into the quarter, his first pass went for an 80-yard touchdown. Four minutes later he completed a 27-yard pass for another. By halftime he had thrown four touchdown passes, and Washington led 35-10. He finished with three hundred forty yards passing as Washington became the first team ever to gain more than six hundred yards in a Super Bowl. Williams was voted Super Bowl XXII's most valuable player, another first.

"Coach was there," Williams said. "I saw him right after the game. He was in the tunnel when I came off the field. We cried together. He said, 'You don't even understand the impact of what you just did.' He told me it was like him looking at Joe Louis knocking out Max Schmeling. That's what he likened it to. And we all know, back then, that fight wasn't on TV for him to see. He listened to it on the radio. But he said it was just like him LOOKING. He was listening to a radio but he was visualizing Joe Louis knocking out Max Schmeling. We both were emotional. We hugged. To the day he died, when he went out to speak, he would tell people the proudest moment of his life was not seeing me win the Super Bowl, but seeing me get up off the turf to get it done after I hurt my knee."

Whenever reporters interviewed Williams during Super Bowl Week, they peppered him with every question they could think of that was even remotely related to being the first black quarterback in the NFL's season-ending spectacle: Did he feel like Jackie Robinson? Would it be easier if he were the second black quarterback in the Super Bowl? Have you heard from Jesse Jackson? Will America root against the Redskins because of you? Has there been much progress in America since the schools you attended were finally integrated? And: Do all of these questions about being the first black quarterback in the Super Bowl bother you? THE question – "How long have you been a black quarterback? – was never actually asked, though it lived on for decades after that Super Bowl. The actual query apparently began with an acknowledgment of his status as a black quarterback, and asked something pertaining to how long his race had mattered, presumably to football fans.

By all accounts, Williams handled the entire interrogation with the kind of poise and patience that would have made Eddie proud. It was exactly what Eddie was trying to prepare his players for, all those years. Williams attempted to have the last word on the subject by collaborating with writer Bruce Hunter in *QuarterBLACK: Shattering the NFL Myth*, his first-person book published in 1990. Washington coach Joe Gibbs did his best to close the issue during his post-game media remarks when he said, "You would hope as we break down the barriers, hopefully we're at the point where most people are looking at people as players and not in colors anymore."

On December 4, 1997, Grambling State University announced that Doug Williams had been chosen to succeed Eddie Robinson as head football coach. Just as the circumstances of Eddie's departure and the role played by Dr. Raymond Hicks were examined and, for the most part, misrepresented, so too was the relationship between Williams and his former coach analyzed as if under a microscope. *The New York Times* and *The Los Angeles Times* were among the newspapers, nationally as well as locally, that covered the apparently awkward transition and strained coexistence. It was reported that Eddie wouldn't move out of his office in the athletic department building, so Williams was stuck in a temporary trailer. They rarely spoke, it was written, and Eddie kept going to practice but watched from his car. Williams dumped Eddie's fabled Wing-T offense, fired some assistant coaches, including Eddie Jr., and cut thirty-one players, mostly walk-ons, who were on Eddie's last squad. "Dawn of a New Era," the slogan adopted to usher in the Williams Years, even meant changing the brand of athletic gear, from Nike to Addidas.

Speaking as a player personnel executive for the Tampa Bay Buccaneers almost twelve years after he began a six-year run as Grambling's head coach, Williams dismissed all suggestion that he and Eddie had experienced any difficulties after he was put in charge of the football program that Eddie had built from nothing. "I had no problem going to the trailer," he said. "When a man's been in one place for fifty-seven years, he can move his stuff as slowly as he wants to. If Eddie Robinson needed that office to do stuff, I didn't have a problem. I saw Coach almost every day. I never said, 'Coach, when are you going to give me my office.' Never. And I never would have." Of terminating Eddie's son from the coaching staff, Williams said, "To this day, we are best friends."

There was an ironic similarity to the public perception of what transpired between Eddie and Dr. Hicks, and portrayal of the interaction, or lack of it, between Eddie and his successor. "It was all people on the outside stirring the pot," Williams insisted. "The day I was announced, Coach and I had pictures taken together at the stadium. He was standing right by me. Coach never, ever, said anything out of the way to me about taking his job. Coach was never anything but helpful. Coach used to come to practice and watch. I used to go and talk with Coach all the time. Coach and I never had a misunderstanding about me coming in."

Williams said repeatedly when he became head coach that he was not following in Eddie's footsteps. "You don't replace Eddie Robinson," he said. "You bronze his shoes and you put them on a pedestal. You wear your own shoes because you can't fill his." Realizing he needed help settling into the job, he turned to Doug Porter, by then retired after a Hall of Fame career of his own.

"My last year on the coaching staff, Doug was a redshirt freshman,"

Porter said. "I got to know him real well during that one year. He and I stayed in contact. When he was in professional football, he and I corresponded and stayed in touch with each other. When I was coaching in Georgia (at Fort Valley State), I had him down as parade marshal of our homecoming parade, had him speak at our banquet, those types of things.

"When he got the head coaching job at Grambling, I had retired and moved back to Grambling. So he and I would sit down and talk about the nuances of being a head football coach. He had been the head coach at Morehouse (for one year), but there was a significant difference in the two programs and in the approach to the programs. We talked about a lot of things that had to do with being a head coach at a program with the visibility of the Grambling program. We talked every day, but not so much about plays and strategy, even though I'd go to practice. We talked about staff, and dealing with his players. And the way you handle the press – that's extremely important."

The popular wisdom about succeeding a legend is that it's always better to be the person who follows the successor. Phil Bengtson, 20-21-1 from 1968-70, was never going to measure up to Vince Lombardi in Green Bay; nor was Gene Bartow, despite a 52-9 record and two berths in the national tournament, ever going to be the equal of John Wooden at UCLA. As great a player as he was, Bill Russell was no Red Auerbach on the bench for the Boston Celtics. There have been exceptions, of course. Ralph Houk succeeded Casey Stengel with the Yankees and won two World Series in three tries, and Tommy Lasorda nearly matched Walter Alston in both longevity and first-place finishes as manager of the Dodgers.

Doug Williams suffered the identity crisis of the former group but enjoyed success akin to the latter. "First of all, I apologize for not being Eddie Robinson," is the way he began his remarks in New York at a press conference for the 28th annual Urban League Classic early in his first season. He had just listened to speaker after speaker rave about his missing mentor at the media event staged to promote Grambling's meeting with

Hampton in the black college football showcase that Eddie started while Doug was still in the eighth grade. Grambling lost that game 28-15 and finished with a losing record – five wins and six losses – in Doug's first season. In his six years as head coach, though, Grambling won three black national championships, three SWAC titles and compiled a 52-18 record that included forty wins in the last forty-eight games. About his only shortfall was the Bayou Classic: he lost five and won only one.

He returned to his NFL roots in 2004 after interviewing for the vacant head coaching job at the University of Kentucky. "I thought I was going to get an opportunity to coach Division 1," Williams said. "I would have loved to. But it didn't happen, so I figured if you're ever going to get a chance to move up in the world, you're going to do it in the NFL, not college football." History would suggest he was probably right. When the 2009 college football season began, the one hundred twenty major college football programs had only seven black head coaches among them – four in their first season. In the NFL, on the other hand, three of the six head coaches in Super Bowls XLI through XLIII were African Americans.

Why didn't Williams continue as Eddie's successor for thirty, maybe thirty-five years? "There was no mountain left for him to climb at Grambling," said Doug Porter. "There will never be another Eddie Robinson," said Williams.

40

ALZHEIMER'S DISEASE is a progressive and fatal mystery that dims both recollection of the past and recognition of the present, relentlessly, heartbreakingly reducing a once-vibrant human being to a feeble, vacant shell. It began attacking Eddie and his brain shortly after he retired, Doris told a reporter in 2004. He felt ill and became forgetful, so she and Eddie visited hospitals in New Orleans, Dallas and Houston, trying to find help. "Eddie Jr. and his wife, the four of us, would just get in the car and go anywhere trying to get something done," she said.

Anguished by her husband's decline, she admitted, "If I let myself, I could cry. But I don't have time to do that. I never thought I would be the strong one, but I have to be now." It was exhausting and frustrating and, above all, so saddening. But having Eddie live anywhere but with her was not even a possibility as long as she was physically able to care for him. "He was always patient and good with his family and, of course, with me," she told a visitor. "He was ready to do everything he could do all the time. I want to be that way about him."

Alzheimer's is named for Alois Alzheimer, the German physician who identified the disease in 1906 by microscopically examining the brain of a 51-year old woman who died after developing memory loss, irrational distrust, and difficulty speaking and comprehending. It is believed that a build-up of protein fragments between nerve cells, called plaques, and twisted protein fibers that form inside dying brain cells, called tangles, combine to contribute to the onset of Alzheimer's Disease. But their exact role still could not be explained conclusively in 2009. The symptoms of Alzheimer's in its early stages aren't always recognizable except by those closest to the afflicted individual. This may have been the case with Eddie.

Rod Paige recalled seeing Eddie in 2003 and being pleased by what he observed. "The last time I saw Eddie," he said, "I was invited to deliver the graduation address at one of the Grambling commencement exercises. As Secretary of Education I had all kinds of invitations to come for similar situations, and I had to decline most of them. I eagerly accepted that one. It was intriguing primarily because of Eddie; I wanted to see how he was doing. When I got there, we had a chance to sit down and talk about memories. He presented me with a football that he signed. I still have it today. It's a treasured memory piece for me. We talked, and I was delighted to find out he was the same old Eddie. I was hearing the same kind of thing, just another version of 'we need to have the coaches teach better and the teachers coach better.' He wanted me to use my position to get that done. He seemed vigorous and attentive. I remember being impressed with how well he appeared with regard to his muscular structure. Eddie had on light clothing and I could tell he was muscular."

Not long after Paige's visit, though, Eddie began experiencing difficulty remembering the names of friends and former players. But even that didn't seem all that unusual. "Eddie was always good at making you think he knew you," said Marino Casem, "even when he was at the height of his career. Eddie would talk to you, and you never would know he didn't know your name. 'Hey, Cat. What's happening? How you doin' man? Boy, it's been a long time. You doin' all right?' Never did it get to the fact that he didn't remember your name. He had Doris so trained that she would get your name. 'You're so-and-so.' You'd answer, and then he would know your name." The difference, to those who knew him best, was that it wasn't that he couldn't put the right name with the right face, as much as he couldn't always place the face to start with.

"I'd come by," recalled Doug Williams, "and Doris would call to him: 'Eddie, Doug's here.' He'd get up and sit up. He'd say, 'Hey Cat, look at this guy. You still leading the Super Bowl?' I'd say, 'Yeah, Coach, we're still out front.' He'd sit there for a while, and then he'd get into a repeat mode. That's when you knew it was time to go. To me, when I stayed five minutes, it was a long time. Because I *knew* Eddie Robinson. I *liked* Eddie Robinson. I knew he had no control over the state he was in. But you just wanted your Eddie Robinson back. It was tough – tough, tough, tough. When you left there, it really hit you. Because you thought about when you were seventeen, eighteen, and here's the man who took you under his wing."

In the fall of 2003, Doug's last season as Grambling's head football coach, Eddie attended a 31-20 loss to McNeese State in September, but wasn't seen at another game that year. John Gagliardi, long-time coach at St. John's University, a Division III school located in Collegeville, Minnesota, about fifteen miles west of St. Cloud, surpassed Eddie's total career coaching victories near the end of the season. But Doris protectively withheld the news from Eddie. And she made sure no one else ever told him his record had been broken. He attended a birthday party for Collie Nicholson in July 2004, and watched Arkansas Pine-Bluff rout Grambling 41-22 in mid-October. But his condition was deteriorating. "He didn't seem to know what happened, and didn't seem to care," Doris told a visitor who accompanied them to the game.

Charlie Joiner could sense the decline without being there to see his former coach. "I always called," he said. "I made sure I called once a month or every couple weeks. In the late stages at home, he'd recognize the name but then he'd forget. He'd fade in and out. It was very hard for me. Because he was such a vibrant, dynamic guy on the phone, a vibrant, dynamic guy in front of people, talking. He could do that, you know. He could really talk."

As late as the 2005 season, Eddie still had moments when he seemed to be his old self. Three of his former players who had returned as assistant coaches brought the team to his house one day to visit. They sang the alma mater, and Eddie participated with a spirit Doris thought she'd never again see. He remembered the words. The team left, but Eddie wanted the coaches to stay. Before they could go, they had to sing the alma mater with Eddie one more time. "I have had a lot of great things happen to me around football," Sammy White, one of those former players turned assistant coach, told a writer some time later. "That's was one of mine. Right there."

What might have been a lasting testament to Eddie's devotion to youth – the Eddie Robinson Foundation – instead became an embarrassment in the last months of Eddie's life. The Foundation's purpose was to perpetuate Eddie's emphasis on education as the key to success by providing college scholarships to high school seniors, eighth grade students who exhibited exceptional potential (provided they maintained top performance in high school), and, by 2001, athletes who completed their collegiate eligibility without graduating. The annual Eddie Robinson Classic football game was the primary source of sustaining funds.

Until 2002 the NCAA allowed college teams to play a 12th regular-season game only if the first game was an NCAA-approved season-opening "classic." But the number of those games had increased to eight over two decades, including the Eddie Robinson Classic. In response to that proliferation, the NCAA decided to allow all schools to play twelve regular-season games, effectively eliminating the special season openers. The loss of revenue generated by the Eddie Robinson Classic had a devastating effect on the charitable endeavor. The Eddie Robinson Foundation eventually went broke, leaving scholarship recipients waiting for money that never came.

By the time the financial problems became known, Eddie was bedridden and barely able to communicate. Doris was handling their affairs. A lawsuit was filed in September, 2006, seeking the return of all of Eddie's memorabilia and prohibiting the Foundation from using Eddie's name or

identity in any form for any future purpose. Although Eddie's stellar reputation lent credibility to the endeavor, he was not involved in day-to-day
operations. Eddie didn't deserve to be blamed for the failure of something
he wasn't personally managing, Doris insisted. "You're talking about somebody who lived right and did everything he could to build a good name,"
she told a TV reporter from Atlanta who broke the story. "I certainly don't
want his name tarnished."

By the fall of 2006, Eddie was spending almost all of his time in the
hospital bed that had been moved into the Robinson home on Adams
Street. He needed help going to the bathroom and changing whatever he
wore. He slept as much as eighteen hours a day. Finally, it was too much for
87-year-old Doris to handle on her own.

"Mrs. Robinson. What a stalwart she was," said Willie Davis, who
stayed in touch to the end. "I knew her well. She probably was the one who
started calling me Big Dave. Up to the very last day, she was just there for
him. Her comment would be, 'Willie, I have loved Coach all my life.'

"I was down there about six months before he passed away," Davis
said. "He was in this assisted living home in Ruston. I went there just to see
him. He would always manage to kid me about recruiting me, and the situation with my mother. 'Ah, Big Dave, I knew what to say, huh?' That was
one of the toughest days ever for me. One minute we're talking about events
like that, and the next minute he's in tears and he's asking, 'Who are you?'
I walked out of there, and I had such a heavy heart. As I flew back to California, that's all I could think of."

Eddie was taken by ambulance to Lincoln General Hospital in Ruston on Tuesday afternoon, April 3, 2007. He died about 11 p.m. that night.

"We used to call him the Wizard," Doug Williams reflected, two years
after Eddie's passing. "You just had to see the vision of Coach Rob coming
down to the practice field with that briefcase in his hand. Everybody used
to say, 'Here comes the Wizard.' It could be raining cats and three dogs, and
we'd all be sitting in the dressing room, hoping that it would just rain all

day. And he'd come around that curve and say, 'Hell, Cat, what're you all sitting in here for? Hell, let's go.' And, I'll be damned – you walk out there and it ain't raining no more.' That's why we called him the Wizard. It was unbelievable.

"He used to tell us all the time, old coaches don't die, they fade away," Williams said. "And when Coach passed away, you're sitting there when it first happened, April 3rd, and you're saying, 'Coach Rob can't die. The Wizard can't die.'"

Requiem

BEFORE EDDIE'S death in April 2007, only five citizens of Louisiana had ever been accorded the honor of lying in State at the Capitol in Baton Rouge upon their passing. He had participated in the first of those when, as a 16-old, he went with Doris to pay their respects to former governor and U.S. Senator Huey Long after The Kingfish was shot to death in 1935. Seventy-two years later, the appreciation and admiration for Eddie was so widespread that he became the sixth person to merit public visitation. An estimated 6,000 Louisianians, whites as well as blacks, whose lives had in some way been positively influenced by Eddie's words, deeds and example, said their silent good-byes and offered private prayers.

In a state that practiced racial discrimination and Jim Crow segregation for more than half his life, Eddie became the second African American to lie in repose at the seat of its government. The first was A. Z. Young, head of the Bogalusa Civic and Voters League, who endured frequent violence in the Bogalusa area while leading marches and demonstrations for fair employment opportunities and voter rights between 1965 and 1967. The 10-day march he led from Bogalusa to Baton Rouge in 1967 is overshadowed in histories of the Civil Rights Movement in the South by events in Selma two years earlier, yet the dangers Young and his followers faced, and the courage they exhibited, was no less. To be accorded equal recognition with a civil rights leader of Young's stature is further validation of Eddie's emphasis on preparing his players to excel when the doors of opportunity swung open rather than joining in the agitation to open them.

"Whether you walked with him in the journey toward equality, or were born into a generation benefiting from his work, you share in the legacy of this great Louisianian," Governor Kathleen Blanco said during an evening memorial held in the House of Representatives chamber. "When he took the reins at Grambling, segregation was still the law in Louisiana. But even that could not stop his determination and belief that in America, anyone could succeed. Over the years Coach Rob leveled the playing field both in football and in life for all of us. With that bright smile and that soft-spoken voice he always said, 'In America, anything is possible. Anything.' Coach Rob loved America. He was a true patriot."

Hundreds of former Grambling football players, from virtually every decade in which Eddie coached, lined the legislative chamber on three sides during a private memorial service. Willie Davis, Charlie Joiner, Willie Brown, Tank Smith, Jim Gregory – they were all there; Adolph Byrd, too, with his daughter Yvonne, and, of course, Shack Harris and Doug Williams. Marino Casem was in the crowd, and Dave Whinham. At one point a football was handed to a player near Eddie's casket. The ball was passed around the room, from player to player, until the hands of every one present who had played for Coach Rob had touched it. Doug Williams was the last player to receive the football. "I don't know who thought of it," he said later. "The players didn't know about it in advance." Doug gripped it and held it up for all to see, then gave it to Doris. Silently, she placed it in the casket next to her husband's body.

"The event in the Statehouse in Baton Rouge was a beautiful and extremely dignified event," said Dave Whinham, "really emblematic of the type of honor that should be received by a great American. And, really, that's what Coach Rob was. In the end, I think that would be at least among the titles of which he would be most proud – that he truly was a great American, and a statesman for our country, representing only the best of what our country has to offer."

Raymond Jetson, a former state legislator who played for Grambling in the 1970s, offered perhaps the best summation of Eddie's life. "Coach" described him but did not define him, Jetson said. "In the aftermath of his death, a lot of attention will be devoted to all the players he sent to the NFL. That's not his legacy. It's the thousands of young men who went to Grambling with no hope of having a life in the NFL. His legacy is the thousands of men who are good fathers and good husbands, good businessmen, good employees and community leaders."

Eddie's funeral was the first event held at the new Assembly Center on Grambling's campus, a perfectly appropriate though unplanned opening. Attendance was estimated at 6,000, including the Rev. Jesse Jackson, who related Eddie's success overcoming racial obstacles to the deeds of figures ranging from Biblical times to the civil rights era, and a representative of George Steinbrenner, who was unable to attend. The Grambling marching band performed, and blues singer Mary Griffin, a native Louisianian who attended Grambling, returned to the musical roots of her father's country church, singing *His Eye Is On The Sparrow,* a spiritual whose chorus goes:

> *"I sing because I'm happy,*
> *"I sing because I'm free;*
> *"For His eye is on the sparrow,*
> *"And I know He watches me . . ."*

The service concluded with Eddie's great-grandson, Eddie Robinson IV, re-enacting one of his great-grandfather's most storied traditions – ringing the trademark cowbell to rouse his players for class. To most, it symbolized Eddie's arrival in a better place.

Acknowledgments

Curiosity led me to this biography. In a 43-year newspaper career I met countless famous and fascinating people. I once interviewed John Wooden, the greatest college basketball coach of all time, while sitting on the edge of the bed in his hotel room; former heavyweight boxing champion Joe Frazier in the back seat of a rushing taxicab; and legendary football coach Paul Brown on a bench outside his motel room in Jackson, Mississippi, before a preseason game there in 1969. I've endured Pete Rose's cockiness, Frank Robinson's glare, and Woody Hayes' ego, among many stars and their trademark features.

But I never met Eddie Robinson. When the biggest name in the history of black college football died, I wanted to know more about him. I looked for a biography, and found there was none. Thus began this exploration of his life in the context of our society's most important period of growth in history. I am indebted to so many individuals for their generous assistance that I worry I will unintentionally omit someone who deserves inclusion in this roll of thanks. Only they will know, if it happens, and to them I offer sincere apologies along with my gratitude.

When I began, I asked Rusty Hampton, sports editor at *The Clarion-Ledger* in Jackson, Mississippi, if he could help me reach W. C. Gorden, whose quote shaped the title and approach of this book. Along with Coach Gorden's home phone number, Rusty told me: "Be prepared to interview one of the nicest men ever – especially in the former football coach category." W.C. Gorden proved to be not only a wealth of information and insight into Eddie Robinson, but also an inspiration whose enthusiasm for this project sustained me throughout. And, yes, I found him to be just as Rusty Hampton predicted. Rusty's help didn't stop there. He and *Clarion-Ledger* columnist Rick Cleveland were instrumental in arranging for me to have access to the microfilm library of *The Clarion-Ledger* and *Jackson Daily News* for research about the historic game between Grambling and Jackson State at Mississippi Veterans Memorial Stadium in 1967. Thanks to them, I discovered the incredible coincidence of the timing of the verdicts in the federal trial of the murdered civil rights workers.

As so many others, I had heard the term "Jim Crow" and knew that it stood for oppressive segregation. But I didn't know the origin of the name or its relationship to the way of life it represented in the Deep South for decades. Dr. David Pilgrim, founder and curator of the Jim Crow Museum of Racist Memorabilia, a teaching lab at Ferris State University in Big Rapids, Michigan, allowed me unlimited time to examine the disturbing 5,000-piece collection of racist artifacts that he has assembled. Dr. Pilgrim, who is Ferris State's chief diversity officer, as well, also generously shared his knowledge and perspectives on racism, the Jim Crow era, and Dr. Martin Luther King and the Civil Rights Movement in an interview that he willingly allowed to exceed its scheduled length. Thereafter, he was responsive to every request for guidance or assistance of any kind. His willingness to help educate an inquisitive visitor was invaluable. It is Dr. Pilgrim's dream to establish a Jim Crow Museum that is open to the public, a project well worth the financial support of all who can afford to help. Thanks, also, to Patty Terryn and Patty Gould at Ferris State for their professional and reliable assistance.

Eddie Robinson's life story could not have been told in vivid detail without the honest, open accounts provided by his former players and coaching colleagues who trusted a stranger enough to discuss often sensitive and personal experiences and feelings. Everyone should have a friend as loyal and true as Marino Casem, who would have done anything for Eddie – and anything to beat him, too. Doug Porter, meanwhile, could qualify as historian for the period he spent with Eddie. The admiration his former players expressed for him might have embarrassed Eddie at times, yet unquestionably he would be proud of the men they became – class acts, all. Indeed, Coach Rob's former players, who exemplify the personal and professional qualities he tried so hard to instill in them, offer the best proof of his far-reaching influence. Willie Davis, Doug Williams, Willie Brown, Charlie Joiner, Nemiah Wilson, Goldie Sellers (and his wife, Peaches), A.C. O'Dell, basketball star Bob Hopkins, Jim Gregory – "Grambling's White Tiger" – and his buddy Charles "Tank" Smith were without exception gracious and totally accommodating. In some cases, they provided contact information for others or arranged the first call. The National Football League alumni organization also was instrumental in the same way – thank you, Jaime Gruber in Fort Lauderdale and Leroy Mitchell in Denver. Special thanks to Nemiah Wilson, who told me about Adolph Byrd and how to find him; and to Adolph and his daughter Yvonne, who welcomed me into his home and put no time limit on our interview. What a remarkable man.

Grant Teaff, executive director of the American Football Coaches Association, and several members of his staff were helpful in numerous ways, numerous times, from providing copies of publications that document Eddie's participation in the organization, including his year as president, and the awards presented to him, to making available photos that document some of Eddie's greatest honors and achievements. Besides Grant himself, I thank Tai Brown, Janet Robertson and Amy Miller for their continued pleasant responsiveness. The AFCA, through them, made this an infinitely richer account. Steve Richardson, executive director of the Football Writers Association of America, couldn't have been more helpful, as well. In addition to recounting events that led to the establishment of the FWAA's Eddie Robinson Coach of the Year Award, Steve also made me aware of Jean Roe Freeling, and led me to R.L. Stockard. R.L.'s rich recollections of life as young black man in the South, his personal reflections on Eddie and his perspective on the Grambling-Southern rivalry all added depth to this effort. Jean Freeling is another who trusted a stranger enough to openly relate her experiences as a student living in the Robinson home. She couldn't have been more gracious. Thank you to all seems insufficient.

Reconciling the high-risk actions of those at the forefront of the Civil Rights Movement in the South with Eddie's unique, measured approach to achieving social progress was critical to the credibility of this book. Congressman John Lewis, who endured more than forty arrests, physical attacks and injuries as a leader of nonviolent direct action during the decisive years of the Movement, was on the floor of the House of Representatives when the scheduled time for his telephone interview with me passed. He considered it important enough that he returned the call immediately upon returning to his office. Beyond gratitude, he deserves respect and admiration for a life of contribution to social progress.

If anyone had reason to be wary of an unexpected phone call from a total stranger, it was Dr. Raymond Hicks, the man who, as president of Grambling State University, will forever be linked to Coach Eddie Robinson's unpleasant departure from that institution. A journalist has no greater respect or appreciation than for the person who does not hide or dodge hard questions or the uncomfortable inquiry. In this case it resulted in a revealing behind-the-scenes look at what actually happened leading up to Eddie's reluctant retirement. A bonus was Dr. Hicks' vivid memory of the student protest on the Grambling campus during his undergraduate senior year.

Acknowledging with detail everyone who contributed to this biography would make a small book in itself. In the interest of some degree of restraint, therefore, sincere thanks go to: Dave Whinham, whose help goes beyond a terrific interview; former U.S. Secretary of Education Rod Paige, for his vivid recollections and insights into Eddie from his previous life in coaching, and Katie Warren of Chartwell Education Group, who set up my interview with Dr. Paige; McKinley High School Alumni Center executive director Eddie Johnson; Thelma Smith-Williams, Sheree Rabon, Claude Lamar Aker, John Williams, Ernie Miles, Luther Ensley, Wilbert Ellis, Doug Ireland, Sailor Jackson, O.K. "Buddy" Davis, and Tom Kelly, for their interviews and the perspectives they provided; Pam Mitchell-Wagner of the Louisiana Press Association; Jason Wahlers of the Tampa Bay Buccaneers; Mike Taylor of the

Oakland Raiders; Jon Kendle of the Pro Football Hall of Fame; Kent Stephens of the College Football Hall of Fame; Jim Hendrickson of the Jackson (Louisiana) Historic District Commission; Sharon Peterson of Southern University; Danelle Gilkes of the Louisiana Workforce Commission; intellectual property manager Sandra Aya Enimil of the *Chicago Defender;* Eric Gaines of *The Pittsburgh Courier;* Dave Plati of the University of Colorado; research librarians at the State Library of Louisiana in Baton Rouge, the Denver Public Library, and Koelbel Public Library in Arapahoe County, Colorado; and former colleagues Jim Delaney, Leslie Juniel, B.G. Brooks and, last but far from least, Mike Madigan, who suggested including maps in the presentation and made numerous other contributions.

Any book ultimately is only as good as the people who work behind the scenes. In my case, Diane Hartman deserves highest praise. A good editor distinguishes between making something different and making it better. Diane's suggestions improved the narrative in subtle but significant ways. She became as invested in the writing and storytelling as the author himself, yet never usurped the writer's creative role. The book is a reflection on her tenacity for facts, supportable conclusions and proper perspective. Scott Johnson's care and talent are displayed in the graphic design of the entire book, front cover to back. Judy Joseph is like automatic pilot when it comes to pulling everything together on behalf of Paros Press, her company.

Finally, my "Doris" (for forty-three years and counting) is named Melanie. She believed in this book from the idea stage, and offered enthusiastic support and encouragement throughout my travels and long hours in a home office that became increasingly cluttered. She has read the entire manuscript more than once, some parts three or four times, and her input challenged me to fill holes and improve the writing. Beyond that, she is what Grant Teaff said Doris was to Eddie. She is my "heart and soul." Our daughter Melissa, her husband Brent and their two fabulous daughters, Erika and Rachel, are constant inspiration. As Eddie was proud of his family, equally so am I of them.

Appendix

LOCATOR MAPS

EDDIE ROBINSON'S
COACHING CAREER

EDDIE'S PROS

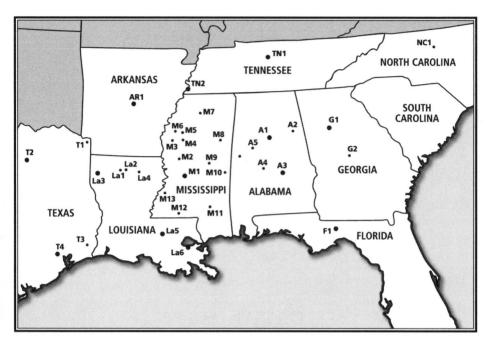

Alabama

A1   Birmingham
A2   Anniston (Freedom Ride attack, 1961)
A3   Montgomery (Rosa Parks, 1955)
A4   Selma (Bloody Sunday, 1965)
A5   Tuscaloosa
A6   Gainesville (Buck Buchanan)

Arkansas

AR1   Little Rock (Central High School, 1957)

Florida

F1   Tallahassee (Florida A&M Univ.)

Georgia

G1   Atlanta (Ebenezer Baptist Church)
G2   Macon (Jim Parker)

Louisiana

La1   Grambling
La2   Ruston
La3   Shreveport
La4   Monroe
La5   Baton Rouge
La6   New Orleans

North Carolina

NC1   Greensboro (lunch counter sit-in, 1960)

Mississippi

M1   Jackson
M2   Yazoo City (Willie Brown, Ben Williams)
M3   Indianola (White Citizens' Councils, 1954)
M4   Itta Bena (Mississippi Valley State)
M5   Money (Emmett Till)
M6   Ruleville (Fanny Lou Hamer)
M7   Oxford (James Meredith, Univ. of Mississippi riot, 1962)
M8   Starkville (Mississippi State Univ.)
M9   Philadelphia (Schwerner, Goodman & Chaney, 1964)
M10   Meridian
M11   Hattiesburg (Southern Mississippi Univ.)
M12   Magnolia (W.C. Gorden voter registration, 1960-62)
M13   Lorman (Alcorn State Univ.)

Tennessee

TN1   Nashville (SNCC formation, 1959)
TN2   Memphis (MLK assassination, 1968)

Texas

T1   Texarkana (Willie Davis)
T2   Dallas (Jerry LeVias, 1965)
T3   Beaumont (Bubba Smith)
T4   Houston

L1   Grambling
L2   Ruston
L3   Shreveport
L4   Homer (Sen. Willie Rainach)
L5   Monroe
L6   Tallulah
L7   Jonesboro (Robert Hopkins)
L8   Dodson (Tom Kelly)
L9   Winnfield (Collie Nicholson)
L10 Natchitoches (Louisiana Sports Hall of Fame)

L11 Lake Charles (Charlie Joiner)
L12 Jackson (Eddie's birthplace)
L13 Port Hudson Civil War battlefield
L14 Zachary (Doug Williams)
L15 Baker (Leland College)
L16 Baton Rouge
L17 Bogalusa (A. Z. Young)
L18 New Orleans (Bayou Classic)

Eddie Robinson's Coaching Career, Season by Season

YEAR	WON	LOST	TIED	SEASONS	CUMULATIVE WON	LOST	TIED
1941	3	5	0	1	3	5	0
1942	9	0	0	2	12	5	0
NO TEAM—WORLD WAR II							
1945	10	2	0	3	22	7	0
1946	6	6	0	4	28	13	0
1947	9	2	0	5	37	15	0
1948	8	3	0	6	45	18	0
1949	7	3	2	7	52	21	2
1950	5	3	1	8	57	24	3
1951	3	5	1	9	60	29	4
1952	7	3	1	10	67	32	5
1953	8	2	0	11	75	34	5
1954	4	3	2	12	79	37	7
1955	10	0	0	13	89	37	7
1956	8	1	0	14	97	38	7
1957	4	4	0	15	101	42	7
1958	6	3	0	16	107	45	7
1959	4	6	0	17	111	51	7
1960	9	1	0	18	120	52	7
1961	8	2	0	19	128	54	7
1962	6	2	2	20	134	56	9
1963	5	3	1	21	139	59	10
1964	9	2	0	22	148	61	10
1965	8	3	0	23	156	64	10
1966	6	2	1	24	162	66	11
1967	9	1	0	25	171	67	11
1968	9	2	0	26	180	69	11
1969	6	4	0	27	186	73	11

YEAR	WON	LOST	TIED	SEASONS	CUMULATIVE WON	LOST	TIED
1970	9	2	0	28	195	75	11
1971	9	2	0	29	204	77	11
1972	11	2	0	30	215	79	11
1973	10	3	0	31	225	82	11
1974	11	1	0	32	236	83	11
1975	10	1	0	33	246	84	11
1976	8	3	0	34	254	87	11
1977	10	1	0	35	264	88	11
1978	9	1	1	36	273	89	12
1979	8	3	0	37	281	92	12
1980	10	2	0	38	291	94	12
1981	6	4	1	39	297	98	13
1982	8	3	0	40	305	101	13
1983	8	1	2	41	313	102	15
1984	7	4	0	42	320	106	15
1985	9	3	0	43	329	109	15
1986	7	4	0	44	336	113	15
1987	5	6	0	45	341	119	15
1988	8	3	0	46	349	122	15
1989	9	3	0	47	358	125	15
1990	8	3	0	48	366	128	15
1991	5	6	0	49	371	134	15
1992	10	2	0	50	381	136	15
1993	7	4	0	51	388	140	15
1994	9	3	0	52	397	143	15
1995	5	6	0	53	402	149	15
1996	3	8	0	54	405	157	15
1997	3	8	0	55	408	165	15

Eddie Robinson's Coaching Career, by the Decade

Decade	W	L	T	Titles	Pro Draft Choices
1940s	52	21	2		0
1950s	59	30	5	1 National, 1 Midwest Conf.	3
1960s	75	22	4	1 National, 5 SWAC	31
1970s	95	19	1	4 National, 8 SWAC	45
1980s	77	33	3	2 National, 3 SWAC	18
1990s	50	40	0	1 National, 1 SWAC	13
TOTALS	408	165	15	9 National, 17 SWAC	110

NOTES:

Titles includes championships won outright and shared.

More than 200 Grambling players appeared on the rosters of pro football teams during Eddie Robinson's tenure. Many signed as free agents and enjoyed notable careers, among them Tank Younger, Pro Football Hall of Famer Willie Brown, Nemiah Wilson, Everson Walls and Charles "Tank"Smith.

Eddie Robinson's Coaching Career, in The Bayou Classic

GRAMBLING VS. SOUTHERN

YEAR	RESULT	SCORE	ATTENDANCE	SERIES RECORD
1974	Won	21-0	76,753	1-0
1975	Won	33-17	73,214	2-0
1976	Won	10-2	76,188	3-0
1977	Won	55-20	68,518	4-0
1978	Won	28-15	72,000	5-0
1979	Lost	14-7	67,500	5-1
1980	Won	43-6	75,000	6-1
1981	Lost	50-20	67,500	6-2
1982	Lost	22-17	71,555	6-3
1983	Won	24-10	58,199	7-3
1984	Won	31-29	51,752	8-3
1985	Won	29-12	57,041	9-3
1986	Won	30-3	58,960	10-3
1987	Lost	27-21	55,783	10-4
1988	Lost	10-3	55,450	10-5
1989	Won	44-30	64,333	11-5
1990	Won	25-13	70,600	12-5
1991	Lost	31-30	62,891	12-6
1992	Won	30-27	71,282	13-6
1993	Lost	31-13	72,586	13-7
1994	Lost	34-7	66,641	13-8
1995	Lost	30-14	67,361	13-9
1996	Lost	17-12	71,586	13-10
1997	Lost	30-7	64,500	13-11

TOTAL ATTENDANCE FOR 24 GAMES: 1,597,193

Eddie's Pros

Grambling players selected in the National Football League college draft (and in the American Football League draft prior to the merger of the leagues).

PLAYER	YEAR	ROUND	TEAM	POSITION	YEARS
Bob Carter	1955	19	Green Bay	OT	†
Willie Davis	1956	15	Cleveland	OT-DE	12
Al Richardson	1957	26	Philadelphia	DE	1
Gehrig Harris	1957	26	Chicago	RB	†
Ronnie Mushat	1958	19	San Francisco	C	†
Jamie Caleb	1959	16	Cleveland	RB	3
Ernie Ladd	1961	15 4	San Diego (AFL) Chicago (NFL)	DT	8
Preston Powell	1961	7 15	Cleveland (NFL) Oakland (AFL)	FB	1
Jerry Robinson	1962	8 11	San Diego (AFL) Chicago (NFL)	WR	4
Clifton McNeil	1962	11	Cleveland	WB	10
Buck Buchanan	1963	1 19	Kansas City (AFL) New York (NFL)	DT	13
Lane Howell	1963	15	New York (NFL)	T	7
J.D. Garrett	1964	8 18	Boston (AFL) New York (NFL)	RB	4
Bob Burton	1963	24	Houston	T	†
Stone Johnson	1963	14	Kansas City	RB	†
Jim Griffin	1964	15	San Francisco	DE	3
Willie Williams	1965	8	New York Giants	DB	9
Mike Howell	1965	8 15	Cleveland (NFL) San Diego (AFL)	QB (DB)	8
Alphonse Dotson	1965	2	Green Bay	DT	5
Frank Cornish	1965	11	Chicago Bears	DT	7
Goldie Sellers	1966	8 20	Denver (AFL) Chicago (NFL)	DB	4
Henry Dyer	1966	4	Los Angeles	RB	4
Leroy Carter	1966	7	Cleveland	WR	†
Charley Washington	1966	11	Pittsburgh	RB	†
Norman Davis	1967	3	Baltimore	G	3
Julian Gray	1967	4	New York Jets	DB	†
Louis Jackson	1967	5	New York Jets	DB	†
Dick Stebbins	1967	10	New York Giants	E	†
Bob Atkins	1968	2	St. Louis Cardinals	DB	9
Essex Johnson	1968	6	Cincinnati	RB	9

Player	Year	Round	Team	Position	Years
Wes Bean	1968	7	Cincinnati	LB	†
Henry Davis	1968	11	New York Giants	LB	6
Harold Jones	1968	12	Cincinnati	OT	†
Charlie Joiner	1969	4	Houston	DB-WR	18
James Harris	1969	8	Buffalo	QB	10
Henry Jones	1969	9	Denver	RB	1
Ed Watson	1969	9	Houston	LB	1
Hilton Crawford	1969	9	San Francisco	DB	1
Richard Lee	1969	12	Boston	DT	†
Roger Williams	1969	13	Los Angeles	DB	2
George Muse	1969	17	Boston	LB	†
Glenn Alexander	1970	3	Buffalo	WR	1
Delles Howell	1970	4	New Orleans	DB	6
Billy Newsome	1970	5	Baltimore	DE	8
Terry Williams	1970	11	Buffalo	RB	†
Samuel Wallace	1970	11	Cincinnati	LB	†
Bill O'Neal	1970	11	Kansas City	RB	†
Robert Jones	1970	12	Philadelphia	DT	†
Cliff Gaspar	1970	16	New Orleans	DT	†
Walter Breaux	1970	17	New York Giants	DT	†
Richard Harris	1971	1	Philadelphia	DE	7
Frank Lewis	1971	1	Pittsburgh	WR	13
Sam Holden	1971	2	New Orleans	T	1
Scott Lewis	1971	2	Kansas City	DE	†
Virgil Robinson	1971	2	Green Bay	RB	2
Joe Carter	1971	4	Dallas	TE	†
Willie Armstrong	1971	5	Houston	RB	†
Coleman Zeno	1971	17	New York Giants	WR	1
John Mendenhall	1972	3	New York Giants	DT	9
Solomon Freelon	1972	3	Houston	G	3
Andrew Howard	1972	4	Atlanta	DT	†
Jack Phillips	1972	11	Atlanta	WR	†
Lee Fobbs	1973	8	Buffalo	RB	†
Matthew Reed	1973	10	Buffalo	QB	5**
Walt Baisy	1973	15	Dallas	LB	†
John Billizon	1973	17	New York Giants	DE	†
Charles Battle	1974	5	New England	LB	†
Bill Bryant	1974	6	Cincinnati	DB	3
Ezil Bibbs	1974	8	New York Giants	DE	†
Oliver Alexander	1974	15	Chicago	TE	†
Gary Johnson	1975	1	San Diego	DT	11
Bob Barber	1975	2	Pittsburgh	DE	4
Jesse O'Neal	1975	6	Houston	DE	†

Player	Year	Round	Team	Position	Years
James Hunter	1976	1	Detroit	DB	7
Sammy White	1976	2	Minnesota	WR	10
Mike St. Clair	1976	4	Cleveland	DE	8*
Ron Singleton	1976	4	San Diego	TE	5
Dwight Scales	1976	5	Los Angeles	WR	8
Robert Pennywell	1976	6	San Francisco	LB	5*
Bobby Simon	1976	8	Houston	T	†
Art Gilliam	1976	10	Denver	DE	†
Doug Williams	1978	1	Tampa Bay	QB	11*
Carlos Pennywell	1978	3	New England	WR	4
Robert Woods	1978	5	Kansas City	WR	2
Bruce Radford	1979	3	Denver	NT-DE	3
Charles Johnson	1979	4	Atlanta	DB	3
Mike Smith	1980	7	Atlanta	WR	1
Joe Gordon	1980	11	Buffalo	DT	†
Mike Barker	1981	10	New York Giants	DT	†
Robert Parham	1981	10	San Diego	RB	†
Arthur King	1982	6	Cincinnati	DT	†
Albert Lewis	1983	3	Kansas City	DB	16
Rufus Stevens	1984	6	Kansas City	WR	†
Robert Smith	1984	2-S	Minnesota	DE	2*
Leonard Griffin	1986	3	Kansas City	DE	8
Sean Smith	1987	4	Chicago	DE	3
Anthony Anderson	1987	10	San Diego	DB	1
Patrick Scott	1987	11	Green Bay	WR	2
Arthur Wells	1987	11	New Orleans	TE	1
Calvin Nicholas	1987	11	San Francisco	WR	1
Curtis Maxey	1988	8	Cincinnati	DE	2
Johnny Carter	1988	12	Denver	DT	†
Bryan Tobey	1989	8	Kansas City	RB	†
Fred Jones	1990	4	Kansas City	WR	4
Clemente Gordon	1990	11	Cleveland	QB	†
Jake Reed	1991	3	Minnesota	WR	12
Walter Dean	1991	6	Green Bay	RB	1
Franklin Thomas	1991	7	Detroit	TE	†
Darryl Milburn	1991	9	Detroit	DE	1
Andrew Glover	1991	10	Los Angeles Raiders	TE	10
Nate Singleton	1992	11	New York Giants	WR	5
Herman Arvie	1993	5	Cleveland	T	4
Stevie Anderson	1993	8	Phoenix	WR	3
Tracy Greene	1994	7	Kansas City	TE	2
Roderick Mullen	1995	5	New York Giants	DB	4
Curtis Ceaser	1995	7	New York Jets	WR	1

Grambling players with NFL service who were signed as free agents (FA)

PLAYER	YEAR	ROUND	TEAM	POSITION	YEARS
Tank Younger	1949	FA	Los Angeles	RB	10
Roosevelt Taylor	1961	FA	Chicago	DB	12
Garland Boyette	1962	FA	St. Louis Cardinals	LB	9
Willie Brown	1963	FA	Denver	DB	16
Leon Simmons	1963	FA	Denver	LB	1
Nemiah Wilson	1965	FA	Denver	DB	11
Sammie Taylor	1965	FA	San Diego	WR	1
Willie Young	1966	FA	New York Giants	OT	10
Woody Peoples	1968	FA	San Francisco	G	12
Al Dennis	1973	FA	San Diego	G	3
Charles Smith	1974	FA	Philadelphia	WR	8
Vernon Roberson	1977	FA	Miami	DB	1
Greg Fields	1979	FA	Baltimore	DE	4*
Everson Walls	1981	FA	Dallas	DB	13
Guy Prather	1981	FA	Green Bay	LB	5
Kerry Parker	1984	FA	Kansas City	DB	2
Joe Williams	1987	FA	Pittsburgh	LB	1
Ed Scott	1987	FA	St. Louis Cardinals	DB	2*
Marvin Ayers	1987	FA	Philadelphia	DE	1
Bennie Thompson	1989	FA	New Orleans	DB	11
Michael Harris	1989	FA	Kansas City	C-G	1
Derrick Ned	1993	FA	New Orleans	FB	3
Michael Samson	1996	FA	Philadelphia	DT	1
Jason Bratton	1996	FA	Buffalo	RB	1
Albert Reese	1997	FA	San Francisco	DT	1

Grambling players who played professional football in the United States Football League (USFL):

PLAYER	YEAR	ROUND	TEAM	POSITION	YEARS
Trumaine Johnson	1983		Chicago	WR	2
	1985	NFL	San Diego/Buffalo	WR	4
Sylveser Moy	1983		Birmingham	G	1
Troy Thomas	1983		Chicago	OT	1
Robert Barber	1983		Washington	DE	1
Jerry Gordon	1984		San Aantonio	WR	2
Reggie Irving	1985		Oakland	G	1

"Years" may reflect time with more than one team.

 * – Includes USFL service following NFL years.

** – 2 years World Football League, 3 years Canadian Football League; no NFL.

 † – Drafted, but no regular season service recorded.

References and Sources

MUSEUMS

College Football Hall of Fame, South Bend, Indiana

Jim Crow Museum of Racist Memorabilia, Ferris State University, Big Rapids, Michigan

McKinley High School Alumni Center, Baton Rouge, Louisiana

National Civil Rights Museum at The Lorraine Motel, Memphis, Tennessee

Pro Football Hall of Fame, Canton, Ohio

BOOKS

Bahrenburg, Bruce. *My Little Brother's Coming Tomorrow*. G.P. Putnam's Sons, 1971.

Carson, Clayborne and Charless R. Branham, Ralph David Fertig, Mark Bauerlein, Tod Steven Burroughs, Ella Forbes, Jim Haskins, Paul Lee, Howard Lindsey, Jerald E. Podair and Jo Ellen Warner. *Civil Rights Chronicle – The African-American Struggle for Freedom*. Legacy Publishing, Publications International, Ltd., 2003.

Cosell, Howard, with the editorial assistance of Mickey Herskowitz. *Cosell By Cosell*. Playboy Press, 1973.

Davis, O.K. *Grambling's Gridiron Glory*. 1982.

Dunnavant, Keith. *The Missing Ring –How Bear Bryant and the 1966 Alabama Crimson Tide Were Denied College Football's Most Elusive Prize*. St. Martin's Press, 2006.

Fairclough, Adam. *Race & Democracy –The Civil Rights Struggle in Louisiana 1915-1972*. University of Georgia Press, 1995.

Frady, Marshall. *Martin Luther King, Jr. – a life*. Penguin Group, 2002.

Halberstam, David. *The Children*. Random House, 1998.

Hansen, Drew D. *The Dream: Martin Luther King, Jr. and the Speech that Inspired a Nation*. HarperCollins, 2003.

Howell, Michael F. *Journey to War's Eve – An Antebellum History of Jackson, Louisiana.* Lockridge Cottage, 2004.

Hurd, Michael. *"Collie J" Grambling's Man with the Golden Pen.* St. Johann Press, 2007.

Lee, Aaron S. *Quotable Eddie Robinson.* TowleHouse Publishing, 2003.

Lewis, John with Michael D'Orso. *Walking with the Wind – A Memoir of the Movement.* Harcourt Brace, 1998.

McMillen, Neil R. *The Citizens' Council: Organized Resistance to the Second Reconstruction, 1954-64.* University of Illinois Press, 1971.

Montville, Leigh. *The Big Bam –The Life and Times of Babe Ruth.* Doubleday, 2006.

Rampersad, Arnold. *Jackie Robinson. A Biography.* Knopf. 1997.

Roberts, Gene and Hank Klibanoff. *The Race Beat – The Press, The Civil Rights Struggle and The Awakening of a Nation.* Alfred A. Knopf, 2006.

Robinson, Eddie with Richard Lapchick. *Never Before, Never Again – The Stirring Autobiography of Eddie Robinson.* St. Martin's Press, 1999.

Sitkoff, Harvard. *King: Pilgrimage To The Mountaintop.* Hill and Wang, 2008.

Staff of the Rocky Mountain News. *Orange Encore – The 1987 Broncos' AFC Championship Season.* Denver Publishing Company, 1988.

The Jackson Assembly, Jackson, East Feliciana Parish, Louisiana. *Yesterday, Today and Tomorrow.* Year unknown.

Wall, Bennett H. and Light Townsend Cummins, Judith Kelleher Schafer, Edward F. Haas and Michael L. Kurtz. *Louisiana – A History.* Harlan Davidson, Inc., 2008.

Wash, A. and P. Webb, eds. *Reflections of a Legend: Coach Eddie Robinson.* Box Square Entertainment, 1997.

Weinstein, Allen and David Rubel. *Story of America – Freedom and Crisis from Settlement to Superpower.* DK Publishing, Inc., 2002.

Williams, Doug with Bruce Hunter. *QuarterBLACK – Shattering the NFL Myth.* Bonus Books, Inc., 1990.

Wilson, Martha (class historian) and members of the senior class. *The Panther,* school yearbook. McKinley Senior High School, 1928.

VIDEO

Breaking The Huddle: The Integration of College Football. HBO Sports of the 20th Century, 2009.

Every Man A Tiger: The Eddie G. Robinson Story. NBC Universal, Inc., 2007.

Grambling's White Tiger. Georg Stanford Brown, director, and Bruce Jenner, producer. Universal, 1981.

Grambling College: 100 Yards To Glory. Howard Cosell, producer, and Jerry Izenberg, director. American Broadcasting Co., 1967.

I-Team: Eddie Robinson Foundation Story, Dale Russell, reporter. Fox 5, WAGA, Atlanta. February, 2007.

Mississippi Burning. Alan Parker, director, and Robert F. Colesberry and Frederick Zollo, producers. Orion Pictures, 1988.

Run That By Me Again: 1973 Grantland Rice Bowl. Kenny Wolin host. Kentucky Educational Television, 1977.

The Black Press: Soldiers Without Swords. Stanely Nelson, producer. California Newsreel, 1998.

DOCUMENTS

Stories and columns dealing with the life, career, retirement and passing of Eddie Robinson published in the *Ruston Daily Leader, Monroe News-Star, Baton Rouge Advocate, The New York Times, New York Daily News, Milwaukee Journal Sentinel, The Washington Post, The Cincinnati Enquirer, The Los Angeles Times, USA Today, The Gramblinite, Sports Illustrated* and *Southern Magazine,* and posted on *ESPN.com* were helpful references in the creation of an Eddie Robinson timeline of significant events and periods. The following documents also were sources of facts and, in many instances, quotations.

Acceptance speech by Eddie Robinson upon receiving Tuss McLaughry Award. American Football Coaches Association Convention Proceedings Manual. 1996.

American Football Coaches Association 2008 Media Guide

Articles including excerpts "Courtesy of the *Chicago Defender,*" from the *Defender* archives. Jan. 1, 1905-Dec. 31, 1995.

CoSIDA Trailblazer Award announcement. College Sports Information Directors of America. 2002.

Civil Rights Address to the citizens of the United State of America by resident John F. Kennedy, June 11, 1963

Eddie Robinson Receives 1981 Stagg Award. American Football Coaches Association Convention Proceedings Manual. 1982.

Eddie Robinson Named Tuss McLaughry Award Winner. American Football Coaches Association newsletter, *The Extra Point.* November-December, 1995.

Grambling College: Where Stars Are Made, LOOK Magazine, Vol. 33, No. 25, December 16, 1969

It's Eddie: Robinson New FWAA Coach of Year Namesake. Article in the September-October, 1997, issue of *The Fifth Down,* newsletter of the Football Writers Association of America.

Letter from a Birmingham Jail by Dr. Martin Luther King Jr., April 16, 1963

Letter to the editor of *The Pittsburgh Courier* written by James G. Thompson of Wichita, Kansas, first published January 31, 1942, reprinted "Courtesy of *The Pittsburgh Courier.*"

Master Coach Seminar Program with Eddie Robinson and Darrell Royal. American Football Coaches Association Convention Proceedings Manual. 1995.

Microfilmed pages from the *Jackson Daily News* and *The Clarion–Ledger*, October 16-22, 1967

Petition for Preliminary and Permanent Injunctive Relief and For Declaratory Judgment, Eddie Robinson and Doris Robinson vs. Eddie Robinson Foundation. Third Judicial District Court, Parish of Lincoln, State of Louisiana. September 5, 2006.

Port Hudson State Historic Site brochure, State of Louisiana Department of Culture, Recreation and Tourism.

President's Column by Blair Kerkhoff. September-October, 1997, issue of *The Fifth Down*, newsletter of the Football Writers Association of America.

Radio and Television Remarks Upon Signing the Civil Rights Bill by President Lyndon B. Johnson, July 2, 1964

Remarks at the AFCA Annual Luncheon by President Eddie Robinson, Toastmaster. American Football Coaches Association Convention Proceedings Manual. 1977.

Solicitation letter. Michael Robinson Watkins, Chairman and CEO, The Eddie Robinson Foundation. 2002.

Southwestern Athletic Conference Eddie Robinson tribute brochure, 1997

Testimony of Fannie Lou Hamer to Credentials Committee of the Democratic National Convention, July 22, 1964

The Baton Rouge Bus Boycott of 1953 . . . A Recaptured Past, exhibit prepared by students at McKinley High School, Baton Rouge, and Louisiana State University graduate students of EDCI 5880, Summer Session 1998, under the direction of Dr. Mary Price

The Drum Major Instinct sermon, delivered by Dr. Martin Luther King Jr., at Ebenezer Baptist Church, Atlanta, February 4, 1968

The Prince Hall Masonic Temple: Taking Pride in Baton Rouge's Black Heritage. Henry Kiely. Preservation In Print, Vol.21, No. 5, June, 1994. East Baton Rouge Parish Library.

Transcripts of Pro Football Hall of Fame enshrinement ceremonies for Willie Davis (1981), Buck Buchanan (1990) and Charley Joiner (1996)

ONLINE RESOURCES

cfbdatawarehouse.com, home page of the College Football Data Warehouse: results by team, coach and season, and other historical information

collegefootball.org, official site of the College Football Hall of Fame

contentdm.auctr.edu, site of A Digital Collection Celebrating the Founding of the Historically Black College and University, maintained by the Historically Black College and University Library Alliance.

databasefootball.com, football statistics and history by databasesports.com

Hesiman.com, official site of The Heisman Trophy

pro-football-reference.com: pro football statistics and history

robinsonmuseum.com, official site of the Eddie G. Robinson Museum

waltercamp.org, official site of The Walter Camp Foundation

Index

The Eddie G. Robinson
Museum

SCHEDULED TO open in 2010, the Eddie G. Robinson Museum was conceived in 1999 to recognize the life and preserve the legacy of the man W.C. Gorden called "the Martin Luther King of football." In 2005, when the Louisiana Secretary of State committed to making the museum a reality, it personified Eddie's belief that, "If you work hard enough, dreams can come true." The former women's gymnasium – where Eddie coached Grambling's basketball teams until 1956 – was chosen as the museum site. In addition to an expansive display of Coach Rob's memorabilia, and contributions from many of his famous former players, the museum design also features a room – named for Doris Robinson – large enough to host banquets or traveling exhibits. There is gallery space, too. Visit the museum website www.robinsonmuseum.com to the learn more. And visit the museum on the Grambling campus to see the full scope of Eddie's career and impact on America, "the greatest country in the world."

DENNY DRESSMAN concluded a 43-year newspaper career in June, 2007. He is a past winner of the Ohio Associated Press Sports Editors' award for Best Sports Column as well as numerous other writing awards, and is a past recipient of the College Football Foundation's Contribution to Amateur Football award. He served as president of the Denver Press Club, the nation's oldest continuously operated press club, in 1986, and was inducted into the Denver Press Club Hall of Fame in 2008. He also was president of the Colorado Press Association in 1993.

He is the author of three previous books, *Gerry Faust: Notre Dame's Man In Motion* (A.S. Barnes, 1980); *Yes I Can! Yes You Can! Tackle Diabetes and Win!* (ComServ Books, 2005), the story of University of Colorado All-American and National Football League star lineman Jay Leeuwenburg, who played nine years in the NFL despite Type 1 diabetes; and *The Diabetes Antidote An Exercise Prescription To Prevent Type 2, To Combat Type 1* (ComServ Books, 2007), a fitness advice book co-authored with Doug Burns, 2006 winner of the Natural Mr. Universe title who was diagnosed with Type 1 diabetes at the age of seven.